The Drum Decade

The Drum Decade

Stories from the 1950s

Edited by

MICHAEL CHAPMAN

 2001
UNIVERSITY OF NATAL PRESS
Pietermaritzburg

Published by the University of Natal Press
Private Bag X01
Scottsville 3209
South Africa
E-mail: books@nu.ac.za

First edition 1989
Reprinted 1991, 1994
Second edition 2001

ISBN 0 86980 985 7

The stories in this anthology are reprinted by kind permission of Mr Jim Bailey, the original owner of *Drum*.

Cover design by Anthony Cuerden
Main cover photograph by Jurgen Schadeberg

Typeset in the University of Natal Press, Pietermaritzburg
Printed and bound by Interpak Books, Pietermaritzburg

Contents

Preface

This selection of stories from *Drum* magazine in the 1950s was originally published a year before the unbannings of 2 February 1990. The intention was to return to publication the urbane, ironic, tough voices of what Lewis Nkosi calls 'the fabulous decade'. *Drum* in the 1950s was a symbol of the new African who, in opposition to apartheid, asserted a city identity. The stories – many of which mingle fiction and fact – represent the substantial beginning of black South African short-story writing. Indeed, the stories have assumed an ongoing significance in both our cultural and social life.

The anthology wished to remind readers in 1989 that despite the grim emergencies of the time, human resilience, a spirit of defiance and freedom, had always been pitted against racial repression. The stories, when read in 2001, provoke new challenges. If according to the media proliferations of style are a feature of post-apartheid identity, the *Drum* writers remind us that 'style' is usually a response to serious and persistent concerns. Or, as the essay at the end of the anthology puts it, to more than telling a story. Or, again, as John Matshikiza, son of the *Drum* legend Todd Matshikiza, puts it in his Introduction to this new edition:

> [These stories] are an invaluable part of our missing store of memories – without which we are destined to have no future.

This elusive relationship between the past and the future suggests the possibility of 'South Africanness'. Apartheid classified people as groups; *Drum* writers valued human beings. To give substance to the concept of South Africanness remains perhaps our greatest challenge.

MICHAEL CHAPMAN

University of Natal (Durban)
2001

Acknowledgements

As in 1989, the publishers join me in thanking the Bailey Estate for granting me permission to republish stories from *Drum* and Mr Jurgen Schadeberg, who most willingly assisted me in my research and provided the photographs in this book. I also wish to acknowledge the University of Natal's financial assistance towards research expenses.

Introduction

It sometimes feels as if I grew up wrapped, like a child from a poor family, in the thick, off-white, cosily newsy pages of *Drum*. Its images seem to have rubbed off on me, like the ink on those reams of cheap newsprint might rub onto the readers' hands, so that, looking back over those flaking pages many years down the line, I have a sense of walking down old familiar streets all over again – which is impossible, because I was too young to have walked down those streets in those times. And yet it is all burned in my memory.

Although that *Drum* was naturally all black-and-white (except for the occasional flash of gaudy red or yellow that was infiltrated onto the cover), its images were more vivid than all the colours of a summer rainbow. *Drum* was larger and more vivid than life because, to my childish eyes, it was a window onto a real world that I could sense and smell all around me, but could only really get to know through the bravado of its pages. Far from being my mantle of poverty, those pages of *Drum* were the wealth of my inheritance, my premature rites of passage to adulthood, before I truly understood the terrible depths of pleasure and pain that adult life encompassed.

That was at the end of the 1950s and the beginning of the 1960s. Official apartheid was ten years old, and growing shrewder by the day. But the writers and photographers of *Drum*, and the readers who lapped up their words and images, seemed to behave as if anything was still possible. They carried themselves with an absurd confidence, as if that drunken wave of freedom that was already pounding across the north and west and the east of the continent would soon be lapping against the shores of South Africa, right up into the violent streets of Sophiatown and District Six, even as far north as the staid, curfew-darkened streets of Pretoria.

I knew the dark side of the life of South Africa through the pages of *Drum* by the time I was six years old: the high life and the bitter end of the gangster; the blunt, *zol*-fired world of the tsotsi, not so many years older than me, but light years ahead in his swaggering confidence, and as fast as a bullet in the black and white sneakers on his feet – glamour I could only dream about. I knew lots about life, and probably lots more about death – like the six Indian sisters, none of them more than teenagers, who had hanged themselves in a death pact in the back yard of their family home in Durban, rather than submit to arranged marriages. The hazy photograph of the six bodies in their pristine saris hanging by their broken necks from a tree just like the tree we had in our own back yard is seared forever into the memory of my retina.

Drum was a fast and fashion-conscious read, something adults dipped into and out of with wolf-whistles, guffaws or bitter comments, depending on what caught the eye: fat-thighed glamour girls posing on the mine dumps like they were St Tropez starlets, socialites at Uncle Tom's Hall, blanketed men on horseback defying authority during the Pondo rebellion – and showbiz, showbiz, showbiz.

What I was not mature enough to explore, and what most of its readers probably also skipped over, were the sections of *Drum* that delved more deeply into the lives behind those racy images. These were the sections given over to more studious journalism, and to writers who dared to grapple with the challenging format of the short story.

As the stories themselves reveal, people were too busy trying to live their difficult lives to be able to stand back and reflect on their own existence. The very conditions that created the pungent stuff of those short stories culled out of their own lives made it all but impossible for the readers to take the short story seriously. There wasn't the time, and besides, it was painful and dangerous to dwell too long on one's own condition. The prophetic voices of the short-story writers were too often lost in the careless din of day-to-day life.

This was the split personality of *Drum* that caused so much contention in its own time, and still gives rise to bitter argument in the politically correct world of today's post-apartheid South Africa. Was *Drum* all glamour and cheesecake, at the expense of providing a proper forum for the most pressing issues of the day, as some black political leaders claimed? Or were the glamour and the racy images a clever way of camouflaging the potent messages contained in the deeper texts that were there to be explored by the more conscientious reader?

There was of course another, more bizarre point of view, expressed by the ruling white National Party: that *Drum* was actually a communist front, encouraging urban blacks to have ideas above their station, whether in the bravado of their lifestyles, the flamboyance of their dress, or in the over-educated English in which they wrote.

The *Drum* of the 1950s, to its credit, was something of all of these things, all at the same time. And its multi-faceted personality, like the multifarious world that it articulated, was distilled in those nuggets of serious journalism, and in the penetrating insight of those short stories that are represented in this collection.

The startling thing is that there is no real dividing line between the two styles of writing: the journalistic and the fictional. Real life in the black town-ships has the monstrously stifling yet banal quality of a B-grade horror movie, while the fictionalised accounts cannot escape from the relentless quality of realism.

Thus Henry Nxumalo's masterfully objective piece of journalism, 'Birth of a Tsotsi', tells a story as compellingly truthful and readable as James Matthews's 'Dead End!' – both recounting the sickeningly predictable journey of the black adolescent lashing out against the mysterious forces of the urban jungle in which he has been cornered, preying on the weakest of his own kind in order to survive, doomed from birth. Nat Nakasa's 'The Life and Death of King Kong', a real-life saga of love and betrayal in a world of prize-fighters, showbiz personalities and petty gangsters, finds its counterpoint in Mbokotwane Manqupu's fictional 'Love Comes Deadly'. Desperation, the losing battle for survival, and a passing moment of glamour in an alienated world: these are the common themes.

The other startling thing is that there is, in a way, no dividing line between those times and our own. Older people like to say that these kinds of things never happened in the old days, and yet here is all the evidence that the petty differences and rivalries that could explode into lethal conflagrations were already with us way back then. We forget that they happened because we have lost our collective memory – the living testimony contained in these stories, buried under the rubble of racial war and fear and carelessness, only now being gradually restored to our banks of memory.

Both Can Themba's 'Mob Passion' and Ezekiel Mphahlele's 'Lesane' dwell on the narrow-mindedness that can lead one ethnic group into an open-ended blood feud with another, destroying all prospect of love, and defying the possibility of unity against a common enemy.

And then there is the endemic violence of people who have been driven from their heritage generations before, living now in 'rows of dilapidated houses that stood cheek-by-jowl as if to support one another in the event of disaster . . .' – dependent on each other, but hating this shared dependence, these narrow confines of the lives of the enslaved, with nowhere to turn but inward upon themselves:

> Saturday. The weekend was around again to bottle up the people's weariness, their anxieties, their pains. They would pick up the bottled mixture the next Monday; a mixture pickled for them to eat up again before they ran for the train on Monday. And so the cycle went on. And when black masses poured out of the trains a strange buzzing noise would begin . . .

It was Saturday. The white man's work was suspended.

And then someone beat his wife and children. A boy dug his knife into human flesh. A boy twisted the arm of a girl. The Zionists sang their half-pagan, half-Christian songs. All so brutally.

(Ezekiel Mphahlele, 'Lesane [The Indian Hawker]')

It was, and continues to be, a brutal life – relieved by flashes of humanity, as in Jordan K. Ngubane's 'Man of Africa' – a brief, heroic moment of self-sacrifice in the midst of a bitter racial confrontation between black and Indian workers in the cane fields of Natal. And it was a life recounted with meticulous honesty, and a passion for language that would convey all the complex feelings that filled those dispossessed yet proud and searching lives.

These stories from 'The Drum Decade' represent more than nostalgia for a bygone age. They are a bridge between the past and the present, remarkably fresh in style and contemporary in the situations and the emotions they convey, in spite of the decades of trauma that have intervened since they were written.

They are an invaluable part of our missing store of memories – without which we are destined to have no future.

JOHN MATSHIKIZA

Johannesburg
December 2000

Rhodesia Road

ALFRED MBEBA

There was a day in a village between Nyasaland and Northern Rhodesia when, as the sun was setting, two young lads saw a number of men passing by who had been away at distant work. The heart of one, Yakusoza, was filled with envy. He longed for a share from the things which he guessed must be in the loads which they carried. His eyes were fixed upon them. His head moved slowly from side to side while one hand went up before his mouth in the gesture of awed amazement.

The other lad, Yakwindula, struck by his silence turned towards him. 'What surprises you so much, Yakusoza?' he said.

'Oh! Those bundles which the travellers there on the path are carrying! If only they were our kin, surely they would throw some little thing to us.'

'True enough,' agreed Yakwindula. 'You are right. Look at the nakedness of us all here in our home! I truly do not know what we shall do now that our grandfather Yamala is old and can only sit about, nodding with age; he who for so long has provided for us . . .'

At this the grandmother, Mbungamawoko, sitting in the warmth of the sun and hearing what was said, looked around quickly. 'What's that you say, Yakwindula? Oh, you young ones! Give honour and show respect for all the acts of your old kinsman. Let him take his rest now and close his eyes; he is too weary to think of what you wear. Should you not go off to work so that you may clothe yourselves by your own labour?'

'Oh, my grandmother,' cried Yakusoza. 'Do you so say! Would you speak badly of us? We truly are keen to go off to work in the south.'

'You will find when you come back that this life of the village just goes on and on, down to the tiniest things. But it is true that naked poverty has fallen upon us and a man should be up and doing. Consider how the cold time of June will soon be on us and all our days go grey!' At once Yakusoza's sisters began taking maize off the cob and breaking it up for roadside roasting. They mushed a lot of groundnuts too. They killed a fowl. All sorts of little things useful to travellers were got ready.

And when the time drew near, together father and mother said, 'Oh, Yakusoza, child of ours; where you are going now is out into unknown country.

Some things there are that you must not do. Have nothing to do with the rudeness of the young or with cocksureness. Never put on any pretended greatness. Do not let self-love deceive you. All these things avoid. Good-bye now. May all go well with you. And when you have spent enough time there, come back to us.'

When the day came for the start it was all flurry and scurry around the huts. People stood about, not knowing whether to do this or that; starting a bit of work only to lay it aside; until the sun was fully up and all went a little way with the travellers.

There were five in the party, three adults and two lads. And for the first ten days or so no kind of trouble at all was met. But when they were well into the country of Chief Mpaseni the flour they carried came to an end; for two days they went without any sort of cooked meal and were very nearly spent. Three nights they slept on the path and on the fourth day they came to the great Zambesi River. At last they were across and at the Government Station of Sipulilo, where all have to get permits to go farther.

At sight of the buildings down went their loads and they rested. But Vicali, senior of them all, disappeared into the bush. He plucked twigs of the bush-plum and mahogany trees. Some he twisted around his forehead. Others he rolled into a bit of dark cloth. What remained, he rolled around in his mouth and chewed; bitter indeed! and his eyes seemed wild as he came back mumbling and muttering as if in dispute with someone. The twigs and leaves were still clutched in his hand.

'What has happened, our father?' the others asked.

'My lads,' replied Vicali, 'ways of life here in Harare you know nothing of. Here we are arrived at Sipulilo and you must listen to me. Not one of you must even spit until we are through this Government place. I have made a charm that the servants of this Government may give us no sort of trouble; not even turn their eyes upon us. This kind of tree-medicine secures happiness. Let us all rub it on our brows.'

And with that he brought out his various objects and taking one piece of twig he broke it in small pieces which he scattered to this side and to that, muttering words as he did so. Opening his eyes he turned to this side and to that and then, after spitting downwards, he said as in prayer:

> If we left our homes with sin on us may it be ended here and now, that we may travel cool in body. May all whom we are to meet, whoever they are, receive us kindly. May the spirits of our forefathers be with us wheresoever it be that we find employment.

As he spoke all were upright but with eyes downward bent. Then he, Vicali, took his charms and rolling them in his mouth and so moistening them, he sprayed slightly each of his friends upon the body.

Coming to the Government Office they showed themselves before the Clerk, who gave them their passes rightaway, though while they were there they saw many others who shook with nervousness when they had to speak to that Clerk. Therefore the travellers thanked Vicali for his wonder-working and he explained to them how to go about finding work.

Among themselves they had some difference of opinion, whether to seek agricultural work among the planters or to take mine work, where, they had heard, big money was to be earned. But what Vicali said was this: 'Divided counsels land you in the fire. Listen now to the real truth. Here we are at the end of our food-money. So I find no good reason for going farther. Let us try to earn at least food-money at the estate of the European called Danzen.' To this they all agreed.

Three days later they reached Muwulve, where many planters from Europe have their estates for different types of crop. It was to a tobacco plantation that the travellers came, one still some distance from Mr Danzen's which Vicali had mentioned, but with their last food just finished they decided against going farther. And when they presented themselves before the white man he sent them off to his African foreman that they might be shown a place to sleep.

When the foreman saw them, he handed out some food and allotted a sleeping hut to them. Next morning when the call to work sounded they all gathered at the owner's office for roll-call. This over, all broke away, each to his own job. As for Vicali and his companions the foreman just left them standing without allotting to them any work at all.

They were much taken aback at this and started off to see the white man. Noticing this, the foreman said, 'There is now work for you,' which made them feel hurt indeed and they just refused to take his word. Instead, they persisted in going to the owner as to make quite certain, and 'Oh yes,' he told them, 'there is some work, but only enough for three,' which spoiled things badly. They had no wish to be separated. So they talked things over until they realized that it really was a case of 'Take it or leave it' if they were not to starve.

So Vicali and the other two grown men went off to hoe, while Yakusoza and the other lad, whose name was Kamuthimbuke, were to be looked after by them in the workers' quarters.

But in a day or two, while the two of them were all at their ease in the sleeping hut, the foreman suddenly appeared and asked them for their work-chit. This put them in fear and trembling. Without a word to say, the foreman took them off to the European. His orders were that they must be off and tie their belongings at once. 'If you are seen again about there,' he said, 'you will be tied up.'

To say that they were downcast is not enough. Their hearts were like lead, and back at the hut they sat down in despair. They asked each other what they could do. It was Yakusoza who put the question; it was Kamuthimbuke who replied, 'Come on, we must put our loads together. It is no place for us here.' As he spoke he was all in a flutter like a hen over her eggs.

But Yakusoza asked, 'Can we go away without taking leave of the others, our friends?'

'Well,' said Kamuthimbuke, 'what do you think yourself? You heard what the European said.'

'True, but I fear their searching for us everywhere when we are gone.'

'Oh then, stay,' cried Kamuthimbuke, 'I am off. Can lightning strike the tree twice? You can stay. I refuse.'

'Friend, it is not that I am blaming you. Far from it. But I wanted to know just what you thought. If that is how it is with you, then I go too.'

Whereat the two threw their things together, more or less anyhow, and got away.

They searched for a job of work among the many planters in the nearby estates. Search as they might, however, a job did not quickly appear. And they were at their wits' end. Sitting under a tree, they began to talk things over. 'We've been over the whole place, haven't we?' said Yakusoza. 'When are we going to find something to do? Do you realise that our food is just about done? What do you think? Have you advice?'

'Well,' said Kamuthimbuke, 'you don't expect to find what you need just right away, do you? Things that turn up just of themselves have no good fortune in them. We have got to put our hearts into this and go on seeking till we find. Come on, let us try that planter's place yonder under the hills.'

And on this they started off once more. It was wearily they were walking, but when they reached the place and met the owner, he wanted his cattle herded and gave them the job.

In the morning a horn would sound and they called it the 'Throw on your clothes' horn. At the sound of it everyone scurried off to his particular bit of work. Yakusoza and Kamuthimbuke opened up the kraal and went off with the beasts to the meadow. An easy job, indeed, this was for them! Had they not been accustomed to it almost from when they began to walk?

As they lay about they began to give names to the various animals; one was Makonongo, another Zimpembe, yet another Ngwetha and a fourth Mancola-cola. But of all the white man's herd the greatest and most powerful was

Makonongo. His horns had a lovely curve and his hump was beautifully rounded and plump. As he paced to and fro, you could almost hear him say, 'Come along; come and have a good look at me.'

Yakusoza took a great fondness to this particular animal and always as it showed its beauties, he would sing this song:

> Oh, Makonongo, you beauty!
> We have found the job!
> We have found the job!
> Look! Can you go and tell our
> people we have found a job?
> Say, 'There are jobs at Harare
> and the boys have got work.'
> Glory! Glory be!
> We have found the job.

And ever as he sang he would break off to whistle and call,

> Vi-i, Vi-i, Co-co-co
> Vo-o, Vo-o, Viyo-o-o,

that beast had so taken his heart. Indeed, Makonongo himself, when he heard that song, would pace and tread as if he were in a dance.

So the lads had great ease and enjoyment there in the glades. And their master came to trust them, for from the very first day they never lost even one of the beasts.

One day Kamuthimbuke got a letter from Vicali, who told him of the illness of one of the others, Yokoniya. He also said that whenever he could find any possible time he would come to visit them. Unfortunately this was never accomplished owing to the great worries following upon the death of Yokoniya.

This death was a heavy blow to all who had known him and his ways; to Yakusoza it was a time of many thoughts. Every memory of his kindly doings and laughter-loving habit was a sharp pain.

Yet while he still sat there, unaware and unheeding, who should arrive there but Yakwindula. 'Odi,' came the voice outside. 'Odini! Come inside,' was the reply and as Yakusoza opened his eyes, there stood the kinsman from home. With a rush Yakusoza had his arms around him and was kissing him! They looked at each other overjoyed.

Laughter and greetings over, Yakwindula offered his comfort in the sorrow.

'Nyirongo! and you, Mkandawiri! One doesn't need to be blood-kin to rejoice in meeting. Only yesterday I went to have a visit with the son of a friend and I heard there the news of death; the death of one well known. I have no wisdom; what to say eludes me; my power is gone. Shall we quietly gaze at each other, o lads of home? I am just come to hold you by the hand.'

And to this Kamuthimbuke responded: 'Yes, indeed, Zgambo; that which you grieve over is true. We are in this too, yet able to do nothing; it is as if something had entered far down within one's ear where it lies beyond one's reach. Yokoniya did not know he was ill for even as much as a couple of days. Gone in the midst of life! On Sunday he felt unwell in his body. On the Monday we had news of his illness. In the evening of Tuesday came news of his death. We have not the knowledge to understand.'

'Ill news, indeed,' said Yakwindula. 'Here we are away in strange country. Better not to grieve; you may call an ill wind upon your health. When the water is spilled there is no way of taking it up again. As one grows, one comes to see things.'

So the food was set out and they ate. And Yakwindula told them all about how things had gone with him in his journey and how he had found work in the town. He described for them all the life of the town and how men found for themselves all manner of employments. But the sun went down and Yakwindula had to make his farewells.

Two weeks later Yakusoza and Kamuthimbuke took a trip to the town as a return visit to Yakwindula. They found their friend awaiting them at the road junction and he took them straightaway to his hut where they rejoiced together far into the dark night. It had been just talk about the ways of the town. Everything simply astounded Yakusoza and Kamuthimbuke as they listened.

When the first light came Yakwindula seized his bucket and went off to the water. Swift-footed.

And yet when he got to the pump he found a long line of people waiting. Said he: 'Would you let me have some water quickly, please. Here I am, your friend, with travellers at my hut to entertain.'

'Oh well, then,' said the others, 'come and draw.'

Very quickly Yakwindula got water and came back to the hut to find his friends still stretched out. He busied himself here and there about the hut and not till all was ready did he awake the visitors; they must wash.

Once they had finished their washing they came back into the hut to find bread all cut in slices and the teapot on the boil. Everything was set out on a table. It was in astonishment that Yakusoza and Kamuthimbuke ate. 'Must not people just throw their money about there?' was their thought. 'This quantity of food must run away with everything.' And they sat on until their friend asked if they would not like to see how the town was built.

First the Post Office where they saw the crowds sending off their letters and parcels to distant places. Then they went to the market and saw the crowds of sellers all over the place. A glance here or there showed sellers of fish, bananas, tobacco, bread! Their eyes stared, their heads slowly moved from side to side. 'We look on marvels here!' they said.

Everywhere people moving to and fro; motors crying 'pe pe-e-e,' bicycles saying 'twee twe-e-e.'

'How,' asked Yakusoza, 'do these people here know where the other man is going to go?'

'Well,' said Yakwindula, 'for a long time they have been growing accustomed so that now wherever a person goes he has his correct way of doing. And here and there are signposts of one sort or another which they all understand.'

On they went among the shops where they saw clothes to break one's heart, gay cloth of all colours, hats and wearing apparel that reduced them to silence. 'Could anyone have enough money ever to buy these things?' said Kamuthimbuke.

'As for me,' said Yakusoza, 'I am speechless.'

Later the friends went down to where they would see something they greatly wished to see; the Railway and the place where the Engines stand waiting; since from their birth they had only heard stories of this famous thing.

They gazed at one or two trains as they went this way and that; pinga-pinga they went and even as you looked they were gone!

Then to the great Station building and what a crowd! what a noise of crying children! Nearby was the place where everyone was buying travelling tickets or despatching parcels or their luggage to distant places.

All that Yakusoza could say was, 'Oh dear! Could one ever finish travel in a world like this!' Even as he spoke an Engine whistled 'Hu-u! uhu-u! hu!' and before their eyes the crowd snatched up their belongings, every man for himself, and besieged the train. Some clambering up, some trying to get down, until it was quite beyond Yakusoza even to look at it.

Yakwindula broke in, 'Come on! Let us be going. The sun is sloping down and we've been long without food.'

But Yakusoza would have none of it. 'May we not go on seeing all the great things that there are here?'

'There is no end to sight-seeing. You could go on and on. But we ought to be going. Darkness draws on.'

'What are you afraid of?' retorted Yakusoza. 'What will we do at the hut, hurrying away there while daylight is still here?'

But Kamuthimbuke said, 'Yes, let's go. You know that it was "I must see more yet" that killed the bushbuck. There are bad folk here and the police might be moving about and take us.' At which Yakusoza moved off with lagging feet.

On the way back they passed a beer-shop. One glance showed a number far on in intoxication, their very eyes running with beer, and uproar everywhere. The tinkling sound of the mingoli, dancers colliding with each other, the drums saying gudu-gudu, the mixed throng of all tribes arrayed in every sort of style, moving on uncertain feet.

Our travellers gazed speechless!

Turning round they saw a young lad who must have put on clothing regardless of cost, a hat on his head, a tie round his neck, a watch on his wrist, squeaking boots on his feet and a pair of spectacles at his eyes!

'What a world!' said Yakusoza. 'So this is what it is like!'

As for Kamuthimbuke all he could say was, 'My mouth is bone dry. I have only eyes to gaze. What takes the eye, though, is this putting on of clothing.'

And then they saw some women, their clothing awry and loose round their breasts, their bodies slim as if they never ate at all, shoes on their feet and cigarettes in their lips. And reeking of scented oils!

'Oh,' was all the travellers said. 'If that's what this land is like no wonder so many leave our home country never to return!'

But even as they watched there was a sudden tumult and cries of 'Jeke! Jeke! Jeke!' They saw two men struggling together, crashing blows at each other. Then one took the other's fist right in the eyes. Shower of stars! And he was down. He lay like dead.

Yakwindula took one look. 'Lads of our home!' he said, 'there is no room for us here! Come on! We must go or we will be called as witnesses in the morning!' So, in silence, they stole away back to their hut.

There they sat and talked until sleep took them, a heavy and noisy sleep.

It was Yakusoza who noticed as he turned over that the light had come and outside it was full day. He waked his friend that they might get their bundles put together and get back to their work.

On their return tramp they discussed everything that they had seen in the Town. Among the hills they travelled in some dread lest some policeman stop them for some Pass or other, but all went well. Thus they got back to the place of their employment before sunset and a lot of the others came to greet them and get food ready for them.

Next morning they were at the cattle-herding again, and now they were singing songs of this sort —

> Oh Father! Won't you write a letter here, to Salisbury!
> Oh Mother! it is you, ah you! that I was with in the days gone by!

Or this one —

> I greet you, my Father; oh I greet you!
> Oh, Kaliyeli! I am only a little boy.
> Mother! my heart is sore.
> Oh, Kaliyeli! I am only a little boy.
> Oh Mother! things sadden me.
> Oh, Kaliyeli! I am only a little boy.

And what they sang turned their thoughts towards home so that they threw up their work and set off back to the village . . .

[March 1951]

The Dignity of Begging

WILLIAM BLOKE MODISANE

The magistrate raises his eyes above the documents and plunges them like daggers into my heart. His blue eyes are shining with a brilliance that sets my heart pounding like the bass of a boogie woogie.

'I'm sick to death of you . . . heartily sick. There is not a Native beggar on the streets whose full story I do not know,' the magistrate said. 'I have watched some of you grow up. There is not one I have not tried to rehabilitate many times. Some I was forced to send to gaol, but they always come back, they come back to the goose that lays the golden eggs.'

These are fighting words, the magistrate sounds as though he is going to put us away for a few weeks. My only regret is that Richard Serurubele has to share my fate. If only the magistrate knew that he is not a parasite like the rest of us, that he is what might be called an exploited beggar. He had been crippled by an automobile, and ever since then his parents have made capital out of it. They use him to beg so they can balance the family budget. They never show him the comfort of love. Relentlessly they drive him like an animal that has to work for its keep and feed. He is a twenty-one year-old lad who drags one foot along. He is an abject sight who has all the sadness of the world in his face; he looks many times older than my mother-in-law.

'You beggars make it difficult for me to do my duty. In spite of my constant failures to rehabilitate you, I always believe in giving you another chance . . . a fresh start you might call it,' the magistrate said. 'But I am almost certain that you'll be back here in a few days!'

The magistrate is getting soft, I can see my freedom at a distance of an arm's stretch, here is my chance to put on my act; a look of deep compassion and a few well-chosen words can do the trick. I clear my throat and squeeze a tear or two.

'Your Honour, most of us beg because we have been ostracised by our families; they treat us as though we were lepers,' I say, wiping off a tear. 'They want us to look up to them for all the things that we need, they never encourage us to earn our own keep. Nobody wants to employ us, people are more willing to offer us alms than give us jobs. All they do is show us pity. We don't want to be pitied, we want to be given a chance to prove that we are as good as anybody else.'

I can see from the silence in the court that everybody is deceived, the magistrate is as mute as the undertaker's parlour. I read pity spelled on the faces of all the people in the court; perhaps the most pathetic face is my own. I am magnificent, an answer to every film director's dream. I know that I have said enough – enough to let me out, that is. The magistrate looks at me compunctiously, I feel like jumping with joy and shouting hallelujah.

'I understand you are matriculated; Nathaniel is the name, isn't it? he said, while turning a page of the report that was prepared by a worker of the Non-European Affairs Department. 'Yes, here we are, Nathaniel Mokmare. The department recommends that you be sent to a place where you will be taught some useful trade. I want you to report to Room 14 at the department's buildings tomorrow.'

This is not what I bargained for, my brilliant idea has boomeranged. Why must I take a job when I can earn twice a normal wage begging? After all, what will the horses do if I must take a job? I must uphold the dignity of begging. Whoever heard of a beggar working? It's unethical, that's all.

'As for you Richard Serurubele, I'll let you go this time, but mark my words, the next time you appear before me, I will have to send you to the Bantu Refuge. Now get out of here, the both of you.'

If the magistrate had seen the big grin on my face as we left the court, he would have thrown my deformed carcass in gaol and deliberately lost the key. He does not see it, so I think I will continue to drain the life-blood of the wonderful people of that big generous city, with the golden pavements. Everything has gone according to schedule, but my friend Serurubele is just about the most miserable man on earth. The trouble with him is that he is one of those people who lack imagination, he always sees the dull side of life.

Serurubele is a fool as well as a hypocrite; if he is forced to beg, I wonder who forces him to hand over everything he receives. His honesty is so appalling it could make a Bishop turn green with envy.

'One of these days I'm going to kill myself,' Serurubele says. 'I can't go on like this, I'm tired of being a parasite. Why did this have to happen to me, tell me Nathan, why?'

How this man expects me to answer a question like this is beyond me. For one unguarded moment I almost told him to send his maker a telegram, and ask him all about it, but my gentler nature sees the harm such an answer can do.

'I don't know, Richard,' I say. 'But things like this happen; it is not in us to question why. Nature has a way of doing things and even then she gives something in return.'

This is one of the times I cannot find something concrete to say. I want to show him that there is compensation for his disability, but I cannot just lay my hands on it. This, I remembered, is what made me leave home.

I left home because my parents did not understand, they almost made me a neurotic. They were afraid to walk freely about the house, everybody sat down as if the house was full of cripples. They treated me like a new-born babe, all the things I wanted were brought to me, I was not even allowed to get myself some water. This excessive kindness gradually began to irritate me, it became a constant reminder that I did not belong, that I was an invalid. It then became apparent that they would soon put the food into my mouth, run my jaws up and down, and push it down my throat. This idea gave me my cue, I packed my things and left.

A new life opened for me. I got myself a wife, a property in Pampoenfontein, and a room in Sophiatown complete with piano. Within two years I had begged well over a hundred pounds. The money has been used wisely. Only one problem confronts me now, I want enough of it to provide for my old age.

I say good night and go to my room. After having something to eat I settle down to do some thinking.

The following morning I am at Room 14 bright and early. A white man with a bored expression is sitting behind a big mahogany desk. I tell him my name. He takes a paper and writes something on it. He tells me to go to that address. The faint showers that were falling outside have become heavier, and as I go out I say something nasty about the weather. A brilliant idea strikes me as a well-dressed lady is walking towards me. She looks like one of those people with a heart of gold. I put on a gloomy face, bend lower than usual and let my deformed carcass shiver.

She stops and looks at me as if she is responsible for my deformity.

'Why, you poor boy, you're almost freezing to death. Here, go buy yourself something to eat.' I feel the half a crown in my hand, give her the usual line of how the Lord will bless, and send her a cartload of luck. From the way she is dressed she appears to have had more than her share of luck.

I play this trick all the way to the address I am given, and by the time I get there I can count well over ten half-crowns. Not bad, I say to myself, at this rate I can become the richest and most famous beggar in the city; to think that the department wants to pin me behind a desk, the idea is criminal.

I find the place and go in. My heart almost misses a beat when I see the large number of people inside. Some, if not most of them, are deformed monstrosities like myself. What could be more sweeter, I say to myself, not even unheard melodies. I can almost see my plan taking shape.

The man in charge starts explaining a few things about the machine. I pretend to be very interested and ask many unnecessary questions, but intelligent enough to impress him. By five o'clock I am running over the key board like a brilliant amateur.

On my way home I go via Serurubele's corner, he is still there and looking as miserable as usual. I suggest that we go home. I lure him to my room and when we get there I begin playing the piano like Rubinstein. Either my rendering is good or my friend just loves bad sounds.

'You can have a house like this and everything that goes with it. It's yours for the taking. Why beg for other people when you can do it for yourself?'

'Don't say such things about my people, I've got to help with the rent and the food,' Serurubele says. 'How do you think I am going to get a room like this? I can't just wish for it.'

'You don't have to, you must plan and work for it like I did.'

Last night I dreamt I was at the race-course and I saw the winning double as plain as I see my twisted leg. I raid my savings in the room and make my way to Turffontein. When I get there I start scouting around for policemen. None are around, and a soothing satisfaction comes with the realisation that I will not have to hide every time I see a police badge. I put a pound win on two and seven, a double in the first leg.

I am too nervous to watch the race, so I decide to walk about and appreciate Nature. Suddenly I feel like someone is watching me. I turn round and look right at Miss Gallovidian, a welfare worker, who has an uncanny habit of showing up at the most unexpected moments. I do not need a fortune-teller to tell me that I am in trouble. She has a notorious record of having safely deposited more than twenty beggars in the Refuge. My only chance is to get out of here before she can find a policeman.

I am going to the gate when I hear somebody talking about two and seven. For a moment I even forget the trouble Miss Gallovidian is going to bring me. I run as fast as a man with a twisted leg can to the Bookie. Only six tickets were sold, everyone was trying to say, only I was not interested. In about half an hour I am at the Building Society where I deposit a sum of £670. After doing that, I take the taxi back to the course. This is my lucky day; another bit of luck like this, then I can retire to my property, and live happily thereafter with my wife. I can destroy my past and start a new life.

But too late!

I feel a gentle but firm hold on my arm. I jerk myself violently and try to hide among the people. I run for a few seconds, stumble and fall on my face. The policeman bends downs, puts bracelets on my wrists, and whispers softly, 'Look, John, let's not have trouble! Come along quietly, and everything will be just fine!'

Under the circumstances I have no choice but to submit. My mother always told me never to resist arrest, let alone striking a uniformed officer of the law. My submission caused me to spend a not-so-glorious weekend in gaol.

I am almost certain that you will be back here in a few days, the magistrate had said. Somebody ought to tell him that he has a greater future . . . reading people's palms. He looks at me and a grin spreads over his pancake-like face. This place must be short of magistrates. Why has it got to be the same one all the time?

'It grieves me, but you leave me no alternative,' the magistrate says. 'Beggars who play the horses are a dangerous nuisance, they misuse the kindness that is showed to them. You have made begging a profession, and it is my duty to curb this occupation of yours. I am forced to send you to the Bantu Refuge.'

The van takes a turn into the grounds of the Refuge. There is nothing to comment about this place; it is completely encircled by trees, which give it an atmosphere of isolation and nonchalance. The van stops in front of the main entrance. The building looks like one of those dull fourteenth-century fortresses, with cobwebs in every closet.

Today I am celebrating my first four weeks at this sanatorium, four weeks of loneliness. No one has been to see me. My first two weeks I spent in entertaining my ego with a daring escape; but now my spirits are dulled by the hopelessness of such an attempt. The nearest town is ten miles away.

I am still ruminating when old man Rantolo comes paddling along on his seat. He is about the oldest man in the Refuge; his face is always sparkling with joy, and he has a way of making people believe that there is good in the world.

'There is someone to see you, Nathaniel, he says he's a friend of yours.'

I thank the old man and go the reception-room. Richard Serurubele is the last person I expected to see, seeing him is a real comfort. I shake his hand as if he is a long lost relation; his dull face lights up, and the firmness of his hand reassures me that the feeling is mutual.

'It's nice to see you Nathan, the town is not the same without you.' His voice does not sound as warm as his face. 'I have a letter for you; I thought it might be important, so I brought it along myself . . . besides, I wanted to see you.'

'Thanks, Richard, I like the way you said that.' I tear the envelope and start reading. Tears flood my eyes as I read the second paragraph.

> Our son Tommy, is dead . . . the doctor said he died from influenza. When it all started I thought he was running a temperature. Gradually the fever made him so weak that he could hardly eat; when the doctor came, it was too late.

Please come home Nathan, I'm frightened. Terry is also acting strangely . . . I can't stand it any more, please come home.

I had always said that only a miracle could get me out of here, but this time I have to go, miracle or no miracle, I just have to go.

'Is anything wrong, Nathan, why do you look so blank?'

'I have lost a son.'

'I'm sorry, Nathan, I wish I could have saved you all this. Things are bad enough without you having to lose your son.'

'What do you mean?'

'Your landlady has locked your room and is threatening to sell your things,' Serurubele says. 'She claims that you have not paid your rent for two months.'

I grab him by the neck and shake him violently. 'My piano . . . will she sell that too?'

He nods his head. I loosen my hold and stare at him viciously. That piano means everything to me, nobody is going to cheat me of it. It is the one concrete proof that I can work for what I want, just like any other man; it represents my entire life.

Serurubele conveys his regrets and goes away. A pathetic image of my wife flashes before me. She must have gone through a terrible ordeal. The being alone must have done her more harm than anything else.

Mr Lherzolite, the superintendent, looks at me with sympathetic eyes, as he reads my letter.

'I simply have to go home, Mr Lherzolite, my wife needs me,' I say. 'Please, sir, I'm trying to make you understand that my son is dead; that my wife is all by herself.'

'Look, Nathaniel, it's not my will that rules here,' he says. 'I only work here, I do not make the decisions. The least I can do is to write to the Welfare Society, telling them of your request.'

This arrangement will take about a week to complete; there is nothing else to do but wait. I thank him and go up to my room, and begin writing a long letter to my wife and to my father.

I choke with joy when I am told to report to Mr Lherzolite in his office. There are five important people in the office, at least they look important to me.

'These gentlemen are going to ask you some questions,' Mr Lherzolite says. 'You will listen to what they have to say, and answer them truthfully. Do you understand?'

I nod and look at their cold faces. The inquisition lasted for about an hour.

'Go and wait outside, Nathaniel,' Mr Lherzolite says.

They took ten minutes to arrive at a decision. Mr Lherzolite calls me in.

'It is the decision of this board that you be sent home. You are not to enter the area of Johannesburg without the approval of the Non-European Department,' Mr Lherzolite says. 'You are forbidden to beg within its jurisdiction. Your parents should be here any day, they are to be responsible for you.'

My wife is waving to us as we enter the gate of the farm. She has not changed a bit. She still has that radiant face, which often caused me to wonder why so beautiful a girl should ever marry a broken-down tramp like me. The day she said yes, I concluded that she was an amnesia case.

She runs to me and throws her arms round my neck. We lock each other in an embrace which isolates us from the rest of the world; her violently palpitating bosom is beating the tempo of a song of surrender. I kiss her long on the neck then our lips meet in the warmth of a kiss. The fire of her lips tells a tale of long, empty nights.

This tender scene is finally broken by a soft pat on my shoulder. My father smiles and beckons for us to come into the house. I ask about my child, everybody starts assuring me that everything is under control, and that a proper doctor has been in to see him.

'Nathaniel, my boy,' my father says, 'I have a surprise for you. If you will please step into the living room.'

Standing in one corner of the room is my good old piano. My suitcase drops down, my mouth gaping like a sea-perch. My heart is beating so fast I feel like dancing the Zulu war and going savage. I rush to it throwing my arms round it in a tender embrace. Everyone is applauding as if expecting a recital from Beethoven's 'Moonlight Sonata'. I remove the top of the piano, rip off the back, and open a little panel hidden between the chords and the left covering.

'This is a day of surprises,' I say casting a quick glance at them, and opening the little packet I took out of the panel. 'It is only fitting that one surprise should follow another.'

I empty the contents of the packet on the small table in the centre of the room. My entire savings heap on the table . . . £183. My father's eyes pop as if in the act of falling out of the sockets.

'This is only cigarette-money, wait and see what I have saved up as the surprise to top all surprises.' I open my suitcase and take out the money I won at the racecourse. 'Do you remember, father, I asked you to stop at the Building Society the day you came to take me from that place? Well, this is the reason I asked to stop there.' This time, even my mother becomes a statue of amazement.

I do not have to ask my father how the piano got here. The conspiracy is all over his face. I find it difficult to hold back my tears when I read the message in his eyes. Welcome home, my son, his eyes said.*

[September 1951]

*Modisane revised sections of this story. The version in *Drum*, as reprinted here, shifts from the ironic tale of the beggar-survivor to an ambiguous celebration of rural homecoming. The later version, as published in the anthology *Darkness and Light* (1958), introduces a 'treatise' on the formation of a Beggars Union and discards the original ending to remain consistently within the ironic mode of the street-wise beggar. (See my discussion of the story on p. 201.)

The Birth of a Tsotsi

HENRY NXUMALO

Of course, tsotsis are made as well as born: they are made every day on the Reef. It is true that when a young boy takes the wrong turning it is partly his own fault; but the amount of crime in a city varies with the well-being or poverty of the mass of its citizens. With the grinding poverty and the sea of squalor that surrounds the 'Golden City', it is not difficult to understand the rest. There is a struggle for existence, and the individual intends to survive.

Young Sibanibani was a case in point. He was illegitimate. His father had picked up his mother and a house on a forged lobolo certificate. But they didn't marry, his father's interest wandered, and he went elsewhere. Sibanibani's mother may have been a gentle girl? – but at the time of his birth she brewed liquor and passed the day with other doubtful activities. To help her, Sibanibani spied out for the police, and so his mother was never caught. He liked it, and that started his career of crime.

For on the Reef the crook starts young. No education, no work, or no pass – that means that a young man must live by night and not by day – and that makes criminals. Able men are frustrated by the lack of opportunity in their lives: soon they find that they can make more money by crime than by honest means: and they turn their talents to sinful and degraded ends. A tsotsi may earn as much as £5 a day; how else could he earn such big money? With that he can look after his girl friends, keep his parents and gamble away the rest.

But it's on the streets where he first gets the wrong ideas. Among kids the 'big shot' is the tough guy who uses a knife, and the real big shot is the killer: he's the Big Guy. 'We are educated in the streets,' says one of our correspondents, 'and we graduate in the reformatories.'

The gangs are classed according to age. The boys of 12 to 16 specialise in pick-pocketing and handbag-snatching: from 17 to 25 or so they go in for payroll-robbing, housebreaking and stabbing. Revolvers, we learn, can now be bought for as little as a fiver, and the studded 'Three Star' knives can be got in shops for 3s. 6d. Knuckledusters are made from anything from a bicycle chain to a studded belt; and everyone knows why tsotsis wear gloves. The latest and most cowardly tool is a short sharp-pointed bayonet: the victim feels it pressing in his side, and unless he gives up his money he feels it pressing harder through his side.

Tsotsis are divided into different gangs operating in different ways. There are the Malume, the railway thieves, who off-load goods trains in the dead of night. 'We mark down a goods train,' one informant tells us, 'and find out what it is carrying in each truck: then we drive on in a car to a slope we know, grease the lines with oil for a stretch which slows up the train, jump on the truck and throw down what we want.'

The Matsisi (Sesotho for bugs) are the pickpockets: and the men who do the hold-ups are the Joavas. Girls take to the life of crime, too: the boys are called tsotsis, the girls, noasisas. The women shoplifters are known as Watchers: and the women decoys in the shebeens are called Spinners . . . Tsotsis often retire at 30 or 50, if they survive. They marry and set up as respectable citizens on their gains: much like some Johannesburg financiers we could name.

Every Saturday morning Johannesburg is thronged with a number of well-dressed African youths in Palm Beach suits, straw hats and white shoes, who walk about the streets looking for their victims. Women who carry handbags in the tightly congested streets are their favourite prey: and with the tsotsis are the noasisas, who are mostly shop-lifters. They wear broad skirts and carry large handbags. Their trick is to enter a shop with a tsotsi: and while he engages the shopkeeper in talk the noasisa helps herself to any articles that may be lying on the unwatched counter.

Very often the shop-lifters haven't the chance to put their stolen articles into the large handbags, and so they smuggle them in between their legs. It is for this reason, among others, that the skirts they wear are tight-fitting at the waist and broad and long at the bottom. They do not wear any bloomers.

Both tsotsis and noasisas live a very glamorous type of life. They make a lot of money, but very few save it. They buy swanky clothes and go to the cinemas almost every day, and entertain each other lavishly.

They go to parties on Sunday, where they are able to impress the shebeen queens with their enormous wealth. For business reasons as well as for fear of reprisals, the shebeens welcome the tsotsis and fear them. Other tsotsis gamble on high card stakes and lose their money as fast as they get it.

A new racket on the Rand is what are called Monday parties. The usual Sunday parties are held by self-help societies, are clean in their motives and are run under an appointed chairman, their object being to augment each other's weekly wages. Monday parties are, however, run by confidence tricksters. The idea is for a friend to invite a well-to-do man, who does not bother very much about working on Monday, to a small party in which a beautiful sex-appealing woman will be present.

This is a like a job, well-planned and implemented. Set hours, own language, etc.

20   *Henry Nxumalo*

She will then pretend to be interested in her victim, who will buy plenty of liquor, take her into his confidence and tell her how much money he has got and where it is.

She will promise him anything, and when she has taken his money will cause a quarrel to be started in some part of the house, after which all the guests will be advised to leave the house in case the police should make a raid.

But should the victim get away with his money before he is robbed, the trickster will arrange for her victim to be followed by a group of thugs, who will terrorise him and either demand the money or rob him. He dare not report the matter to the police, for fear of reprisals.

To speak broken Afrikaans is one of the methods by which tsotsis identify each other, but each group has its own common vocabulary in the presence of strangers.

To speak English is a great setback for anyone coming into contact with tsotsis. It is considered to be a sign of showing off one's education, and a means of pretending to be a teacher. Tsotsis say teachers have the knowledge, but they the sense!

Many apparently motiveless crimes may have concealed motives; some shopkeeper has refused to pay protection money; or the gangs are quarrelling among themselves: perhaps one gang has taken a rich victim from the other's territory – and then they start fighting.

There are big-timers and small-timers. The big-timers often have Indians or Europeans behind them, who plan large-scale robberies with care and science. The small-timers, the usual run of cowards, are amateurs. Let us get the gen from one of these, a Coloured 'king' of Kliptown:

'Ek praat my nooit verby nie,' declared one of the so-called kings of Kliptown, in the lingo of his type – a tough youngster who knows more about the ways of making money on the soft than one would suspect for a boy of his age.

'I am a tsotsi, it is true. I don't care to work. Working at a regular job does not pay. I can make more money by stealing – at least most of my friends do. That is why they don't work.

'But that is nothing. On the whole it is quite easy to get fixed up with a pass. In fact the real criminal has nothing to fear on that score. It is easy to get either a Chinaman or an Indian to take out a pass for you so long as you are able to find the pass fees. Some African businessmen also help sometimes.

'There are no organised Coloured gangs as such in Kliptown. Although the boys may meet and plan their operations they are mostly lone wolves. Their operational base is by a church on the main road; from there they move all along the bus stops, particularly on weekends. They rob, drink and smoke dagga.

'Around Suikerbossie – on the East Road – is one of the most notorious spots in Kliptown. Assaults, drink, stabbings and loose women – these can be had there. This is the Coloured tsotsi boys' happy hunting ground.

'At Dukathole, also in Kliptown, you will find mostly Africans, representative of all the tribes you can think of. There they drink, play dice, smoke dagga and enjoy the company of bad women. Nearly every hut there is a shebeen – specialising in "Barberton" and "Korean" booze.

'Tamatievlei just on the ridge behind Sansouci bioscope is another bad spot. There are to be found the Bashoeshoe, notorious for fighting among themselves for the favours of their womenfolk.

'The Chinese are the greatest sinners insofar as supplying illicit liquor is concerned in Kliptown. Customers come from all the neighbouring townships and locations. They sell liquor from distilleries operated by their countrymen. Innocent looking shops are known to have a big turnover in liquor. A contributory factor to the success of these hooch merchants are the stokvel parties, parties when the guests pay for the liquor – the devil take the hindmost. Nearly every location and township has these clubs where weekend debauchery has a lot to do with the large numbers of murders and assaults.'

We cannot give the accounts of all our informants, including one who had stabbed three people before he was caught shoplifting at the age of 13; but here is a typical story, of Jeremiah Majola, who tells us just how his shameful career came to an end at the age of 15:

'I was born in Randfontein and my parents moved to Alexandra when I was still very young. I went to school when I was 10 but already I had heard about picking pockets and snatching handbags.

'Our heroes were the boys who could steal and stab. The more stabbings they did, the bigger they were. The "biggest shot" of all was the one who had killed somebody – either with a knife or a gun.

'These boys used to have a lot of money and they were able to have a good time with the girls and buy them many presents. It was not long before I wanted to be a tsotsi.

'I was about 13 when I committed my first crime. My friend and I were drinking pineapple brew in Alexandra. It is made with mtombo, pineapple, sugar, oats, carbide and so on.

'The quick-service brew is made at 6.30 in the evening and can be swallowed just after. A glass jar for carrying fruit full of pineapple brew costs a shilling. I used to get drunk after about a gallon.

'The first time I got drunk my friend and I decided to go and steal something. We went over to the Inanda Club. It was a Sunday afternoon and all the white people were watching the game they play with horses. We each had a six-inch knife.

'I saw some Africans working near the club house and said: "Hey folks, I'm looking for a job."

'They told me to come back the next morning and see the boss.

'As I talked to them I looked in the door of the secretary's office and saw a lady's handbag and a grey sports jacket lying on a chair. I went in and took them.

'I was walking away when one of the stable boys shouted at me to put the things back in the office. I told him to come and get them himself and threw the bag and the coat on the ground. As he bent down to pick them up I stabbed him with my knife three times in the back – one up near his neck, the other in his ribs and the other in his buttocks. My friend and I picked up the things and ran away.

'We crossed the road near the club and saw a servant girl in the back yard of the house belonging to Mrs—. My friend asked the girl for a drink of water and when she went to the tap to get it I walked into the kitchen door.

'I was looking for money, but could find none. But in one of the bedrooms, under a pillow, I found a Baby Browning gun. This was better than money.

'I took it out to my friend. "Listen," I said, "I've got something very important. I'm going to make money out of this." And I showed him the gun. There were five bullets in it.

'We went to work at Bramley. Always we had something to drink or smoked some dagga to give us a big heart.

'Every Friday and Saturday we held up somebody at Bramley. Mostly they were Europeans, and nearly always in daylight.

'Why did I do it? Because I wanted to be a big shot among my friends and my girl friends. I wanted a lot of money to have a good time and give my girls a good time. Sometimes I made £50 in one day with the gun. I would spend it all in three or four days and then go and get some more.

'When I leave Diepkloof I am going straight. I hope to get a good job. I have stabbed 15 or 16 people – sometimes when I robbed them and sometimes when one of my friends didn't have any money to buy me drink. But all that is finished now.

'I think the best way not to start stealing and stabbing is not to make friends with a boy who has got a bad spirit. He says to you, "What a fool you are. You only can make a few pounds a month while I can get £50 a day and all the girls I want."

'It's not our parents' fault. They don't even know we are doing it. Sometimes they think we are working or still at school. We always sleep at our homes.'

Well, there is his tale; a tale of wasted and degraded life. Decent citizens struggle to keep our African society straight, the police struggle, and reformatories like Diepkloof make great and noble efforts to turn young prisoners into good and upright citizens. Diepkloof takes in 600 youths: but there are perhaps 20 000 tsotsis, probably more, along the Reef. All these efforts are good, right and useful: but the roots of crime are to be found in the deep social evils that breed wickedness wherever they are found in the world.

[November 1951]

Crime for Sale
[An Escapade]

ARTHUR MOGALE

[ARTHUR MAIMANE]

'Look, Moollah, you don't want me to hold private bioscope shows for the police, do you?'

'No! damn you?'

'Neither do I, chum. So let's have the thousand quid, hey? That's fair enough!'

'I tell you I ain't got it now! I'll send it first thing Monday mornin'.'

'Now you're talking, ole boy. And, by the way, why Monday? Have you got another big 'un lined up for the week-end? You hurt my ego, Moollah; why don't you invite me; then we can have a quiet movie, me and you, afterwards?'

'If I see you anywhere near my jobs, Chief, you'll never aim another damn movie camera! You'll look like you've been through a meat-grinder when I'm thru with you! I'm gonna get you one day!'

And with this most flattering remark he rang off. I put the phone back with a sigh. I took the cigarette out of my mouth and walked out of the telephone booth . . .

Yes ladies and gentlemen. This is me. O. Chester Morena, Private Detective, and what not. These uneducated crooks call me 'Chief'. Anyway, that's what my last name means.

Me, I'm smart. I know all the angles. I've been plenty places. They kicked me out of university during my second year, and my father kicked me out of the family. I became a gangster, pick-pocket, robber and all-round crook. But I played it scientifically. Still, after a few years I decided the old saying 'crime doesn't pay' was correct. I joined the police force in Pretoria – where I wasn't known.

After a year's excellent service I sent in my resignation. After I'd convinced the Inspector I meant it, and told him my plans, he pulled a few strings to get me a private detective licence – and one for a gun.

Of course, you all know such creatures don't exist in Johannesburg. Well I don't exist either – except on paper.

My first two months in this crook-infested Golden City I spent finding out who the big boys in the underworld were. And making love to their women. I suppose what they used to tell me in high school about me being a 'pretty-boy' was right, 'cos all these women fell all over themselves to get next to me. They would come in handy when I was all ready with my plans to rake in all the golden pavement stones folk in the country say Joh'burg is lined with. And whilst doing this, I also hired myself a room in every location. And a small room in Rosenberg Arcade in town.

I then went shopping. I bought the smallest cine camera in town. And one of the biggest books. Photography has always been my hobby, you know. But now it was going to be my business. I cut out the middle 100 pages of the book so my camera could fit snugly in. The lens peeping through a small hole was flush with the back cover of the book. And the 2-foot release cable snaked out of the book and hung from my buttonhole.

It took me two days' hard work to learn to aim my camera-book at a two-by-two target.

Then the following Saturday I took a stroll in town. I found them on the corner of Eloff and Kerk Streets admiring Levison's window-dressing: Fingers and his 'G.I. Joes'. With my big book under my arm, I also admired . . . and waited. I looked them over. There were four of them. Fingers wore a gaberdine coat over a brown suit. Joe and Eddie were in suits too, and carrying newspapers. I never knew they could read. Boykie, the get-away-man, was sitting on a delivery tricycle dressed in a khaki uniform.

After some time a Cadillac parked behind the bloke on the tricycle. A lady carrying a big but empty shopping bag walked out. She waited at the robot. Fingers was right beside her, arms swinging. I was behind them, with the other three behind. Boykie was all of a sudden carrying a bulky parcel in his hands.

I pressed the button at the end of the release cable. I could hear the steady whirr of the motor as I recorded the event on film.

Fingers had no thumbs on him. As we reached the middle of the street, the zip to the bulging side-pocket of the lady's shopping-bag was half-open. We waited for the robot across the street. As she moved to cross, Fingers pulled out the thick purse. He swung his arm back, and Eddie pushed me slightly as he took the purse. Boykie walked past him still carrying the parcel. Eddie dropped it into his tunic pocket. I stopped the camera.

At the Cleghorns entrance she stopped to pull out the purse. She looked with quick-rising fear at her empty hand. She screamed and fainted. I walked back to her car and told her chauffeur. He was mildly interested. After telling me her name and address – and accepting my cigarette – he walked across to the crowd.

I strolled on. I left the peanut boys alone. It was amusing to watch their different techniques of pick-pocketing. Then I went to Rosenberg Arcade. To my dark-room. After lunch I was the only audience at the *prèmiere* of the biggest movie scoop. 'Easy-Money-Land, here I come!' I chuckled as I walked out to my car. It was a run-down coupe, but I knew in a few months I would be driving the sleekest car in town.

I drove to the morning victim's home. After showing her my licence and explaining I saw her robbed that morning, I told her I might be able to help her recover the money – it was £43. After giving me the okay and telling me it wasn't so much the money that mattered, but the eliminating of pickpockets from the city's streets (which I hoped would never be) she asked me:

'By the way, how did you know where I lived?'

'Ah, madam,' I said looking very knowing – which I am anyway – 'How I came to know I cannot say; but it shows that I *am* a good detective, doesn't it?'

She muttered a good-bye and left me on the stoep. As I drove away I was thinking of the mere ten quid she was offering me for the job. Well, I thought, I would see how much nimble Fingers and Co. offered me.

I wanted to find the boys before they had spent all the money at the many midnight parties Sophiatown specialises in. So I was on the prowl for them soon after nine that evening. After half a dozen wild-goose chases, I found them in Edith Street.

I parked the jalopy outside and sent a boy in to call out Fingers. He was 'nice' as he belligerently looked into the car through the far window. The car was filled with the smell of gin and brandy as he spoke.

'What do you want from me, bub? Make it fast too, because the boys might finish the "straight" before I get back!'

'You won't smell it, wise guy. We are going for a little ride, me and you. And don't dare call me "bub". I could knock your teeth down your throat for that,' I said. 'Anyway, let's not waste time on pleasantries. Nice job you pulled in town this morning, eh, Fingers? How much of the £43 is left?'

'Say, who are you, anyway?' he asked, beginning to sober up.

'They call me "Chief." I'm a private detective – if you know what that means.'

He didn't. He thought I was from Marshall Square, so when I asked him to come in for a ride, he flopped into the seat next to me.

I drove to a quiet and dark corner. I stopped. I pulled back the floor carpet, revealing white canvas between our feet. I screwed the small projector on to the stand clamped to the seat rest. I connected the flex-ends to the car battery and switched off the light.

I started the projector. The show was on! He got the surprise of his life when he saw his work of the morning on the canvas. I switched it off at the end. His face had come apart in the dark.

'She's offered me twenty quid to bring you in,' I lied. 'She hasn't seen this — yet; but if you don't give me thirty she will. AND the police.'

'Now be a sport, brother!' The words fell over each other. 'Me and the boys have spent £6 on liquor already; and if we give you thirty, we'll only have seven left. Make it the twenty she offered you!'

'You just be damned glad you haven't seven years' hard labour each, "brother"!' I mimicked. 'Let's have it!'

He still had enough liquor in his head to feel brave. He made a grab for the projector. I clipped his knuckles with the .25 I'd been carrying in my lap since calling him out. I jabbed him with it in the ribs.

'Don't you go being brave, wise guy. It's loaded, and I have a licence for it. I could plead self-defence, you know! Give.'

I put it back in my lap. He was scared.

'I don't want it to seem like robbery chum,' I said. 'Give us the money now, will you? Then you can have the film you seem to love so much!'

The last sentence made up his mind. We made the exchange. With a curse he stepped out and slammed the door shut. With a smile I drove away. I turned down the first street. It was Gold Street. Yes, that would be the name of all my streets from now on!

[January 1953]

Crime for Sale
[Another Escapade]

ARTHUR MOGALE

[ARTHUR MAIMANE]

Now what would Shadow be doing in this part of town? I thought as I saw him in a warehouse area of town. He was essentially a pick-pocket; so I thought there was a catch somewhere. I followed him from across the street.

He stood for a minute watching workers remove bales on the pavement into a warehouse. He walked back two blocks to a car. That was an improvement, I thought, the fingers racket must be paying well. I hadn't been wasting my time filming their penny-ante snatches since I got on to the big-time warehouse burglars. He rummaged in the backseat, came out with a white overall, walked into an empty lot, and came out wearing the overall. He walked back to the warehouse.

There was a delivery bicycle near the warehouse entrance. Without any ado he wheeled it to one of the bales. He looked like any of the workers in his white overall. He examined the label. He passed on to the next and examined its label. He asked one of the workers to help him load it on to the bicycle. With a casual wave of the hand he pedalled towards his car.

I laughed myself weak. I hadn't heard of anything as simple and brazen as that! I wasn't even sorry I didn't have my camera-book with me. Even if I had, I think I wouldn't have filmed it. He deserved to go off scot-free with such audacity.

That was an historic moment. The first of a rash of similar snatches the city was to suffer from. With each warehouse employing scores of Africans, who could know them all? There was a variation, though. One used by the less brave.

They would 'case a joint' then hire the nearest rickshawman, offering him a large sum, about a pound, if he would go to such a warehouse, pick up one of the bales on the pavement, and deliver it at some address – which was usually some deserted spot where he got his pound and the bale went to the locations.

This variation was too tedious for me, so I concentrated on the braver boys . . . and did I clean up!

I decided to widen my scope after these 'pick-ups' quieted down. I spent Friday and Saturday nights in Ferreirastown, Vrededorp and Doornfontein. At the organised gambling schools. Many an 'honest' citizen with a reputation as good as gold – the innocents thought – visited these 'schools' at the same time that I did.

They wanted to see how much Lady Luck loved them. She, like most women I've met, loved me better still. Some made a pile on the glass-topped tables, some didn't. Those who didn't slunk home after midnight, making up the tragic story the wife was to hear. How he had gone to one of the pal's homes for a game of chess, and on coming back had been bound, gagged, and robbed.

Those who made a pile stamped out of the room with a smug look on their faces. They normally never got very far with it. Either on the stairs or in a dark alley the look would be wiped off with a tyre lever or gun barrel. They had a true story to tell the wife about the robbery!

After establishing myself as a gambler who never won – it wasn't surprising with the glass-topped tables that mirrored the poor innocents' cards so the McCoys knew their hands before they did – I always left after these lucky few who had held their cards a little closer to their chests. I made sure they got home safe!

I didn't want to lose a client. I would invariably have a movie to show him just how he won the night before. And as they never wanted their trusting wives to see just what good card players they were at games other than casino, they would give me a cut to burn the film. So they could go home with a light heart – and wallet – I burnt the films before them.

This not wanting to lose a client got me into trouble now and again. I remember the night I unobtrusively escorted one of Joh'burg's biggest noises out of the danger area.

Trouble began on the stairs. I was walking behind him with my camera-book under my arm. There was a door on the landing. As he passed the door it opened. An arm shot out and dragged him in by the collar. Not quite in, because with one leap I was behind him. I had my mauser in hand and brought down its barrel on the arm's exposed wrist. Hard! I heard the bone crack. There was one helluva scream from the closet.

Mister Big Noise was scared stiff.

'Make it fast, Hero!' I whispered in his ear as I hustled him down the remaining stairs. He could feel the mauser still in my hand and thought I was another of the robbers. At the bottom we found the rest of the farewell party. Two Coloureds and an Indian.

'Now you wouldn't try anything funny, would you boys?' I said casually, with my right hand still behind Big Noise. They looked at the big book I was carrying. Probably they thought I was just another book-worm, and they tried to give me the bumsrush. I shot the Indian in the thigh from round Big Noise's body, pushed Noise into the first Coloured, and brought the barrel down on the second's neck. The first one just pushed Big Noise aside and jumped me from the side. I stepped back, and as his fist shot past, I chopped his forearm with the edge of my flattened palm. He screamed as it went numb. It was an old judo chop. As his arm went down, I sank a left in his stomach. He came down.

I caught him in the face with my knee. He knifed backwards and landed on his head with a loud thud.

Big Noise was already at the door. I picked up my camera-book and ran after him. His car was three blocks away in a more respectable area. He was puffing like a bellows when he got there. I had to drive him a few blocks – to my car – before he had deflated enough to drive.

I was waiting for him outside his office the following evening. Being winter, it was quite dark. But he recognised me.

'Thank you very much, son,' he whispered as he crowded me, pushing a fiver into my hand.

'Oh, no sir!' I said politely as I refused the fiver and followed him to his car. 'I can't accept the money yet. After all, what I did was in my own interests.'

This puzzled him. He looked at me. I smiled. I opened the car door for him. 'May I drive you a little way – again?'

He was too puzzled, and I think a bit scared to do more than nod. I parked the car in a quiet one-way. We hadn't spoken a word. I opened the case I'd been carrying. I hung the screen on the back seat of his long '38 Buick, I plugged the projector to the ignition wires I disconnected behind the dashboard. I closed the fancy curtains over the windows.

'Young man, what's all this?' Big Noise spluttered. 'You take over my –'

'Yes, your car!' I cut in. 'But this will interest you more. Take a look at how you won the sixty quid last night!'

With that I switched on the projector.

'Well, what do you think of it?' I asked him as I turned it off. 'Good, isn't it? Don't you think I ought to get an Oscar for this one?'

For a moment more he was dumb. His eyes were still fixed on the screen. I pulled it away. I began rolling it.

'What . . . what are you going to do with that film? Give it to me!' Anyway, that's what I think he said. He spoke so doggone fast, all I could understand was the grab he made for the projector. I jabbed his paunch with the rolled-up screen. He jerked back.

'No hurry, sir! If you are so in love with the film, you'll get it! Only you'll have to buy it.'

He was relieved. 'How much!' he breathed.

'I'll be fair. You won sixty last night. Peanuts. Your income is over a thousand. Not bad, but nothing much. So, can I have £600? – two hundred being of course for the help I gave you last night.'

He had gasped when I said six hundred, so I added the encouragement. 'Or perhaps you would like me to show the film to the missus? It's so good I reckon she'd buy it!'

'No! damn you!' he shouted as he fumbled for his cheque book.

'No thanks!' I said. 'No cheques for me. I'll pick up the cash tomorrow.' I stepped out of the car with my case and was gone.

Well, if you haven't left off reading this with disgust, you must be thinking I'm the meanest villain you ever heard of – though I was blackmailing criminals only. Gambling is a crime, isn't it. And I think I agree with you. I'll tell you why.

You see, I kept on changing my lodgings everytime I thought the fly-boys were getting to know my latest. I was a mug to rent a room in the house of one of these 'decent' Shebeen Queens who go to church every Sunday morning.

I didn't tell you, did I, that I kept a duplicate roll of every film I 'sold'? Well, I did. And I was afraid to leave them in the Rosenberg Arcade darkroom. So I kept them in a strong-box in my lodgings.

Now this queen I was living with. I reckon she got rather brave and wouldn't pay the uniformed boys the agreed cut. So a raid was organised. They searched every room and box. They got enough brandy, gin, whisky and beer to intoxicate the whole Force.

And they got all my films. What they saw when they examined them caused the sensation of the century in this country. What with all those films and one of the gambling big-noises being brave enough to give evidence, I couldn't escape. I reckon that will teach me to play everything straight. I'll never keep anything back on my clients in the future. I'll sell them everything plus the developer. Well, I better be getting along. Here comes the prison warder!

[March 1953]

Mob Passion

D. CAN THEMBA

There was a thick crowd on Platform Two, rushing for the 'All Stations' Randfontein train. Men, women and children were pushing madly to board the train. They were heaving and pressing, elbows in faces, bundles bursting, weak ones kneaded. Even at the opposite side people were balancing precariously to escape being shoved off the platform. Here and there deft fingers were exploring unwary pockets. Somewhere an outraged dignity was shrieking stridently, vilely cursing someone's parentage. The carriages became fuller and fuller. With a jerk the electric train moved out of the station.

'Whew!' sighed Linga Sakwe. He gathered his few parcels upon his lap, pressing his elbows to his side pockets. He did not really have any valuables in these pockets; only long habit was working instinctively now.

Linga was a tall, slender fellow, more man than boy. He was not particularly handsome; but he had those tense eyes of the young student who was ever inwardly protesting against some wrong or other. In fact at the moment he was not a student at all. He was working for a firm of lawyers in Market Street. He hoped to save enough money in a year or two to return to university to complete an arts degree which he had been forced by 'circumstances' to abandon.

People were still heaving about in the train but Linga was not annoyed. He knew that by the time the train reached Langlaagte, or Westbury, most of these folks would be gone and he would be able to breathe again. At Braamfontein many people alighted; but he was not thinking of his discomfort any more. He was thinking of Mapula now. She had promised that she would be in time for this train. That depended, of course, on whether she had succeeded in persuading the staff nurse in charge of the ward in which she worked to let her off early.

The train slowed down. Industria. Linga anxiously looked outside. Sure enough, there she was! He gave a wolf-whistle, as if he were admiring some girl he did not know. She hurried to his carriage, stepped in and sat beside him. They seemed not to know each other from Adam. An old man nearby was giving a lively account, in the grimmest terms, of the murders committed in Newclare.

At Westbury the atmosphere was tense: Everybody crowded at the windows to see. Everywhere there were white policemen, heavily armed. The situation was 'under control', but everyone knew that in the soul of almost every being in this area raved a seething madness, wild and passionate, with the causes lying deep. No cursory measures could remedy; no superficial explanation could illuminate. These jovial faces that could change into masks of bloodlust and destruction without warning, with the smallest provocation! There is a vicious technique faithfully applied in these riots. Each morning these people quietly rise, and with a business-like manner hurry to their work. Each evening they return to a Devil's Party, uncontrollably drawn into hideous orgies. Sometimes the violence would subside for weeks or months, and then suddenly would flare up at some unexpected spot, on some unexpected pretext.

At Newclare, too, from the train all seemed quiet. But Linga and Mapula knew the deceptive quiet meant the same even here. The train rushed on, emptier. Only when they had passed Maraisburg did these two venture to speak to each other. Linga was Xhosa and Mapula Sotho. A Letebele and a Russian! They had to be very careful! Love in its mysterious, often ill-starred ways had flung them together.

Linga spoke first.

'Sure you saw no one who might know you?' he asked softly.

'Eh-eh,' she replied.

She fidgeted uneasily with the strap of her handbag. His hand went out and closed over her fingers. They turned simultaneously to look at each other.

A sympathetic understanding came into Linga's eyes. He smiled.

'Rather tense, isn't it?' he said.

She looked past him through the window.

'Witpoortjie!' she exclaimed. 'Come, let's go.'

She rose and went to the door. The train stopped and they went out. Together they walked to a bridge, went over the line and out by a little gate. For some two hundred yards they walked over flat, stubbly ground. Then they went down a mountain-cleft at the bottom of which ran a streamlet. They found a shady spot and sat down on the green grass. Then suddenly they fled into each other's arms like frightened children. The time-old ritual, ancient almost as the hills, always novel as the ever-changing skies. For a long time they clung to each other silently. Only the little stream gurgled its nonsense; these two daring hearts were lost to each other. The world, too – good, bad or indifferent – was forgotten in the glorious flux of their souls meeting and mingling.

At last Mapula spoke – half cried: 'Oh, Linga! I'm afraid.'

'*Here where the world is quiet?*' he quoted, with infinite softness. 'No, dear, nothing can reach and harm us here.' Then with a sigh: 'Still, the cruellest thing they do is to drive two young people like guilty things to sneak off only to see each other. What is wrong with our people, Mapula?'

She did not answer. He lay musing for a long time. She could see that he was slowly getting angry. Sometimes she wished she could understand the strange indignations of his spirit and the great arguments by which he explained life. Most times she only yearned for his love.

'They do not see! They do not see!' he continued vehemently. 'They butcher one another, and they seem to like it. Where there should be brotherhood and love, there are bitter animosities. Where there should be co-operation in common adversity, there are barriers of hostility, steeling a brother's heart against a brother's misery. Sometimes, 'Pule, I understand it. We have had so many dishonest leaders, and we have so often had our true leaders left in the lurch by weak-kneed colleagues and lukewarm followers, that no one wishes to stick his neck out too far. Where is the courage to weld these suicidal factions into a nation? The trouble is, very few of us have a vision comprehensive enough of our destiny! I believe *God has a few of us to whom He whispers in the ear*! Our true history is before us, for we yet have to build, to create, to achieve. Our very oppression is the flower of opportunity. If not for History's Grand Finale, why then does God hold us back? Hell! and here we are, feuding in God's dressing-room even before the curtain rises. Oh! – ' He covered his face and fell into her lap, unable to say any more.

Instinctively Mapula fingered his hair. In God's dressing-room, she thought, What does it mean? But his anguish stabbed at her heart. Trying to forget herself she only sought within her a tenderness to quell the bitter wretchedness she had heard in his voice.

'Linga, no! Let me show you something else – something that I understand. It is not so long before you and I can marry, I dream about the home that we are going to have. I . . . I want that home, Linga. You taught me that woman's greatest contribution to civilisation so far has been to furnish homes where great men and great ideas have developed. Moreover, there's our problem. Let us rather think of ways of handling my father. No, no; not now. Let us think about the present, about *now*.'

Thabo was running faster now that he was nearing home. His mind was in a whirl; but he knew that he had to tell his father. The lopsided gate was in the far corner, so he smartly leaped over the fence where it was slack. He stopped abruptly at the door. He always did when there were people. But now he soon realised these people were his two uncles – Uncle Alpheus and Uncle Frans. Somehow great news always brings a glory of prestige on the head of the bringer. Thabo felt himself almost a hero now; for these two men were diehard stalwarts in the Russian cause. Uncle Alpheus was a romantic firebrand while

Uncle Frans was a scheming character of the power-behind-the-throne variety. They were complementary to each other: together a formidable team.

'Father, where is he?' hissed Thabo, breathing hard. The excitement in his voice aroused everyone.

'Holy Shepherd! What's the matter, boy?' cried Uncle Alpheus.

'Mapula, Mapula. She loves with a Letebele.'

'What!' exploded Uncle Alpheus. 'Where is she?' Then more calmly: 'Come'n, boy. Tell us everything more quietly; your father is out there?'

'J-J-Jonas t-t-tells me – J-Jonas is a boy who works with me – Jonas tells me that Mapula loves with a Letebele. They always meet at the hospital; but never in the sitting-room. He hopes to marry her.'

'Never!' barked Alpheus. Just then the door burst open. A party of men carried in the limp form of Thabo's father. He was unconscious and blood streamed all over his face. Beyond them, just outside the door, a crowd had gathered. Everyone was at once asking what had happened. As the news spread, ugly moods swept the crowd. Ra-Thabo was carried into the bedroom and tended by the women. Alpheus and Frans returned to the fore-room and conferred.

'What now?' Alpheus asked Frans.

'Of course, we must revenge. You will talk to the people – the women. Talk fire into them. Connect it with the Mapula business; that'll warm them. Suggest drugs – a Letebele must use drugs, mustn't he? I'll be in the house. Just when they begin to get excited I'll arrange to carry Ra-Thabo out – to the hospital, you know. See if we can't get them bad!' He smiled cheerlessly.

Outside, the crowd – mostly women – was thickening. Even in the streets they could be seen coming along in groups, blanketed men and women. From the house Thabo and his little sister, Martha, joined the crowd. It was obvious that their uncles were going to do something about it.

Alpheus stepped on to the little mud wall. He raised his left hand and the blanket over it rose with it. This movement was most dramatic. In a few moments the crowd moved closer to him and became silent. Then he began to speak. He began in a matter-of-fact voice, giving the bare fact that Ra-Thabo, their leader, had been hurt. Warming gradually he discussed the virtues of this man. Then he went on to tell of how this man had actually been hurt. Neither confused fighting nor cowardly brutalities rose in the mind as this man spoke, but a glorious picture of crusaders charging on in a holy cause behind their lion-hearted leader. Oh, what a clash there was! The Letebele were pushed beyond Westbury station. There the heroes met a rested, reinforced enemy. For a moment all that could be seen was the head of Ra-Thabo going down among them. The clang of battle could be heard; the furious charge could be seen, in the words of this man who was not there. The Basothos fought desperately and won so much ground that their all but lost leader could be rescued and carried back home. And what finds he there? Alpheus's voice went down softer and heavier, touching strings of pathos, rousing tragic emotions which the hearts present had never before experienced. There was an automatic movement in the crowd as everybody strained forward to hear. In awful, horror-filled whispers he told of Ra-Thabo's daughter giving herself to a Letebele. The thing is not possible! he hissed. It would not have happened if the maid had not been bewitched with drugs. Are they going to brook it! he cracked. No! all the throats roared. Are they ready for vengeance! Now! thundered the mob. Someone in the crowd shouted '*Mule!*' Then the women took up their famous war-cry, chilling to a stranger, but driving the last doubting spirit there to frenzy and fury.

'*Ee!–le!–le!–le!–le!–le!–le!–Eu! Eu! Eu!*'

Now they were prancing and swaying in uninterpretable rhythms. A possessed bard in their midst was chattering the praises of the dead, the living, and the unborn; his words clattering like the drumsticks of a fiend.

'Let us go past Maraisburg and attack them from the rear!' yelled Alpheus over the din.

At that moment the door of the house went open. The mob, which had been on the point of dashing out, recoiled. The sight they saw stunned them. Frans and two other men were carrying out Ra-Thabo, besmeared with blood. Thabo saw Uncle Alpheus leaping with trailing blanket and yelling 'To Maraisburg!' Again he leaped over the fence into the street. The mob followed hard on his heels.

'*MULE!*' '*MULE!*' '*MULE!*'

As the last blanket swept round the corner, Frans turned back to the injured man. His two helpers had also been drawn in by the irresistible suction of the mob-feeling. With a smile he said to the unhearing Ra-Thabo: 'I'll have to get a taxi to take you to hospital, brother.' Then he carried him back into the house.

'All Change! All Change!' And more brusquely: 'Come'n. *Puma! Puma!*'

Linga and Mapula hurried out. News had arrived that trouble had started again at Newclare; more seriously than usual. All trains from Randfontein were being stopped here and sent back.

Shrugging, Linga drew Mapula away, and arm-in-arm they strolled along the platform, out by the little gate, into some suburban area. For a time they walked on in silence. Then Mapula spoke. 'I hope I'll get back in time,' she said.

'Then let's walk faster. We might get a lift outside the suburb.' They walked into the open country. Linga knew that if he could only find a certain golf-course somewhere around here, he would know where the road was.

Meanwhile, they had to stumble on over rough country, and Mapula's cork-heeled shoes were tormenting her toes. She limped on as stoically as she could. Linga did not notice her suffering as he was looking out for familiar landmarks. Those trees looked suspiciously like the golf-course to him.

When they reached the trees Mapula said: 'Linga, let us rest here; my toes are suffering.'

'All right,' he replied. 'But I must look for the road. Let's look for a cool place where you may rest while I search for the golf-course.'

'Mm.'

He led her amongst the trees. She sat down and pulled off her shoes. When he thought he saw a shadow of distress flit across her brow he bent down, took her hand, pressed it and muttered: 'Back in a moment, sweet.' He rose slowly, looked at her indecisively, then turned away slowly and walked off.

He did not search far before he noticed a torn and faded flag. The hole was nearby. Suddenly he emerged from the cluster of trees, and came upon the road. But his attention was caught by a horde of Russians pursuing a woman who came flying towards Linga. This spelt trouble for the Letebele. But in a flash he thought of an idea. He spoke fluent Sesotho and believed he could pass for a Mosotho, possibly as a Russian. He quickly drew a white handkerchief from the pocket of his trousers, tied it round his head. This made him look like an active supporter of the Russian cause. Skirts flying, the woman sped past him. Facing the mob he shouted: 'Helele!'

All its wrath spent, the mob crowded round out of sheer curiosity. Some were even in a jocular mood now; one playing lustily on a concertina. But here and there Linga could see deadly weapons snatched up in their hasty exodus from Newclare. He spoke to them in fluent Sesotho, taking his idiom from Teyateyaneng. He asked if he was on the road to Newclare; he said that he worked in Roodepoort, but was going to Newclare because his uncle there wanted more man-power in the house. Won't they please tell him where this road was?

'Che! It is no Letebele this; this is a child of our home,' remarked Alpheus.

'Kgele! You speak it, man,' said a burly fellow. Then everyone directed Linga to Newclare.

Just then Mapula came running, shoes in hand and stockings twisted round her neck.

'Linga! Linga, my darling! What are they doing to you!' she screamed as she forced her way through the crowd. Linga stiffened. When she reached him she flung her arm around him and clung to him with all her strength, crying all the time. Then she saw her uncle, stupefied like the rest of them, standing there. She ran to him and begged him to save her lover. He pushed her aside, walked up to

Linga, and stood before him, arms akimbo.

'Ehe! So you *are* a Letebele after all. You lie so sleekly that I can understand why my daughter thinks she loves you.' Then he swung round, his blanket trailing in an arc. 'Friends, we need go no further. This is the dog that bewitched my brother's child. Let's waste no time with him. Tear him to pieces!' The mob rushed upon Linga: *'Mmate! Mmate!'*

'Uncle! Uncle!' cried Mapula. But even as she cried she knew that nothing could be done. She had courted the contempt of her people; and she understood now that all her entreaties were falling upon deaf ears. Whether from convenience or superstition – it did not signify which – she was considered the victim of the Letebele's root-craft.

Suddenly from the scuffling mob flew an axe which fell at her feet. In a flash she knew her fate. Love, frustrated beyond bearing, bent her mind to the horrible deed.

Mapula acted. Quickly she picked up the axe whilst the mob was withdrawing from its prey, several of them spattered with blood. With the axe in her hand Mapula pressed through them until she reached the inner, sparser group. She saw Alpheus spitting upon Linga's battered body. He turned with a guttural cackle – He-he-he! He-he-he! – into the descending axe. It sank into his neck and down he went. She stepped on his chest and pulled out the axe. The blood gushed out all over her face and clothes. With that evil-looking countenance she gradually turned to the stunned crowd, half lifting the axe and walking slowly but menacingly towards the largest group. They retreated – a hundred and twenty men and women retreated before this devil-possessed woman with the ghastly appearance. But then she saw the mangled body of the man she loved and her nerve snapped. The axe slipped from her hand and she dropped on Linga's body, crying piteously: 'Jo-o! Jo-o! Jo-o! Jo-na-jo! Jo-na-jo!'

Someone came and lifted her up. Someone else was dragging Alpheus's bleeding corpse by the collar so that his shoes sprang out one after the other.

The crowd was going back now. All the bravado gone, they were quiet and sulky. Only the agonised wailing of Mapula could be heard. Every breast was quelled by a sense of something deeply wrong, a sense of outrage. The tumult in every heart, feeling individually now, was a human protest insistently seeking expression, and then that persistent wail of the anguished girl, torturing the innermost core of even the rudest conscience there. The men felt themselves before God; the women heard the denunciations of thwarted love. Within they were all crying bitterly: 'Jo-o! Jo-o! Jo-nana-jo!'

[April 1953]

Mr Drum Goes to Jail

HENRY NXUMALO

Last month Drum *published an article on 'My Time in Jail' by Manilal Gandhi. Mr Gandhi described how prisoners at Germiston Jail, Transvaal, were knocked, kicked, slapped and 'treated like beasts'.*

Mr Gandhi's allegations in Drum *were widely publicised in the Press, and were supported by a number of statements from ex-prisoners, and also by a former warder. The allegations were, in turn, denied by magistrates, by the Director of Prisons, and by the Minister of Justice.*

Many people have called for a commission of inquiry into conditions in prisons. The Director of Prisons has agreed to conduct an investigation. But that is not enough.

Drum *decided to conduct its own investigation. We believed that only by sending a member of our own staff to jail could we be certain of an accurate report.*

So Mr Drum went to jail. The account below is an accurate, carefully checked account of five days spent in Johannesburg's Central Jail. Everything described was seen by Mr Drum in person. There is no hearsay, no second-hand description. And the facts contained in this account can be supported by witnesses. The story speaks for itself:

I served five days' imprisonment at the Johannesburg Central Prison from January 20 to January 24. My crime was being found without a night pass five minutes before midnight, and I was charged under the curfew regulations. I was sentenced to a fine of 10s. or five days' imprisonment.

Two constables arrested me at the corner of Rissik and Plein Streets. I was taken to Marshall Square Police Station, charged, searched, given two blankets and locked up in the cells together with 37 others. The night was long. The prison doors kept clanging as more prisoners trickled in during the night. The cell itself was dark. I couldn't tell the day from the night. Only the familiar shout of the young constable carrying a noisy bunch of prison keys told us it was morning.

We had roll-call, breakfast, got back our personal effects and were packed like sardines – over 40 of us – in a truck and delivered to the cells below the magistrate's court. When we got off the truck into the cells below the courts, one elderly-looking prisoner was a little slow to climb off. The prisoners were jostling to get off at once and blocking the way, and when the old man reached

Blacks treated differently than whites

the ground he nearly missed the direction the other prisoners were taking. He looked about and S. saw him. He hit him with his open hand on the temples and told him to wake up.

Before we appeared in court I asked one of the black constables to allow me to phone my employers and my family. He said: 'Go on, voetsek!' Meanwhile white prisoners in the opposite cells were phoning their families and their employers without trouble from a wall telephone near the warder.

After our cases had been heard by the magistrate, we were sent back to the cells. Convicted prisoners who couldn't raise enough money to pay their fines employed various methods to get money. They either borrowed from those who had much less or bartered their clothes, promising to release their benefactors as soon as they were out. Discharged prisoners took messages to relatives of convicted prisoners.

This lasted about two hours; we were checked and taken to Johannesburg Central Prison by truck. We arrived at the prison immediately after one o'clock. From the truck we were given orders to 'shayisa' (close up), fall in twos and 'sharp shoot' (run) to the prison reception office. From then on 'Come on, Kaffir' was the operative phrase from both black and white prison officials, and in all languages.

Many of us who were going to prison for the first time didn't know exactly where the reception office was. Although the prison officials were with us, no one was directing us. But if a prisoner hesitated, slackened his half-running pace and looked round, he got a hard boot kick on the buttocks, a slap on his face or a whipping from the warders. Fortunately there were some second offenders with us who knew where to go. We followed them through the prison's many zig-zagging corridors until we reached the reception office.

Pen taken

The reception office had a terrifyingly brutal atmosphere. It was full of foul language. A number of khaki-uniformed white officials stood behind a long cement bar-like curved counter. They wore the initials 'PSGD' on their shoulders. When they were not joking about prisoners, they were swearing at them and taking down their particulars. Two were taking fingerprints and hitting the prisoners in the face when they made mistakes.

Five long-term prisoners attended to us. One came up to me and said he knew me. I didn't know him. He asked for cigarettes, but I didn't have any. Another told us to take off our watches and money and hold them in our hands. These were to be kept separate from our other possessions. Another asked me for 2s. 6d.; but I had 5d. only and he wasn't interested. He noticed I had a copy of *Time* magazine in my hand and asked for it. I gave it to him. He hid it under the counter so the warders couldn't see it. Later he asked me what paper it was, how old it was and whether it was interesting. After we had undressed, one long-term prisoner demanded my fountain pen.

'That's a fine pen you've got, eh?' he asked. 'How about giving it to me?' I said: 'I'm afraid I can't; it's not my pen, it's my boss's pen.' 'Hi, don't tell me lies, you bastard,' he said, 'what the hell are you doing with your boss's pen in prison? Did you steal it?' he asked. I said I hadn't stolen it. I was using it and had it in my possession when I was arrested. 'Give it here. I want it for my work here; if you refuse you'll see blood streaming down your dirty mouth soon!' I was nervous, but didn't reply. 'Look, you little fool, I'll see that you are well treated in prison if you give me that pen.' The other prisoners looked at me anxiously. I didn't know whether they approved of my giving my pen or not; but their anxious look seemed to suggest that their fate in prison lay in that pen. I gave it away.

Hit on mouth

We were called up to have our fingerprints taken by a white warder. Before taking the impression the warder made a loud complaint that the hand glove he uses when taking impressions was missing. He swore at the long-term prisoner who assists him and told him to find it. The other white prison officials helped him find the glove. He was a stout, middle-aged man, apparently a senior official. He took my impression, examined it and then complained that my hands were wet. He hit me on the mouth with the back of his gloved hand. I rubbed my right thumb on my hair and he took another impression.

From there I ran down to the end of the wide curved desk to have my height taken, and stood beside the measuring rod, naked. The long-term prisoner taking my height asked for my name and checked it against my ticket. He asked for my address and tribe. He then recited something very long to the white official who was writing in a big book opposite him.

My surname and address were wrong. But I dared not complain at that stage for fear of getting more blows. The only words I recognised throughout the recitation was my first name and 'five foot, baasie,' which is three inches below my actual height. Though I was near the measuring stick, he hadn't measured me; nor did he measure the other prisoners. He merely looked at them and assessed their height at sight. When finished with a prisoner, he would throw his ticket on the floor for the prisoner to pick it up and get on with the next one.

We were then taken to the showers in another room. There was neither soap nor a towel. After a few minutes under water we were told to get out, and skip to get dry. Then our prison clothes were thrown at us − a red shirt and a torn white pair of short pants. They looked clean; but the side cap and the white jacket which were issued to me later were filthy. The jacket had dry sweat on the neck.

From then on we were barefoot, and were marched to the hospital for medical examination in double time. Another long-term prisoner lined us up, ordered us to undress and turn our faces to the wall, so that we would not pollute the medical officer with our breath when he came to examine us. While we were being inoculated, another prisoner, apparently being hit by someone for some reason, suddenly ran into the others at the end of the queue and there was a general shuffling round of places. We were then told to face front and make urine. Three prisoners were detained and sent to the hospital as V.D. suspects. Whether the white official in khaki uniform was a doctor or not, I was unable to tell. He didn't examine me. There was a mix-up of prison clothes after that shuffling round and changing of places, so that many prisoners couldn't find their clothes. Everyone picked up the clothes nearest to him. Some said the clothes they were wearing had been worn by the prisoners detained for V.D.

Kicked in stomach

After this we were marched down to the main court of the prison in double time. Here we found different white and black warders and long-term prisoners, who took charge of us. Again we undressed and had our second shower in 30 minutes. I was unable to make out my own clothes after the shower and the skipping. The African warder kicked me in the stomach with the toe of his boot. I tried to hold the boot to protect myself, and fell on my face. He asked if I had had an operation to my stomach. I said no. He looked at me scornfully. I got up, picked up the clothes in front of me and ran to join the others squatting on the floor.

After another roll-call we were marched to the top of the court to collect our food. The dishes were lined in rows and each prisoner picked up the dish nearest to him. The zinc dishes containing the food were rusty. The top of my dish was broken in three places. The food itself was boiled whole mealies with fat. We were marched to No. 7 cell, given blankets and a sleeping mat and locked in. We ate. The time was about 4.30 p.m. Clean water and toilet buckets were installed. But that water wasn't enough for 60 people. The long-term prisoners warned us not to use the water as if we were at our own homes. An old man went to fetch water with his dish at one stage and the long-term prisoner in charge of the cell swore at him. The old man insisted that he was thirsty and continued scooping the water. The long-term prisoner took the water away from him and threw it all over the old man's face.

There was a stinking smell when prisoners used the toilet bucket at night without toilet paper. At 8 p.m. the bell rang and we were ordered to be quiet and sleep. Some prisoners who had smuggled dagga and matches into the cell started conversing in whispers and smoking. The blankets were full of bugs; I turned round and round during the night without being able to sleep, and kept my prison clothes on for protection against bugs.

Filthy hands

We were up at about six o'clock the following morning. I tried to get some water to wash my dish and drink. The dish was full of the previous night's fat, and I didn't know how I was going to do it. But the long-term prisoner shouted at me and ordered me to leave the water alone. I obeyed. He swore at me in Afrikaans, and ordered me to wipe the urine which was overflowing from the toilet bucket with a small sack cloth. I did so. He said I must wipe it dry; but the cloth was so small that the floor remained wet.

He told me to find two other prisoners to help me carry the toilet bucket out, empty it and clean it. It was full of the night's excrement. There were no volunteers, so I slipped to a corner and waited. He saw me and rushed at me. 'What did I tell you, damn it; what did I say?' He slapped me on my left cheek with his right open hand as he spoke. He said he could have me put in solitary confinement if he wished. He could tell the chief warder that I had messed the floor and I would get an additional punishment. I kept quiet. I had done nothing of the sort. Finally he ordered two other prisoners to help me.

We emptied the bucket and washed it as the other prisoners were being lined up in readiness for breakfast. One of my colleagues tried to wash his hands after we had emptied the bucket. The white warder saw him and slashed him with the strap part of his baton. The dish containing my porridge – and many others – still had the previous night's fat. It had been washed in cold water. The breakfast itself was yellow porridge with half-cooked pieces of turnips, potatoes, carrots and other vegetables I could not recognise. No spoons are provided; so I had my breakfast with my stinking soiled hands. I didn't feel like eating, but feared that I would be inviting further trouble.

'Tausa'

After breakfast we were divided into many work spans (parties). I spent my first day with a span cutting grass, pulling out weeds with my hands and pushing wheelbarrows at the Johannesburg Teachers' Training College in Parktown. We walked for about half a mile to our place of work, and I was one of two prisoners carrying a heavy, steel food can, which contained lunch porridge for a party of 16. Two warders escorted us: one white and one black. Once I slackened because we were going down a precipice; my fingers were sore and the burden was heavy.

The old white warder who was carrying a big rifle slashed me on my bare legs with the strap of his baton and said, 'Ek donder jou, Kaffir.'

We returned to jail at 4. We were ordered to undress and 'tausa', a common routine of undressing prisoners when they return from work and searching their clothes, their mouths, armpits and rectum for hidden articles. I didn't know how it was done. I opened my mouth, turned round and didn't jump and clap my hands. The white warder conducting the search hit me with his fist on my left jaw, threw my clothes at me and went on searching the others. I ran off, and joined the food queue.

Hit every day

One night I didn't have a mat to sleep on. Long-term prisoners in charge of the cells sometimes took a bundle of mats to make themselves comfortable beds, to the discomfort of other prisoners. In practice, a prisoner never knows where he will sleep the next day. It is all determined by your speed in 'tausa', food and blanket queues. Invariably a prisoner is always using another prisoner's dirty blankets every night.

In the four days I was in prison – I got a remission of one day – I was kicked or thrashed every day. I saw many other prisoners being thrashed daily. I was never told what was expected of me, but had to guess. Sometimes I guessed wrong and got into trouble.

Long-term and short-term prisoners mixed freely at the prison. For example the famous A– D–, of Alexandra Township, who is doing a '10-year sentence for various crimes', was one of the most important persons in prison during my time. He was responsible for the in and out movements of other prisoners and was respected by prisoners and warders. Though I was a short-term prisoner, I, too, took orders from A–.

It was a common practice for short-term prisoners to give their small piece of meat to long-term prisoners on meat days for small favours such as tobacco, dagga, shoes (which are supposed to be supplied to Coloured prisoners only), wooden spoons – or to ensure that they were always supplied with sleeping mats.

Many other prisoners shared the same fate. There are no directions or rules read or posted in prison. At least I didn't see any. Thrashing time for warders was roll call and breakfast time as well as supper time. For long-term prisoners it was inside the cells at all times. Long-term prisoners thrashed more prisoners more severely and much oftener than the prison officials themselves, and often in the presence of either white or black warders. All prisoners were called Kaffirs at all times.

On the day of our discharge we were mustered in a big hall at breakfast and checked. There was an open lavatory at the corner of the hall. Six men used it, and when the seventh one went a long-term prisoner swore at him and told him to keep his stomach full until he reached home. He said the man belonged to a tribe he detested: a tribe which had killed his brother. After that none of us could use the latrine.

We were then marched to the Reception Office for our personal effects and checking out. The long-term prisoners officiating there told us not to think that we were already out of prison. They kicked and slapped prisoners for the slightest mistake, and sometimes for no mistake at all; and promised them additional sentences if they complained. In the office there was a notice warning prisoners to see that their personal belongings were recorded in the prison's books correctly and exactly as they had brought them. But I dared not complain about my pen which was commandeered on my arrival, lest I be detained. Even the prisoner who took it pretended not to know me.

'Any complaints?'

Before we left prison we were told the Superintendent would address us. We could make complaints to him if we had any. But the fat Zulu warder who paraded us to the yard for the Superintendent's inspection said we must tell him everything was all right if we want to leave prison.'This is a court of law,' he said. 'You are about to go home, but before you leave this prison the big boss of the prison will address you. He will ask you if you have any complaints. Now I take it that you all want to go to your homes – to your wives and children – you don't want to stay here. So if the big boss asks you if everything is all right say, "Yes, Sir." If he says have you any complaints say, "No, Sir." You hear?'

In a chorus we said 'Yes.'

Just then one prisoner complained that his Kliptown train ticket was missing from his things. It was a season ticket. The Zulu warder pulled him aside and said, 'You think you're clever, eh? you'll see!' He put him at the tail-end of the parade. The Superintendent came and we answered him as instructed. Most of us were seeing him for the first time. The Zulu warder said nothing about the complaint of the man from Kliptown. Later as we were going to collect our monies from the pay office, the man from Kliptown was escorted to the Reception Office to see the famous fierce discharge officer, C. C. said the man's papers showed that he was charged at Fordsburg and appeared in Johannesburg. The fat Zulu warder said in broken Afrikaans: 'He's mad, sir.' He gave the man a hard slap in the face with his open hand and said: 'You're just wasting the boss's time, eh? On your way . . . voetsek!' And the man sneaked out.

One by one we zigzagged our way out of the prison's many doors and gates and lined up in two's in front of the main and final gate. We were ordered to leave prison quietly and in pairs when the small gate was open. If we blocked the gate we would be thrashed. We were to come out in the order of the line. The man on the left would go out first and the one on the right would follow. The gate was opened. We saw freedom and blocked the gate in our anxiety. If they thrashed us we couldn't feel it . . . we didn't look back!

What Should Be Done . . .

This account by Mr Drum describes nothing extraordinary in South Africa. Most Africans living in towns can expect to be sent to jail sometime during their lives. Every year nearly a quarter of a million people in South Africa are sent to jail, out of a total population of 12 million. (In 1951, the last year on record, it was 245 950.) The events in Mr Drum's story are common knowledge to many of our readers.

Mr Drum's account makes it clear that prisoners are in fact 'treated like beasts', that they are degraded, humiliated, and leave jail in a worse moral state than when they went in. This prison does not cure criminals; it makes them.

But this is not the purpose of imprisonment. Prisons are not only meant to punish, but to reform. The law intends prisons themselves to be law-abiding, correctly-run institutions.

The treatment described by Mr Drum, and scores of other ex-prisoners, is contrary to the spirit and to the letter of the prison regulations.

The prison regulations should, according to Act 13 of 1911, 'be placed in conspicuous parts of every convict prison or gaol in such a manner as to be legible to officers, convicts and prisoners therein.' Mr Drum never saw these regulations in jail, nor did the other prisoners.

Regulations demand that searching should be conducted with due regard to decency and self-respect. We have shown how searching is conducted.

Regulations demand (No. 475) that 'Convicts shall wash their hands and face on rising in the morning and in the evening before supper.' Mr Drum was not able to wash at any time, after his admission.

Regulations demand (No. 410) that as far as possible all classes of prisoners shall be kept separate from one another, and that (No. 411) 'Penals will not be allowed to mix with, sleep with, eat with or talk to men in the other classes.' Mr Drum ate, worked and talked with murderers and hardened long-term prisoners, who gave orders to him and other petty offenders.

How have these appalling conditions come about? Why have prisons been allowed to become breeding places of barbarity, crime and vice? Why can the regulations be openly flaunted?

It is simply because prisoners have no effective means of redress. They dare not complain; they know that if they do so, they will very likely be beaten, punished, or refused remission.

Magistrates and visitors have stated that they interview prisoners in private, and ask them for complaints and receive none. But Mr Drum has shown how prisoners are intimidated even before they are asked for complaints. They are at the mercy of the warders and the long-term criminals who are given power over them.

Everyone must wish for the bestial treatment described in this article to be stopped.

It can only be done if the prisons are properly supervised and inspected, and if prisoners are able to make complaints without fear of punishment.

In 1947 the Penal Reform Commission, presided over by a well-known Judge, Mr Justice Lansdown, expressed dissatisfaction with conditions and treatment in prisons. In particular the Commission stressed the importance of allowing prisoners full opportunity for complaint.

'Much care and discretion,' says the Commission (paragraph 695) 'on the part of the inspectors, superintendents, gaolers and visiting magistrates is necessary to ensure not only that every inmate of the institution inspected shall know and be given the opportunity to make complaints, but that he should have the assurance that this is a matter of right which can be exercised without hindrance or fear of consequence.'

The Commission recommends that 'Inspectors of prisons should be appointed whose sole attention is directed to the duties of the position . . .'

Drum *believes that only by appointing such inspectors and giving them exceptional powers can the appalling abuses in prisons be put right. They should be allowed free access to prisons, without warning, and opportunities to observe normal prison routine. The breaches of prison regulations are in fact so frequent that only careful warning and preparations beforehand can have concealed them so long from inspectors.*

At the same time, the system by which long-term prisoners, who are hardened criminals, are put in a position of authority over petty offenders should be abolished immediately. The Lansdown Commission agrees (par. 194) 'that these (long-sentence) prisoners are apt to abuse the temporary authority given them and to deal harshly with the entrants to the prisons, hustling them in order and even, in some cases, accompanying this by blows. Any such practice of employing prisoners in such positions of authority should cease forthwith . . .'

Obviously no institution can be run in a law-abiding way, when the most hardened criminals are given responsible positions.

On leaving the jail, prisoners should be carefully questioned as to whether they have complaints, and it should be made clear that there can be no possibility of reprisals.

A Commission of Enquiry should be appointed immediately to investigate the many complaints made by prisoners, and to find out how these abuses have been allowed. Mr Drum would be glad to co-operate fully in supplying a great deal of information, and providing sworn evidence.

The present state of prisons is degrading a large section of the population, bringing the law into disrespect, and breeding more criminals. No country can afford such folly. It must be stopped.

[March 1954]

Under the Blue-gum Trees

DYKE H. SENTSO

At first, a deep-rooted suspicion and mistrust and then a fear, ugly and profound. Men went about their daily work with their ears a-cocked, their eyes wide open. A rustle among the leaves, a whisper in the night . . . and men's hearts stopped still with misgiving. An unguarded word here, a misplaced word there and men strove feverishly to interpret them into an intelligible whole. Suspicion sprouted and grew . . . But nothing happened. The people waited with their breaths held in. Two years, four years . . . Perhaps the fears were unfounded, the doubts misplaced. The people waited still. Ten years, fifteen . . . thirty . . . all was still . . . Ha! . . .

But suddenly the suspicions were redoubled and a fear, stark and naked throttled the hearts of men. They slept with their hearts in their throats, pistols under their pillows. During the day they practised shooting locusts . . . at night locusts shot them. In the cities they barred and barricaded their doors and windows . . . in the farms they hedged in their homes with barbed wire and thin-meshed wire netting, and allowed huge dogs to saunter arrogantly within their yards. Then men slept better, with pistols for cushions and dogs for guardian angels . . . Such was the time when our story begins . . .

Once at home, loneliness descended upon the family with implacable force. Japie Genade went aimlessly from room to room, then he went outside only to re-enter the house. When he went outside again, he watched his son chasing butterflies in the garden; with unseeing eyes he saw him trample one flower after another and he was startled as much as the boy when his wife suddenly called out: 'Gert, get out of the garden!' Gert looked once at his mother and then he vanished round a corner of the house. A smile creased Japie's face. Saturday, he thought, Saturday!

He paced the verandah slowly with his hands behind his back. Just what could he do? The idea came like a flash. He walked briskly into the house.

'Ma,' he said, 'I am going to tell Moiloa to collect all the sheep tomorrow for counting.' And before his wife replied, he was already well on his way towards the stable.

It was most gratifying to see how the six dark men, some with hands held aloft and others clutching their tattered hats in their hands, jumped up respectfully to greet him. It was even more gratifying to see how they vied with each other to speak to him. Genade looked about him deliberately and felt secretly proud that when he looked at them, little black faces vanished around corners and big heads were jerked back quickly at doors and windows through which they were peeping. He got down from the horse and mingled with the people. Soon a glassful of cold drink and cakes were brought to him. He drank off the drink at a gulp and munched at the cakes happily . . .

'You see,' said the old man, 'he is a pure white man.' Genade did not hear. He was watching the antics of the leader with obvious enjoyment. He raised one leg to imitate him, then suddenly he dropped his foot. The words of his wife came to him. You could dance too, she had said, but remember, you are white! Suddenly he left the crowd and stood apart by himself. He was no longer part of these people. He was now a mere onlooker . . . foreign. His beaming face sobered abruptly. He walked to his horse and mounted it. He was going home.

He turned his horse and rode through a subtle aroma of cooking porridge and meat which issued from the fires in the reed enclosures. As he rode, he heard the deep rumble of men's voices fade slowly away. He heard the prattle of children's voices and the happy laughter of the women die slowly out. He stopped his horse then, seized by a strong desire to return to the people and to mingle with them as he had done a few minutes ago. He had felt very happy then, the people loving him the more for his action, but now . . .

He looked at his home. His wife was there, he knew, . . . cooking. Perhaps even then, the wireless was playing. But a wireless was such poor consolation for company. When his wife and he wanted company, they had to go to town or visit their neighbours. He could go to Karel even now, but it was impolite to pester one's friend with visits. He turned his horse and looked longingly at the stad. Why could he not return there? It was so simple and yet so difficult . . .?

A voice suddenly spoke close by, frightening him and when he turned round Moiloa was standing below him with his hat in the air. 'Good day, Morena!' he was saying.

'O, is it you? Moiloa, where do you come from? Among the trees . . .?'

'No, Morena . . . from beyond them . . . from the graves.' Japie nodded understandingly. 'But you go to your son's grave often, Moiloa. Is that good?'

'It is good Baas. When I have been to his grave I feel well. It is as if he tells me what to do. You see he was my eldest son. When he died I was left alone. My other son is only twelve years. If I should die what will happen to my children?'

Genade did not answer this question. Indeed he did not know how to answer it, so he changed the subject. He told Moiloa about the sheep and then: 'O, ja, next Saturday I want you to get ready to go with me to Baas Meyer's farm. There will be a great show there. Is that clear?'

'It is clear Baas . . .'

'Well, goodbye' . . . Genade trotted slowly homewards.

When Moiloa arrived at the village, the men were drinking and talking in a room specially reserved for the purpose. They did not see him come and when he approached, they were talking about white men. Justice was speaking.

'A white man does not understand humble stammering respect. He mistakes it for stuttering stupidity . . . and when once he thinks you are stupid, he makes you work like a donkey. Now I never allow that . . . I show him at once that I am not as stupid as he thinks.'

When Moiloa joined them, a sudden guilty silence fell over them. Moiloa was their farm captain but they did not trust him. There were stories current about Moiloa . . . that he agreed to everything he was told, that he curried favour and above all that he had been the cause of many dismissals on the farm. Jantjie felt alarmed that he had been overheard. He spoke quickly, trying to recover lost ground.

'You know,' he said, 'Genade is a very good man. Little wonder that his workers stay long here and work well for him. Look, I have been here five years and I have no intention of leaving yet.'

'Yes,' agreed another, 'you are right. Genade is a very good man. I have never worked for any one farmer for more than four years, and yet I have been here six years. I do not know what will cause me to leave here.'

'Brother,' said Moiloa, 'you must not speak like that. There are many things to cause you to leave here.'

The men sat bolt upright and looked at each other slyly. 'Like what?' they shouted in chorus.

Moiloa filled his pipe deliberately, lit it and smoked in silence for a while. Then he asked abruptly: 'Have you ever been to Baas De Beer's farm?' Every one of them had been there. 'Well, what did you see there?'

They had seen many things. They had seen sheep and cattle and a new house being built and lands filled with sunflower.

'Did you see the number of ruins there?' The men looked at each other and tried to recollect how many empty huts they had seen, but they failed. Moiloa told them. 'Six,' he said, 'six! They did not leave because they wanted to. De Beer did not chase them away. Something else did . . . a roaring . . . two, three roaring monsters which do in a day what thirty men do in ten days.'

'What are they?' they asked.

'Go and see them for yourselves. They roar continuously during the day and when night falls, they put on their lights and continue to roar. At night they look like so many ghosts in the mealie-lands and do the white farmers love them! You will see what will happen when they come,' he warned.

The men looked at each other again. 'Moiloa is talking in parables,' one said. 'What did you say?' asked another. The first one replied, 'Moiloa is talking in parables.'

'Nothing,' said the second. 'Moiloa is delving in deeper tricks!'

The mistiness of dawn dissipated slowly and 'The Orchards' opened her silvery gates wide in anticipation and welcome to the many cars that would soon pass through to see the show. Above the main gate, in artistic lettering ran the simple words 'The Farmers' Show'.

In a big open space under a row of trees nestled fifteen brand new tractors, and in the morning sun were ranged in careful order all kinds of farm implements. There were planters and windmills; ploughs and trailers; milk-separators and Diesel engines; everything from shellers and waterboring machines to windchargers. Mr Hoarding stood at the entrance and welcomed the first visitors to his show. 'The Orchards' hummed with life.

Moiloa clambered down from the rear of the van and stood silent at what he saw. A new type of tractor was pulling a new type of plough which was turning the soil with the least effort. Another tractor was turning in circles in the least possible space and Mr Hoarding was running here and there making explanations wherever he went whilst a loudspeaker kept up a running commentary.

At noon a pause was declared and whilst the people sipped their coffee or enjoyed their tea, a lecture was given. Moiloa did not understand everything that was said but he did grasp one or two things. He heard, for instance, that all those implements were intended to raise the output of every farm to a maximum, but that they would lower the cost to a minimum. That with three tractors pulling the latest ploughs and only three Native labourers, more work could be done than by employing forty labourers, and that now farmers could go to bed with the knowledge that their farms were freed from that great curse of the farmer . . . a lot of idle hands!

Moiloa led a few friends from one exhibit to another and when they had seen everything, he led them aside and swept his hands from side to side. 'These, my friends, are wonderful inventions!' he said.

'Ha!' they said, with their hands on their mouths as they expressed amazement.

'But these things are the things I was telling my friends at home about. You see them yourselves. They do a hundred men's work in one day! They do a hundred men's work in one day! They are very good my friends but some of us will be the sorrier for their presence!'

Genade came beaming to Moiloa then. 'I am going to buy two tractors,' he said.

'How many Morena?'

'Two, Moiloa!'

'Ja,' said Moiloa.

'You do not seem to be pleased Moiloa?'

Moiloa rubbed his face with his hands uneasily. 'I am pleased Morena,' he said.

Back at the Huis, the little white boy looked east and then looked west. He looked down, scratched his head and then looked up. The Saturday sun shone brightly down at him. He turned his head from side to side and wished he had gone with his father to the show. Anyway it did not matter much for soon his father would be back and then they would go to town. Meantime what to do? His eyes rested on the towering leaves of the blue-gum trees and an idea shone through his eyes. Yes, he had found a solution to his regular Saturday problem of what to do with twelve hours of no school, no arithmetic and no real work to do. He rushed into the yard and when he came out he was holding a catapult. He ran into the plantation whistling.

The little black boy was already in the plantation. When he saw the little white boy, his face spread in a happy smile of welcome. 'Why are you running Gert?' he asked in broken Afrikaans. The little white boy placed two fingers on his mouth and jerked his index finger towards the Huis.

'My mother,' he said, 'she always says I spoil her garden.' And then without further thought on the matter he asked: 'Where are the birds?'

The birds screamed wildly among the branches, their eyes wild with fear. They flew from branch to branch, from tree to tree but still the pebbles missed them by fractions of an inch. Some hid in their nests, others flew into the air but not knowing where to go, they landed again on the trees to scamper away panic-stricken again when the pebbles hit against the branches with a thud!

'Gert,' said the little black boy, 'these catapults are no good . . . they miss too much.'

'Ja,' said the white boy, 'they are no good . . .' He stopped a little and thought a while. Suddenly he began running. Over his shoulder he shouted: 'I am coming!'

In a little while he was back, but the little black boy gaped in surprise.

'It is a gun,' he said, 'where did you get it?'

'Still,' said the white boy, 'it is my father's.' The black boy came nearer to examine the gun and then suddenly he retreated. The white boy laughed. 'You are afraid!' he said. The black boy continued to retreat. The white boy called to him. 'Man, it cannot shoot . . . it has no bullets . . . look!'

There was a shattering report and both boys fell down like broken trees. The white boy rose and looked at his mate. Blood was gushing out through a small hole above the left eye. Gert turned then, and fled with bulging eyes, out of the plantation towards his home.

Japie Genade saw his son running out of the plantation from the van which was then coming towards home. He saw his wife, too, rush out of the house and run towards the boy. He pressed the accelerator hard and the van shot forward. He saw his son point to the plantation. Then his wife saw him. She ran towards the van. He shouted from the van: 'What is it?'

'Gert,' he said, 'he has shot a boy.'

'Where . . .?'

'In the plantation.'

Moiloa heard the words from the rear of the van. When the van stopped he was running towards the plantation followed hard by Genade . . . In the plantation, they stopped suddenly and looked . . . the little black boy was lying as he had fallen. The two men looked at each other . . . no words passed between them . . . then the white man stepped forward and touched the boy. A tear rolled quickly down his cheek . . . Moiloa nodded.

'There is no more life in him,' he said, and he stood there and looked at his master, then he looked at his son and then he just stood there . . . stunned.

There was no voice under the blue-gum trees, no breeze when they lowered the little coffin into the grave beside his brother. There was no tears, the tears had dried up. People just stood near the little mound and dropped their heads. Only one person cried . . . Japie Genade.

When the first tractor arrived, Genade drove it himself and was very excited. He showed it to his boys. 'It cost me a lot of money. A lo–t of money,' he said impressively. The men looked at it. It was red as the setting sun and roared like a charging bull. 'The other is not like this,' he said. 'It is as blue as the sky.'

The men clustered around the tractor. Then they shook their heads sadly. One asked, 'Do you remember what Moiloa said?'

'I remember, my brother.'

'Well, those monsters have arrived.'

The men shook their heads and went their ways. The following morning early, one neighbour peeped through the window of his house and spoke with a hushed voice. 'Have you heard that the Ditsebes are going away?'

'I have heard brother. Moiloa is at it again . . .'

'No,' said the first. 'It is not Moiloa's action . . . this is retrenchment!'

A few hours later two young men walked towards the mealie-lands. They spoke little, then . . . 'Have you heard that Moiloa is going away?'

'No, why . . . has he quarrelled with Genade?'

'No, they have not quarrelled. Genade said it was very difficult to part with Moiloa but his financial position compelled him to retrench all the old hands.'

'What did Moiloa say?'

'He asked Genade whether his action was not caused by the fear that he Moiloa would one day kill him because his son (Gert) had shot his little boy? Genade denied this vehemently.'

'Well, do you know where he is going to?'

'I do not know, my brother.'

The men fell into silence and then they shook their heads sadly. 'Haai,' they said. Then after a while:

'Perhaps tomorrow it is you.'

'Perhaps tomorrow it is you.'

And beyond the blue-gum trees, in the misty greyness of the morn, before two raised mounds of cold earth, an old man spoke softly with the tenderness of the depth of his heart. 'Farewell, my sons!' he said.

When Moiloa reached home, his wife looked at him. The look spoke and he understood. 'Excuse me,' he said, 'but I am an old man now and I love the quiet and the peace.' His face twitched, there was sorrow in his eyes. He spoke softly: 'I hoped too much. I hoped that someone else would move instead of me.' His children looked at him. There was fear and doubt in their eyes.

'Don't look at me like that my children, don't look at me like that. Where is the horse? I must go and look for work once again.' The eldest girl of eight years came running to her father. 'Let me go and look for work, father.' Moiloa smiled and then he sobered. 'I will go my child!'

'Can you give me work, my Baas?'

'I cannot give you work, my man. I am using tractors. Can you drive a tractor? No, but you are old and you cannot drive it. Go to Baas Adams. Perhaps you will get work there . . .'

'Can you give me work, my Baas?'

'I cannot give you work, my boy. I have bought another Jeep and I am using Jeeps. Have you been to Baas Michael? Try him. Perhaps he has work for you.'

'Come Bless, the journey is long, the quest uncertain. Do not tire so soon. Remember, the children at home are waiting . . .!'

'Can you give me work, my Baas?'

'I cannot give you work, my friend. I am in the co-operative and the tractors of the co-operative are many and they have drivers too. Baas Viljoen wants hands. Go to him!'

Even Bless had heard. He pricked his ears and was impatient to go. 'There, Bless, there is work for us in front.'

'Can you give me work, my Baas?'

'Yes. I can give you work. I have work for many hands. Come, let us make a contract. I will give you twenty shillings a month and food and water. Have you any cattle? Yes . . . I will use them on the farm and your daughters and your sons too!'

'For twenty shillings, my Baas . . .?'

'For twenty nice, shiny, round shillings. Come, surely that is good pay. Times are hard and I want to buy tractors too!'

'But I got thirty shillings where I worked and it was insufficient.'

'I cannot give you so much. It is too much for me . . . and for you too. Look, you are old and you cannot do what you used to do. Will you work?'

The sun was sinking fast in the west but the sun had sunk in Moiloa's heart. Twenty shillings . . .?

'I must tell my wife and my children first, Baas, but twenty shillings is little money.'

'It is not little, my friend. It is a lot of money and there are many people who want work!'

The sun had set when Moiloa reached home. The sun would never rise in Moiloa's heart. A fire was burning low in the house and when he sat and cupped his chin in his hands, the fire burned lower still. There could never be another day. It would always be darkness and night. The children sensed the sadness and shifted closer to each other. Moiloa bent his head and brooded. Wood was put into the fire . . . there was smoke and silence, the one worse than the other. Suddenly Moiloa raised his head. His voice was confident, there was hope in his eyes.

'I am going to apply for a stand in the location tomorrow!'

The flames leaped up in the fire. The wood crackled and cracked. The little children giggled and tittered and Moiloa's wife looked at her husband with a song in her heart. Yes . . . the location. That was what she wanted. That was what every farm labourer strove for . . . that was her ambition. She repeated the little word to herself: '. . . location . . . location . . .' This was living!

'Can you give me a stand in the location, Baas?'

'A stand in the location? Who are you? Where do you come from?'

'I come from Baas Genade . . . Baas Japie Genade.'

'O, yes, I know him . . . why did you leave him? . . . but no, I cannot give you a stand in the location.' He repeated the words. 'I cannot give you a stand in the location.' Another white man had entered and had heard. He looked at Moiloa. His heart wept for him.

'Why can't you give him a stand in the location?'

'Why can't I give him a stand?' The first man repeated incredulously, '. . . Why . . . ? Because who is going to work on the farms if all these poor people come to the locations? . . . Besides the locations are full already . . . filled with old idle hands, and they are supposed to be labour reserves for the towns!' The other white man was not satisfied. They argued, they almost wrangled. Then suddenly the one gave in. 'You know,' he said, 'it is unfair . . . it is unsympathetic . . . but,' he said, 'what can I do? It is against the law!'

Moiloa had heard and had understood. There was no hope for him here. No haven for him there. He must go back to the farms and seek a new home. He looked forlornly about. The question hit him hard . . . where? He felt very tired and there was something wrong with his knees. He could scarcely get on the horse . . .

'Baas Viljoen, will you take me on?'

'O, is it you? Let me see. Yes . . . but I have since found out that I cannot pay you twenty shillings. I will give you eighteen shillings. Will you work?'

There was a queer film in the eyes, a queer trembling of the voice, as if it was hard to speak . . . 'I will work, Baas!'

The branches and twigs of the mimosa trees brushed and crackled loudly as a dry branch was broken here and a twig was picked up there. Then suddenly the woman, with a bundle of firewood on her head, stopped short in her tracks, and listened. Before her, a man, with hands held aloft and looking steadfastly above him, was praying . . .

'Please, Lord, take me to your land of promise and rest where there is neither want nor care . . . where there is neither sorrow nor night . . .'

The woman did not wait for the man to finish his prayers. She retraced her steps carefully and when she reached her home she made fire as if nothing had happened. When her husband came in, he found breakfast ready for him, and as he began to eat in silence, his wife abruptly spoke. 'Moiloa, I want to die . . .!'

He was shocked and for a moment he could not speak. Then . . .

'What did you say?'

'I said I want to die.'

'Why do you want to die?'

'Because I think it is wrong for me to live a life of despair and have no hope for the future . . . it were best that I should die.'

'But how can you die? What about the children and what about me? Do you lack anything . . . are you not satisfied with your lot?'

She did not answer him immediately. Instead she put more fuel into the fire.

'You do not want me to die?'

'I do not want you to die?'

She turned then and looked steadily at her husband. 'What is it?' he asked.

'I am sorry, but this morning you were praying to die. Is that right?' He was ashamed and embarrassed. It was only natural and human that he should attempt to deny it but when he looked at his wife, true light dawned on him.

'I am sorry, my dear. I did not realise how my prayer would affect you. Please pardon me . . . I shall work and hope . . .!'

Mr Japie Genade was very happy . . . doubly happy. It was the happiness of success. He had just parted with his last guest who had congratulated him on his recent election to the Town Council. Mr and Mrs Genade sat on the verandah of their new home in town and enjoyed their happiness in silence.

Mrs Genade thought of her previous home on the farm. She had lived well there. But many times she had been very lonely. When her husband was away, she had suffered from a terrible fear . . . the fear of being alone with many black people around her. Her husband had often reprimanded her for it, but the fear had remained real to her . . . Her husband had told her that it was imaginary . . . black people were faithful and when treated well could always be relied upon. But she read newspapers and in the newspapers were many stories . . . like the ones she had read in her old history book a few years ago at school . . . They must be true! On the farm there were jackals, too, but she did not fear these. People too told strange eerie ghost stories . . . but these did not frighten her . . . her fear was the fear of black people. That was why she had kept her husband's gun . . . the one her son had used in the accident . . . in the corner of the kitchen, behind the dresser. There it was within easy reach in case of an emergency, but the emergency never came. What came instead was tragedy and remorse . . . She thought of the incident . . . the shiny buttons of the police uniforms . . . the stricken faces of the white and black people . . . their questions . . .

'Where was your husband?'

'Why was the gun kept within such easy access?'

'Were the boys friends, did they often play together?'

She shook herself free from these thoughts . . . all that was over now . . . she had a lovely house in town and many friends. A policeman passed her house every day on his regular beat . . . this was living!

'Ma,' said Genade, 'that was a neat little deal I made, eh? Twenty thousand pounds with surface rights to the farm . . . Ha! . . . I always thought there was gold on the farm . . . It brought me in a tidy little sum and I now can think of that little business I always dreamed to build for myself. It will be pleasant to live here.'

His wife did not answer him. She was much too happy for that. She remembered the nice words that people had spoken to her during the day . . . how people looked at her when she walked in the street. She could almost hear them: 'That is Mrs Genade, you know, the wife of Mr Genade who sold his farm for twenty thousand pounds! She had always desired a mink . . . perhaps . . .'

A dark old man passed in the street. Genade stared at him. 'Moiloa,' he called . . . 'Moiloa!' The man stopped and looked at them, 'Did you call?' he asked. He came nearer. Genade saw his mistake then. The man was not Moiloa but he looked very much like him. 'I am sorry,' he said, 'but I thought you were a certain servant who once worked for me.' The black man went on his way.

But this incident had spoiled the day for Genade. He wondered how Moiloa was faring. His son, he remembered, had killed . . . he corrected hurriedly, had been the cause of Moiloa's son's death. He remembered, too, that it had been found to be accidental shooting at the inquest and that Moiloa had felt the same and had shown no animosity. He remembered vividly Moiloa coming to him after the inquest . . .

'It is all over now,' he had said. 'I am very glad . . . one does not always want to talk about a sad thing, and to remember that they were such friends.' Genade remembered these words and he decided.

The following day he found Moiloa hard at work, with the sun beating down on him. The oxen looked at him with anticipation, they thought he had come to release them. No sweat ran down Moiloa's face. Perhaps he had no more sweat left in him. Moiloa looked at Genade . . . Could it be him? Yes, it was. Genade had not changed, but the clothes and the car . . . Genade spoke.

'I have come to fetch you. You know I live in town now. I have sold the farm.' Moiloa was radiant with happiness, but he did not lose his balance.

'Where will I live, Baas? I cannot live in a little room at the back, you know . . . I have a family and some animals. Can you get me a stand in the location?'

Genade raised himself up . . . to the height of a rich man. 'I will see about that,' he said.

'It will be difficult,' Moiloa warned.

Genade raised himself to his full height . . . the height of a rich town councillor.

'With me,' he said, 'many things are possible. You know that, don't you?'

Moiloa knew, and he knew, too, that with white people, many things were possible . . . were made possible . . . But that did not matter at the moment. What mattered was that he would get a stand . . . his life's ambition.

'Thank you very much,' he said . . . and then 'Thank You very much.'

[April 1954]

Dead End!

JAMES MATTHEWS

The messengers walked past the council room on tiptoe. The noise of the strife within reached to the end of the passage. The group around the table were on their feet, unmercifully attacking the lone speaker, who managed with dignity to let his voice be heard above the uproar.

'Gentlemen, believe me, if you could only see the utter misery and wretched conditions under which these people have to live. Now winter is at hand, and the ensuing rain will add to their discomfort. In our tourist booklets we are apt to describe our city as fair but forget to add the hideous blot which mars its fairness. Gentlemen, Windermere is our duty.'

'Duty! Bah!' they roared. 'Our duty is to the city, to beautify it, to protect it, and not the welfare of a pack of Natives! Let them go back to where they came from or let those for whom they labour, look after them.'

He bowed his head before their onslaught.

The voice of the chairman ended their baiting.

'Gentlemen, the meeting is adjourned until tomorrow morning, same time.'

The heat from the sun drew the moisture from the puddles in the road, cracking the edges. On a piece of sacking in a doorway, a bitch was sprawled, surrounded by a quivering mass of hungry puppies, each hanging on to a teat, their sides contracting and expanding with the vigour of their sucking. A striped pig lumbered in their direction, changed its mind and went off to investigate the pile of refuse stacked at the side of the road.

Inside the shanty a youth was stripped to the waist. He speculated his bony chest, shrugged and pulled on his jersey. A tattered windbreaker was put on over the jersey and he was dressed. At the edge of the dresser a zoll was dangling.

He took a deep pull, filling his lungs with it. He let it out slowly, the dagga smoke forming into intricate patterns. He had to hold on to the dresser as a coughing spasm wracked his body. He felt dizzy and took another puff. Opening a drawer he took out a gun, stashed beneath the clothing. He gazed at the gun and fondled it, then slipped it in at the side of his waist, the jersey covering it. He took a hat from behind the door and with a final glance at the mirror, he left.

His canvas shoes sloshed through the wet mud, grey sand-flies fluttered up at each step and sank back to the gaping holes. The grunting pig moved reluctantly as he passed. Skirting the waterlogged footpath, he made his way to the gravel road. He passed innumerable shanties like his own. In the doorways the occupants were lounging. Through a window came the tinny sound of jazz music from a gramophone. He could hear the throb of the drums.

In the doorway a girl was swaying. A tight sweater was pulled over her hips, accentuating the breasts, the tips pointing to the sky. He watched the movements of her body. She returned his gaze. His mouth formed a word. She withdrew from the doorway and pulled down the sack which served as a door. He pulled his narrow shoulders back, holding his body tight. He swaggered as he walked. He knew she was watching him. He turned his head. She didn't pull back. He walked on whistling. She would not forget him. Not this one. He had read the invitation too clearly in her eyes.

At the bus terminus a dice game was in progress. He idled over and watched. He knew most of the players and returned their greetings. He took some small change from his pocket and waited his chance. A four came up. He took everything he had and faced the player.

'Cover this; no four.'

The player grunted his assent.

The dice rolled. It turned up eight, then six, then ten, box cars, then a one. The other dice rolled on. It turned a three, his heart sank, then it rolled over, it was a four, a two, then it settled on a six. The dice stood six to one. With a smile he raked in his winnings.

It was his turn to throw. He picked up the dice and caressed them with his fingers. He shook them softly and threw. A six and five smiled back at him. He doubled his money and threw a seven. He covered all his bets on a five and came through with a four and one. The game was almost finished. He had most of the money in front of him. He had to make a three-way point. No one was eager to cover him. He rolled a seven and the dice passed him.

He withdrew from the game and counted his stake. His hal-a-duf had brought him over three pounds. He grinned. He could afford to be generous. He watched them play for what little was left and after a few turns the game broke up.

One of the small fry was dispatched for some dagga and a half-jack brandy and soon they were lighting zolls. The small fry had their own zoll.

The tiny living room was crowded. Couples occupied the chairs, the wheezing old sofa, overflowed to the ground, sitting with their backs to the wall. He threaded his way carefully and made his way to the kitchen.

In the kitchen, a middle-aged woman was busy at a small petrol tin, scooping jugs of skomfaan, the mixture bubbling in the tin. She moved ponderously as she shifted the jugs to the table. Her black face was wreathed in smiles at his entry.

'You've been away a long time. I thought you had forgotten all about your poor auntie.'

'You ought to know better, Auntie. Turn around and close your eyes, I have a present for you.'

He pulled her around so that she faced the wall, she twisted in his grasp and squealed like a child being teased. 'Now quit your fooling and hand it over like a nice boy.' He made her plead for a few minutes longer, then produced a small bag which he dangled in front of her face. She grabbed at it and waddled to a chair.

Squeaks of delight came from her as she dug her fingers into the depths of the bag and transferred a powder-coated turkish delight to her mouth. He grinned as she stuffed herself, the powder forming a halo round her mouth. With a last lick at her fingers, she finished off the bag, throwing it to the floor with a sigh.

'Auntie, have you got something for me to drink? – and I don't mean this dishwater you're serving.' He looked with distaste at the bubbling brew. 'It's a wonder how they can still get it in.'

From behind the stove, she produced a half flask of peppermint brandy.

'Here, how's this for a pleaser?'

'Do I drink this alone?'

She looked at him quizzically.

She called out, 'Lena!' From the living room came a girl. She was dressed in a brown dress which hugged her in the places which brought the blood rushing to his temples. She looked over-ripe. He could not guess her age; she had the appearance of a young girl but her eyes belied it, showing an ageless wisdom.

His auntie said, 'Do you like it?'

He had to swallow deeply before he could reply.

With an amused smile she spoke to the girl. 'He has a bottle and he is lonely.'

He followed the girl. She took him down the passage and up a few steps which led to the roof. Underneath a pigeon loft was a mattress and two blankets.

He was shy. The nearness of the girl excited him, he could smell her, the woman smell, prickling at his nostrils, tearing at his chest.

The girl handed him the bottle. His head shook as he poured. He swallowed his fast and poured another, sipping it a bit slower. The liquor warming him, making him more bold.

He placed the bottle out of reach and slipped his arm over her, his hand searching for her breast. His fingertips caressed her nipple. He could feel her breast, straining against the fabric of her dress. He pressed his mouth on hers, her tongue darting in and out of his mouth like a small snake, setting him on fire. He pushed her down.

Afterwards as they leaned apart, gazing at the sky, he questioned her. 'Do you come up her often? Have you known many men?'

'Your aunt calls and I obey.' Her voice sounded as if it was not part of her.

He was angry at her reply and felt as if he was betrayed. He pulled her towards him. 'From now on you belong to me, understand?'

After a short walk, he reached the centre of the town and he made for the theatre district. Cars were parked in rows. He left these and walked round the block. On the other side of the block was a side street. He waited his chance. He walked past each car, pressing at the handles. They were locked. Then one sagged beneath the weight of his hand. He swung the door open and slipped behind the wheel. Luck was with him, the key was in the ignition switch. He pulled out the brake and the car rolled down the slight incline on its own weight. Switching on the engine, he pulled away.

The car was a late forty model, of the kind which would not draw undue attention. He went down Dock Road, in the direction of the foreshore. The car rolled smoothly on the Marine Drive, the tyres singing as it made contact with the asphalt. He felt elated at the thought of the powerful engine at his bidding. He pressed down on the accelerator and the car leaped forward. From the corner of his eye he could see the telephone poles falling behind like wheat being cut by a giant sickle.

He noticed that the petrol gauge showed a quarter full and made for the main road. Nearing Woltemade, he spotted a garage and pulled in. The attendant was fast asleep in the little office next to the petrol pumps. He hooted a few times. Rubbing the sleep from his eyes, the attendant moved towards him.

'Fill it up.' He barked at the attendant.

The attendant stumbled to the rear of the car. Unscrewing the cap, he pushed the snout of the pump into the gaping hole, the petrol falling with a gurgling sound. The attendant was too slow and the petrol overflowed before he could shut it off. He wiped it dry with a greasy rag which protruded from the side of his overall.

A plan formed in his mind as the attendant advanced for the money.

'Have you got change for a fiver?'

The attendant nodded in the affirmative and jerked his head in the direction of the office. He followed the attendant to the office, and as the attendant reached out his hand for the money, a gun was jammed into his stomach.

'Where is the money?'

The attendant pointed to a large leather wallet lying on the desk.

'Now move over and face the wall.'

He opened the wallet. There were a few bills and some silver. He scooped them into his pocket. Spying a tin of scotch tape, he pulled off a few strips and applied them to the phone. With a warning to the attendant, he backed to the door. Slamming the door, he ran to the car and with a roar of the engines he pulled away.

He smiled as he thought of the scotch tape. It was a clever move. The attendant would have to waste a few minutes before he could ring the police. At his get-away, he had travelled to the north. He swung the car down a side street and made for the national road. In a few minutes he was headed back to town. Only half an hour had elapsed since he took the car.

He remembered the girls in tight dresses. He had more than enough money now and besides he had the car. They would sing a different tune when they heard the jingle of silver. He could pick and choose now. He sent the car in the direction of the waterside cafe they frequented.

The huge barnlike place was filled. Grouped around tables sat an assortment of loafers; further apart were seated the workers from the docks and the fishing sloops. Round the blaring jukebox, the girls were wiggling their hips beneath their tight dresses, to the timing of the music. He felt syrupy as he watched the swaying hips. He moved nearer to them.

The jukebox stopped. He pushed past them and took a handful of silver from his pocket. Dropping a coin in the slot he pressed three buttons and the music blared. He jangled the money in the palm of his hand. Like hounds on the scent, they moved closer to him.

A police-van pulled up at the entrance, the driver alighted and entered the cafe. All talk stopped, the occupants stood as if they were holding their breath. The jukebox ignored the silence and blared a plaintive wail, the singer mourning a lost love. The driver favoured them with a disdainful glance, his eyes washing over them. The eyes rested on him, he was choking. The eyes moved on and he could breath again.

The shortwave radio in the police-van began to crackle, the driver's companion took down the call and reported to the driver. He was near enough to hear as the driver mumbled the message. 'Car stolen. Light blue Dodge. Licence number CA 88640 . . . Stolen early this evening.'

He was panicky. Suppose they went outside and checked his number plate? It was the only car outside.

Something in his behaviour as he left the cafe must have drawn their attention. As he slammed the door of the car he saw them rushing out of the cafe. Their cries died in his ears as the car shot forward. As he gained the corner, the van pulled out. He had a clear road, he pressed down on the accelerator, feeding petrol to the whining engine, the car felt as if it was flying. Despite his speed, the police van held him and was gaining. He spotted a corner and swung round it on two wheels, praying that it would not prove a dead end.

He went up a steep incline. Near the top the engine missed a beat. He whispered, 'Don't fail now. You've got to keep on.' The engine picked up and he was over. Further on were two turnings, the van was close behind him. He turned to the left and to his horror the road ended after a few yards. He had to pull up sharply to avoid smashing into the wall. The police-van screeched to a halt, blocking off his escape. He jumped from the car, gun in hand.

He called out, 'Don't shoot, white man.'

His voice was lost in the roar from their guns. He waved his arms about, the gun catching the light. The gun went off, surprising him with its noise. His finger seemed glued to the trigger, each shot jerking his hand back. It all seemed unreal as if it was happening on a screen and he was an interested spectator.

Something struck him which shoved him back. He looked with amazement at the blood pouring from his chest. He poked a finger at the hole, the blood ran over it, it felt sticky. Another bullet struck him. He did not feel it. From a distance he could hear a soft popping noise. He wondered what caused it. He felt tired and wanted to sleep but something was keeping him back. He was annoyed as he tried to recall what it was. He sank to his knees. His last conscious thought was, 'How rich and red my blood is. I must cover myself in its warmth.' Above the moon hid itself behind a cloud in sorrow.

'Gentlemen, the meeting is in session.'

'Mr Chairman, Gentlemen, in reply to our colleague's plea of yesterday, I regret to say, he lost in a vote of twelve to five and the council will proceed with the plans regarding the foreshore.'

He shook his head at the words. In front of him lay a newspaper. The glaring, black headlines screamed their story.

NATIVE YOUTH KILLED IN GUN BATTLE WITH POLICE

After a stirring chase in a stolen car, which ended with him being trapped in a cul-de-sac, he was killed in the ensuing gun battle. It is believed he is the same native who held up a service station attendant earlier in the evening.

[September 1954]

Love Comes Deadly

MBOKOTWANE MANQUPU

A velvet pall, which had silently and smoothly slid over the light of day, hung over Alexandra Township. And under its softness, and the myriad of tiny stars that flickered like diamonds in a lovely evening frock, hid the filth and wickedness of this slum area. In this evening frock, the Dark City, as it is called, could compete for loveliness with any other town and hold its own.

Children's voices had quietened, and the softening of voices from the homes and shebeens were a sign that the embers of the day's revels were slowly dying out. Now and again there would sound the heavy banging of a door: and a solitary figure would drunkenly venture into the dark, lonely and menacing streets, singing a slurred ditty of wine, women and anything else. The words of the ditty wouldn't be very polite; but who cared?

Barney turned the page of his novel, chuckling as he read Lemmy Caution's salty description of a 'fly-baby'. And his mind roved from the pages of the book to where his girl was probably crooning a song of broken hearts at the Café de Castanito.

A light knock at the door brought his mind back to his surroundings. He listened intently, and decided the knock had probably been at the next door. He hadn't finished reading a paragraph when there was another light tap on the door.

'Who's there?' he asked.

The reply was 'Joe sent us.'

He wondered what his friend would be wanting from him at that time of night. He stood up to open the door. He had just shifted the bolt when the door was pushed open, knocking him back. He had not recovered his balance when, without a word, two men, with long shining knives in their fists, charged at him and started stabbing him in the neck and chest. With a groan and a sigh, he collapsed on the floor and into a widening pool of his own blood.

'Now that's a good job!' one of the men said, looking down at the bleeding thing on the floor.

The bigger of the two knelt down to make sure Barney was dead. Then he stood up and nodded to the other one, and they filed out of the room.

As he closed the door, the next door opened and a woman, carrying an empty jam tin that served for a mug, came out. She was laughing foolishly as she came out of the door and over to the bigger of the two men, and asked: 'Barney's friends?'

'Yes,' the man said, noting that his friend was cowering as far as he could from the woman.

'It's the first time I see you here,' the woman said, looking closely at them.

'Yes; we only come on business.'

'You sell back-door goods?'

'Sure. That's our business.'

'Ah!' the woman exclaimed, 'Then you're just the people I want to see. I am sure you can help me. You see, I have a boy at school, and he . . .'

'That's it!' he said with a trace of impatience in his voice. 'We've got just the stuff you want. It's a pity we're in a hurry now. We'll come and see you on Saturday.'

They turned to leave, but stopped when the woman knocked on Barney's door. The big one asked her what it was she wanted from Barney.

'I want to know the time,' she said. 'My husband has sent me to ask Barney what time it is.'

'You don't need to bother Barney. The time's twenty minutes past eleven.' She thanked him and they waited till she drifted off into the yard.

The woman walked over to the corrugated-iron fence, and after removing a lot of dirty sacking, a tin of liquor was visible. She filled the mug with the beer, and tottered back to the door, humming a church hymn under her breath.

She stopped at her door. She had forgotten the time, and her husband would be angry when he found out. She sipped from the tin, smacked her lips and shuddered as the poison reached her stomach. Then she walked over to Barney's door and knocked.

There was no reply.

She knocked again. And again there was no reply. The third time she knocked, she called: 'Barney? Are you there?' and tried the door-knob. The door opened.

She looked in. And a scream tore through the velvet pall into the dark, insensate night. It was a sharp, prolonged cry of fear, of hurt, of sorrow and of all the bitter memories stored in a suffering heart.

A match flared, and then a light flickered in a window across the street; then another sliced through the dark from a half-opened door. Men and women erupted into the street, heading for the scream, followed by children and dogs, jumping over fences and crawling through holes in the broken fences. Kicking and stumbling over empty tins, they all rushed to find out what this unearthly scream was for.

Men wearing white armbands and carrying torches, sticks, knobkerries and sjamboks hurried to the door, pushing the others aside. In the room they found a sobbing woman kneeling in a pool of her tears . . . and the crumpled body of what had been a young man in the prime of his life, lying in a pool of blood.

'They have killed my Barney . . .' the woman wailed.

Kitoe, leader of the area's Civic Guards, leaned against the wall and said: 'What is Township coming to?' Then he ordered that somebody be sent on a bicycle to the police-station to tell the police about the tragedy.

'Such things make me cry for Shaka,' Kuzwayo said. 'He would have collected all the men of the age-group of the guilty ones and killed them!'

'Yes,' Kitoe agreed, 'as long as the sentences of the courts are small, crime will march on undaunted.'

'Heavy sentences won't stop crime,' said Moreti, a school-teacher member of the Guards. 'Look at it this way,' he went on quietly. 'You always preach that crime was unknown in our ancestors' days because sentences were heavy. But that is not altogether true: poverty was unknown, and there was no idleness – and so there was no crime.'

'So you say,' Kitoe answered angrily, 'but some of these tsotsis are from well-off homes.'

'It is not the fault of the boys,' Moreti answered, 'for how can a good potato stay good among rotten ones? How can these boys stay good when they are surrounded by evil? Would you be the good man you are today if you had grown up in a place like this, where illicit liquor is sold openly, where prostitution goes on day and night without even the decency of closed doors, where one is killed for no reason at all, where . . . Goodness! Why do I have to tell you things you know?'

At the far corner of the café was a raised dais. On it was no band, but only a piano. Gray felt like laughing when he looked at the pianist: the pianist was a short, stocky man with broad shoulders hunched over the keyboard like a gorilla.

The formal dress-suit he was wearing made him look the more bizarre. He looked tired; his legs were folded round those of the stool, like a child.

The café was quiet. The lights had been dimmed, and everybody's eyes were on the dais, eagerly waiting for the act to begin. The man at the piano spread out his fingers over the keyboard and they danced delicately on the ivory pieces. A quick tempo tinkled from the piano and filled the room; then the tempo slowed down into a soft, haunting melody which charged the room with tension and made even the gorilla-like pianist look more human.

A spotlight focussed on the curtained corner of the dais. The curtains parted, and a ravishing beauty, dressed in a flowing black frock, floated on to the dais. It was Jacqueline, and she came out singing like a nightingale. Her voice, a rich admixture of soprano and alto, fell over the enchanted audience like a sweet lullaby, and the words and music seeped into their hearts as she sang the song 'Conflict':

> One September noon,
>   When all the world was gay;
> When winds had gone and
>   Spring was soon,
> With passions all in rage:
>   I fell in love!

With expression, she pulled and strained the words till a feeling was communicated to the listeners and they were enchanted. She sang the chorus:

> Our souls craved, our hearts ached;
> Our yearning lips were baked:
> To satisfy the mad desires
> We settled for a kiss!
> The conflict was a flame,
> Devoid of any shame:
> 'Cause . . .
> Halfway across the journey,
> Our lips were warmed by wine!

As she closed the song with that made ending, the whole house burst into spontaneous clapping of hands and cheering, not wanting her to leave the stage; but she made way for 'The Peppermints', an act by three men who looked like they came from the 'Know How To Dress Shop'.

Gray saw the man he had sent with a message for her go through the door that went to her dressing-room.

'Mr Gray?'

Gray looked up and she was standing at his table. Mumbling something, he rose and offered her a chair. And he started off: 'Please; I won't waste your time and mine as I'm a busy man, too. In brief, I am from Marshall Square and have been assigned to your late boyfriend Barney's murder. I'm handling the case. I came here to see you and try and get some assistance from you.'

A look of sorrow flitted over her face when he mentioned Barney's name; only for a moment. She spoke: 'Sure; I'll be happy to help track down Barney's murderers.'

'That's the spirit,' Gray encouraged her, lighting a cigarette after she had refused one he offered her. 'All I want from you now is about your affair with Barney, and anything strange you noticed about him lately.'

'It was nothing much,' she said, with a faraway look in her eyes. 'I met him in a bus on my way to Alexandra, and he helped me carry my parcels and even took me home. Before a fortnight, we were in love. He was a quiet sort of man, and seemed lonely; and when I asked him anything about himself, he would try and make me forget it with sweet talk. I knew nothing about his family, because he didn't want to talk about them.'

'What were his likes?' Gray asked. 'Did he have any side-lines besides his job?'

'Not that I know about,' she answered. 'He used to like taking me to the movies, the zoo and maybe soccer matches – which were his favourite.'

'He did nothing unusual for you during the last month?'

'No.' She still had that faraway look in her eyes.

'Did you know that he backed the horses heavily?'

This question wiped off the faraway look from her eyes and brought surprise to her face: but she recovered quickly and said she did not know about it.

Gray asked: 'Then where did you think he got the £500 from?'

'Which £500?'

'Which he gave you.'

'You're crazy!' she said, 'I know of no £500: whoever told you that was mad and didn't know what he was talking about.'

'Come, come now,' Gray quietly said, 'don't make things difficult for yourself. He told us so himself. And he wouldn't lie about you, would he?'

She was shocked, and looked at him with unbelieving eyes. 'I don't get it,' she said after a moment. 'I thought he was dead before anybody found him. How could he have told you? What are you trying to sell me, mister?'

'That a diary is a very handy thing. Barney kept one, and in it, under the date of September 19, he mentions how he won the double at Benoni and gave you the £500 to keep, and how he kept £22 to buy himself clothes. That, lady, was only a fortnight before he was killed by the murderers you hired!'

'Hey! I don't know anything about any murderers!' she said with fear in her voice. 'Sure, I had the five hundred; but I didn't hire no killers!'

'But I thought you knew nothing about the money?' Gray asked.

'Well, I thought it didn't concern you,' she said lamely, 'I was going to tell his parents about it.'

'When?' he asked. 'His parents were here to fetch his body, and you didn't make a move to meet them. Don't make me laugh! Anyhow, you can tell that story to the judge.'

'There won't be no judge to tell any stories to, wise-guy!' a soft voice behind him said. 'She ain't going to see no judge and you ain't taking her nowhere, see? I'm levelling a torpedo at your spine, and if you do anything funny I'm liable to pump you so full of lead they'll need twenty guys to carry your coffin. You just turn around now and walk like a nice kid to the door, and no tricks!'

'Chocolate,' Gray said without looking round. 'Where do you think you'll wind up with all these killings? Sooner or later the law will catch up with you as it always does, and you'll be snivelling to the papers to have your sentence reprieved after you're given sentence.'

Gray stood up, with Chocolate close behind him. Jacqueline hip-swayed on to the dais, and started a song called 'Lucifer, here I come!'

Gray moved slowly, and noticed that a waiter was coming towards him with a full tray. He stopped as if to let the waiter pass, and as the waiter did, he shot out his leg and tripped him. The waiter fell in a heap on the floor, the tray crashing over the nearest table.

Before Chocolate knew what was happening, Gray had pivoted round to face him. Chocolate's right hand jerked up in his jacket pocket, then stopped. He decided not to pull out the gun in the crowd. His hand then came out empty, and he rushed at Gray. Gray picked up a bottle of sauce from a table and hit Chocolate in the face with it. As Chocolate staggered back, he turned round to face another man rushing at him with a screwdriver in his fist.

Gasping and panting, Gray looked over the heads of the crowd towards the dais. Jacqueline was nowhere to be seen. He elbowed his way through the crowd and made for her dressing-room. The room was empty, but a window was open. He looked through the window and saw her running down the street carrying a suitcase.

'Stop!' he shouted as he climbed through the window.

She looked back, then ran on even faster. She kept looking back as she ran across the street. There was the bright glare of headlights, the screech of tyres as a car rocked round the corner at speed . . . a scream and then a body hurled high in the air. It landed on the pavement with a sickening thud.

Later Gray was telling Solly about Jacqueline. 'Her last song was "Lucifer, here I come",' he said. 'But one thing I know is that old Lucifer won't be so happy to see her.'

'Why?' Solly asked.

'My dear man,' Gray said, 'a dame like that is liable to start a strike in hell! Lucifer will find himself up against a wench who'll promise a better standard of living to the inmates and lead them in a revolt to overthrow the established government of that joint.'

Solly's eye popped.

And Gray thought that there was still a lot of trusting Barneys in Johannesburg; and while there are still so many Jacquelines making eyes at the Barneys, Marshall Square will be kept busy.

[January 1955]

The Suitcase

BRUNO ESEKIE

[EZEKIEL MPHAHLELE]

One of these days he was going to take a desperate chance, Timi thought. He would not miss it if it presented itself. Many men had got rich by sheer naked chance. Couldn't it just be that he was destined to meet such a chance?

He sat on a pavement on a hot afternoon. It was New Year's Eve. And in such oppressive heat Timi had been sitting for over an hour. An insect got into his nostril and made him sneeze several times. Through the tears that filled his eyes the traffic seemed to dance about before him.

The grim reality of his situation returned to him with all its cold and aching pain after the short interlude with the insect. Today he had been led on something like a goose chase. He had been to three places where chances of getting work were promising. He had failed. At one firm he had been told, 'We've already got a boy, John.' At the second firm a tiny typist told him, 'You're too big, Jim. The boss wants a small boy – about eighteen, you know.' Then she had gone on with her typing, clouding her white face with cigarette smoke.

At the third place of call a white man had put down his price in a sandy voice, 'Two pounds a week.' 'Three pounds ten a week,' Timi had said. 'Take it or leave it, my boy,' the white man had almost whispered his final word, and snorted to close the matter. In spite of himself Timi chuckled softly when he was outside, not knowing what tickled him.

He was watching the movements of a wasp tormenting a worm. The wasp circled over the worm and then came down on the clumsy and apparently defenceless worm. It seemed to stand on its head as it stung the worm. The worm wriggled violently, seeming to want to fly away from the earth. Then suddenly the worm stretched out, as though paralysed. The winged insect had got its prey. Timi felt pity for the poor worm. An unequal fight, an unfair fight, he thought. Must it always be thus, he asked – the well-armed and agile creature stings the defenceless to death? The wasp was now dragging the worm; to its home, evidently.

He remembered he had nothing to take home. But the thought comforted him that his wife was so understanding. A patient and understanding wife. Yes, she would say, as she had often said, 'Tomorrow's sun must rise, Timi. It rises for everyone. It may have its fortunes,' or 'I will make a little fire, Timi. Our sages say even where there is no pot to boil there should be fire.'

Now she was ill. She was about to have a baby; a third baby. And with nothing to take home for the last two months, his savings running out, he felt something must be done. Not anything that would get him into jail. No, not that. It wouldn't do for him to go to jail with his wife and children almost starving like that. No, he told himself emphatically.

A white man staggered past him, evidently drunk. He stopped a short way past Timi and turned to look at him. He walked back to Timi and held out a bottle of brandy before him, scarcely keeping firm on his legs.

'Here, John, drink this stuff. Happy New Year!' Timi shook his head.

'C'mon, be – be a s-sport, hic! No p-police to catch you, s-s-see?'

Timi shook his head again and waved him away.

'Huh, here's a bugger don't want to have a happy New Year, eh. Got-to yell then.'

The white man swung round, brandishing his bottle as he tripped away.

If only that were money, Timi thought bitterly.

He remembered it was time he went home, and boarded a bus to Sophiatown. In the bus he found an atmosphere of revelry. The New Year spirit, he thought; an air of reckless abandon. Happy New Year! one shouted at intervals.

Timi was looking at a man playing a guitar just opposite him across the aisle. Here a girl was dancing to the rhythm of the music. The guitarist strummed away, clearly carried away in the flight of his own music. He coaxed, caressed and stroked his instrument. His long fingers played effortlessly on the strings. He glowered at the girl in front of him with hanging lower lip as she twisted her body seductively this way and that, like a young supple plant that the wind plays about with. Her breasts pushed out under a light sleeveless blouse. At the same time the guitarist bent his ear to the instrument as if to hear better its magic notes, or to whisper to it the secret of his joy.

Two young women came to sit next to Timi. One of them was pale, and seemed sick. The other deposited a suitcase in front between her leg and Timi's. His attention was taken from the music by the presence of these two women. They seemed to have much unspoken between them.

At the next stop they rose to alight. Timi's one eye was fixed on the suitcase as he watched them go towards the door. When the bus moved a man who was sitting behind Timi exclaimed:

'Those young women have left their case!'

'No, it is mine,' said Timi hastily.

'No. I saw them come in with it.'

This is a chance . . .

'I tell you it's mine.'

'You can't tell me that.'

Now there musn't be any argument, or else . . .

'Did you not see me come in with a case?'

I mustn't lose my temper, or else . . .

'Tell the truth, my man, it bites no one.'

'What more do you want me to say now?'

The people are looking at me now. By the gods, what can I do?

'It is his lucky day,' shouted someone from the back. 'Let him be!'

'And if it is not his, how is this a lucky day?' asked someone else.

'Ha, ha, ha!' A woman laughed. 'You take my thing, I take yours, he takes somebody else's. So we all have a lucky day, eh? Ha, ha, ha!'

She rocked with voluble laughter, seeming to surrender herself to it.

'Oh, leave him alone,' an old voice came from another quarter, 'only one man saw the girls come in with a suitcase, and only one man says it is his. One against one. Let him keep what he has, the case. Let the other man keep what he has, the belief that it belongs to the girls.' There was a roar of laughter. The argument melted in the air of a happy New Year, of revelry and song.

Timi felt a great relief. He had won.

The bus came to a stop and he alighted. He did not even hear someone behind him in the bus cry, 'That suitcase will yet tell whom it belongs to, God is my witness!' Why can't people mind their own affairs? He thought of all those people looking at him.

Once out of the bus he was seized by a fit of curiosity, anxiousness and expectancy. He must get home quickly and see what is in the case.

It was a chance, a desperate chance, and he had taken it. That mattered to him most as he paced up the street.

Timi did not see he was about to walk into a crowd of people. They were being searched by the police, two white constables. He was jolted into attention by the shining of a badge. Quickly he slipped into an open backyard belonging to a Chinaman. Providence was with him, he thought, as he ran to stand behind the great iron door, his heart almost choking him.

He must have waited there for fifteen minutes, during which he could see all that was happening out there in the street. The hum and buzz so common in Good Street rose to a crescendo; so savage, so cold-blooded, so menacing. Suddenly he got a strange and frightening feeling that he had excited all this noise, that he was the centre around which these angry noises whirled and circled, that he had raised a hue and cry.

For one desperate second he felt tempted to leave the case where he squatted. It would be so simple for him, he thought. Yes, just leave the case there and have his hands, no, more than that, his soul, freed of the burden. After all, it was not his.

Not his. This thought reminded him that he had done all this because it was not his. The incident in the bus was occasioned by the stark naked fact that the case was not his. He felt he must get home soon because it was not his. He was squatting here like an outlaw, because the case was not his. Why leave it here then, after all these efforts to possess it and keep it? There must surely be valuable articles in it, Timi mused. It was so heavy. There must be. It couldn't be otherwise. Else why had Providence been so kind to him so far? Surely the spirits of his ancestors had pity on him; with a sick wife and hungry children. Then the wild, primitive determination rose in him; the blind determination to go through with a task once begun, whether a disaster can be avoided in time or not, whether it is to preserve worthless or valuable articles. No, he was not going to part with the case.

The pick-up van came and collected the detained men and women. The police car started up the street, Timi came out and walked on the pavement, not daring to look behind, lest he lose his nerve and blunder. He knew he was not made for all this sort of thing. Pitso was coming up the pavement in the opposite direction. Lord, why should it be Pitso just at this time? Pitso, the gasbag, the notorious talker whose appearance always broke up a party. They met.

'Greetings! You seem to be in a hurry, Timi?' Pitso called out in his usual noisy and jovial fashion. 'Are you arriving or going?'

'Arriving.' Timi did not want to encourage him.

'Ha, since when have you been calling yourself A.J.B.?'

'Who says I'm A.J.B.?'

'There my friend.' Pitso pointed at the large initials on the case, and looked at his friend with laughing eyes.

'Oh, it's my cousin's.' Timi wished he could wipe the broad stupid grin off the large mouth of this nonentity. He remembered later how impotent and helpless he felt now. For Pitso and his grin were inseparables, like Pitso and his mouth. Just now he wished he wouldn't look so uneasy.

'I'm sorry, Pitso, my wife isn't well, and I must hurry.' He passed on. Pitso looked at his friend, his broad mouth still smiling blankly.

The Chevrolet came to stop just alongside the pavement. Then it moved on, coasting idly and carelessly.

'Hey!' Timi looked to his left. Something seemed to snap inside him and release a lump shooting up his throat. 'Stop, jong!' The driver waved to him.

There they were, two white constables and an African in plain clothes in the back seat. Immediately he realised it would be foolish to run. Besides, the case should be his. He stopped. The driver went up to him and wrenched the suitcase from Timi's hand. At the same time he caught him by the shoulder and led him to the car, opening the back door for Timi. The car shot away to the police station.

His knees felt weak when he recognised the black man next to him. It was the same man who was the first to argue that the case was not Timi's in the bus. By the spirits, did the man have such a strong sense of justice as to call God to be witness? Even on New Year's Eve? Or was he a detective? No, he could have arrested him in the bus. The man hardly looked at Timi. He just looked in front of him in a self-righteous posture, as it struck Timi.

Timi got annoyed, frantically annoyed. It was a challenge. He would face it. Things might turn round somewhere. He felt he needed all the luck fate could afford to give him.

At the police station the two constables took the case into a small room. After a few minutes they came out, with what Timi thought was a strange communication of feelings between them as they looked at each other.

'Kom, kom, jong!' one of them said, although quite gently. They put the case in front of him.

'Whose case is this?'

'Mine.'

'Do you have your things in here?'

'My wife's things.'

'What are they?'

'I think she has some of her dresses in it.'

'Why do you say you *think*?'

'Well, you see, she just packed them up in a hurry, and asked me to take the case to her aunt; but I didn't see her pack them.'

'Hm. You can recognise your wife's clothing?'

'Some of it.' Why make it so easy for him? And why was there such cold amusement in the white man's eyes?

The constable opened the suitcase, and started to unpack the articles singly.

'Is this your wife's?' It was a torn garment.

'Yes.'

'And this? And this?' Timi answered yes to both. Why did they pack such torn clothing? The constable lifted each one up before Timi. Timi's thoughts were racing and milling round in his head. What trick was fate about to play him? He sensed there was something wrong. Had he been a dupe?

The constable, after taking all the rags out, pointed to an object inside. '*And is this also your wife's*?' glaring at Timi with aggressive eyes.

Timi stretched his neck to see.

It was a ghastly sight. A dead baby that could not have been born more than twelve hours before. A naked, white, curly-haired image of death. Timi gasped and felt sick and faint. They had to support him to the counter to make a statement. He told the truth. He knew he had gambled with chance; the chance that was to cost him eighteen months' hard labour.

[February 1955]

the very thing Timi didn't want to happen did.

The Departure

PETER CLARKE

It was evening and the first stars were out and everything was kind of quiet the way things become when night starts settling down. Already people were relaxing and talking on their balconies after having finished supper when Benny came down past the houses in Cardiff Road with a bundle of wood on his shoulder and his dog, Rinty, running alongside of him.

He didn't have to look to see that they were staring at him as he passed because he could feel it, the same way that he could feel when there were people talking about him. And they were talking about him. They always did.

'There goes that James kid. He's not all there, you know.'

'. . . and so young too. Twelve. What a pity, hey.'

'And they say he's very headstrong too. Must really be a burden for Uncle Herb. That poor old man really had a raw deal when he took him on.'

'M-mm. I wonder if they can't do anything about it, get him into a Home or something? I wouldn't feel safe with him around, he might just get mad all of a sudden and what with that terrible temper . . .!'

'You're telling me. It's a good job the children keep away from him too or else I wouldn't know where I'd be with all the worry.'

'God, yes, hey, and I said only the other day . . .'

That's the way it goes, he thought bitterly, always talking about me, always, always talking about me. It makes me sick. It was always the same thing. People thought he was mad. Of course they didn't say so to his face but he knew it all right.

Some of the kids said it though, but they always made sure that they were a good distance away when they said it, especially since the time he had caught hold of Billy Witton and banged his head so violently against a wall that the blood ran. He could still remember the bright redness of the living blood as it seeped beneath his fingernails and stained the fresh whiteness of his clean shirt when his fingers accidentally touched it. Oh yes, they kept away from him all right but it didn't worry him.

Often he wondered why it should have happened to him. 'I don't know,' he said, 'it's crazy.' And in a way it was. It made him seem normal in a crazy way and made everybody else seem crazy in a normal kind of way. It was all so very confusing. He was always wondering about it and the question was always popping up in his restless mind, 'Am I really mad as they say, am I really mad?' – and there was always the same indeterminate answer, 'I don't know!' It worried him and forced him to think of things which could provide suitable solutions and so prove that he wasn't mad. 'Augie never said I was and he should know and Rinty doesn't think so either. But then dogs don't speak, do they?' But as far as he was concerned Rinty was different. Benny had had Rinty for a long time and they understood each other so well that it was as good as speaking. Sometimes he wondered if Rinty was really not speaking. Often, when his tongue lolled out, it looked as if he was.

Augie could speak to animals and make them understand and the strangest thing was that they never ran away from him. Even birds, they wouldn't fly away when they heard his voice. They only sat and listened as his voice went on and on. Thinking of it, Benny knew what made them listen like that to Augie. It was the goodness in him.

'That is why he was my friend,' Benny said, 'and he still is. But then I suppose you'd think it funny me saying that when Augie isn't alive any more. He's dead, you know. I killed him although of course they said I couldn't have. But I did.

'I still see him up in the forest sometimes and then we speak to each other. I always liked him though most everybody else didn't. I don't think they liked him because he was ugly and he didn't have a family and his clothes were nearly almost always raggedy and shabby. Uncle Herb was one of those who didn't like him. He was always calling him ugly names like "You guttersnipe" and "You dirty little bastard" and "You filthy bundle of rags".'

Only once Benny saw Augie cry and that was after Benny received a thrashing from Uncle Herb for playing with him. Uncle Herb was furious that day.

'Look, Benny,' he yelled, 'how many times haven't I told you not to play with that filthy bastard and you keep on, keep on, keep on. I'm tired of telling you the same old thing over and over and I'm not telling you again to keep away from him.'

He was really very angry. Benny could see that, as he came towards him, at the same time unbuckling his belt which had a heavy brass buckle. Benny was standing in a corner of the front room then, that dark front room with the eternally drawn curtains and the heavy brown furniture that he hated so much and there was no way of escaping from Uncle Herb. His big hands tore so hard at Benny that buttons popped off and, his braces loose, the trousers slipped down his legs while the belt lashed at his bare backside. He screamed and screamed at the top of his voice because it seemed Uncle Herb was becoming mad with anger the way the buckle was biting into his flesh.

Benny felt he could have died then if suddenly he wasn't calm enough to think and his hand grabbed at Uncle Herb's long, straggly, greasy grey hair and hung on until he felt quite nauseous smelling its horrid oily odour and got sick, vomiting all over Uncle Herb's head and on to Aunt Martha's carpet. Only then Uncle Herb stopped. By then Benny was so weak he couldn't get his fingers loose from Uncle Herb's hair as he lay on the floor and Uncle Herb had to pry them loose one by one. He was calm enough then to see that he could have killed Benny and he was so shaken that he knelt there behind an overturned chair shaking like a leaf in a breeze, while Benny lay crying with his hands knotted into fists in the air and his trousers still around his ankles.

They were both scared at what had happened so suddenly that they didn't move from where they were on the floor and they stayed that way for what seemed hours and hours until finally Benny stopped crying and Uncle Herb, wiping his head, got up, kind of sheepishly and mumbled, 'I'm sorry, Benny, I'm really very sorry. I'm sorry, Benny . . .', until it sounded painful to Benny's ears and he shouted, 'Shut up, shut up, I hate you, I hate you,' while he pulled up his trousers and held it with one hand while with the other hand he grabbed up one of Aunt Martha's silly ornaments, a porcelain woman with a band of painted flowers, and threw it blindly at him. He ducked and it banged against the green-striped wall paper and splashed into billions of tiny bits that scattered all over that part of the room.

Rinty saw him running up Cardiff Road to the mountain and followed, he always did, when he saw him heading in that direction. That's why he liked Rinty. You needn't tell him a thing and he'd know what to do. That's why he followed him. He was a smart pal, that dog.

Benny was tired already when he reached the field, so tired that he could only fall into the stink white and yellow daisy bushes and crawl into their shelter, staying there quietly until he was sure nobody had followed. He stood up carefully and went to the grass hut. It wasn't a grass hut really. Just dead branches that Augie had arranged into a hut and over this he had carefully woven other branches, live ones with leaves. Nobody walking around there would say it was anything but a big bush because there was nothing to give it away. Even the entrance was so placed that the other children would not notice it.

Augie was there of course, just as Benny thought he would be, and he was surprised to see him looking the way he did. He had to explain but he burst out crying before he could finish. Augie put his arm around his shaking shoulders and when Benny looked he was crying too, not openly as Benny was, but just a little. He didn't say anything then, not until they were both calm again and then he said, 'Oh, Benny, my friend, my friend.'

Augie was like that, he didn't say much but when he did he often said things that were beautiful. But then, Benny thought, it's because of the way he was. You know how I mean. He was ugly but inside his heart he was beautiful and kind. It couldn't be seen on the outside, it was in the inside, and his ugliness was only the wrapping that covered it up like paper around a parcel.

Everybody said Augie was ugly. Once Uncle Herb said he looked like his father, who was a big, black French Moroccan sailor and not a bit like his mother who was a street-woman and who was small and light-complexioned. They both disappeared before Benny could remember. Because he never saw them and Augie never spoke about them he never wondered about them. With him, Augie just happened to be there, in the same way that waves beat on the shore and clouds come along in the sky and you see them there without wondering where they come from and it doesn't worry you. They're there and that's all. That's the way it was with Augie and Benny.

Augie was thirteen and big and strong for his age whereas Benny was eleven and small. He was very much darker coloured than Benny too, almost black, with thick lips and a flattish nose and narrow, almost slant eyes. His pitch-black hair was thick and very curly because he did not always bother to comb it. Whenever Benny saw him he always seemed to be wearing the same things but he got so used to seeing him wearing them that after a time he didn't even notice them. Only once he saw Augie wear shoes and that was the day of his grandmother's funeral when he was lent a pair of shoes by one of the neighbours. The shoes pinched and one could see that they were painful. Afterwards, the child, whom those shoes belonged to, refused to wear them again, not even after his father beat him for it. They had to give the shoes away. That's the way children were with Augie.

Even in school. He went to school for only a few years, up to Standard Four, but he didn't enjoy it because he couldn't seem to learn, besides it irked him to have to sit and to be shut up like that in a classroom the whole day. And another thing, children didn't like to sit next to him because they said he was dirty. Benny didn't want to sit next to him either simply because he didn't like the way he looked but the teacher forced him to sit there so he did. He wasn't so bad after all and Benny got to like him. Benny was lonely for a friend, as lonely as Augie then, and so after a while he didn't mind at all having to sit next to him. Besides, Augie spoke about so many interesting things which he normally never heard about and which made him much more interesting than anybody else that Benny knew, even the cleverest grown-ups. And the places on the hills that he'd been to, even though merely about the town, sounded as wonderful to him as if they were foreign places in strange lands because he had never yet been to those parts.

Augie said, 'I'll take you there one day, Benny, if you like. Would you?'

'Of course,' Benny said, 'of course.' He was so eager to go that he could hardly even wait. 'When will we go? Let's go right after school today, as soon as the bell goes.'

'All right.' Augie hardly ever seemed to have anything to do after school anyway. 'We'll go then. I'll wait for you up in the mountains.'

'But how will I know you're there?' Benny asked, wondering on that point.

'I'll know.' It was the way Augie said it that made him know for sure that he'd be there without fail. He had the kind of voice one trusts without question.

That same afternoon they went up the mountain to the brook above the waterfall, tracing their ways through paths that Benny didn't know existed, between thick, scrubby bushes and over huge rocks to which they clung with only fingers and with a lot of air beneath them. If they dropped they would have fallen on to rocks in the river bed and been killed. Augie wasn't scared at all although Benny was. He just said, 'Aw, it's nothing at all,' rubbing his finger across his nose. 'Just put your hands and feet where I put mine and don't look down or else it'll make you nervous.'

'What about reptiles?' There were long, deep shadows between rocks, most of them big enough for snakes and lizards and things to nest in.

'What's reptiles?' he asked, clambering over a rock and holding aside an Afrikaner bush for Benny to come by. The scarlet flowers on the long green stalks looked like tongues of flame in the shadow.

'Snakes and things, man.'

'Not here. They'll be gone after the sun. They don't stay in one place all the time.'

They reached the heights above the waterfall. Looking down Benny wondered that they had come up what seemed nothing but a plain wall except for clumps of bushes and ferns tucked here and there between folds of rock. How were they going to get down again? He turned around. Augie was splashing his arm in the brown water of a pool, cutting it beneath the surface with his hand. Tadpoles scattered when he moved his fingers anywhere near them.

He looked happy kneeling on the hard rock with his arm under water and he could have stayed that way for ever, holding that moment with his arm under water and his knees paining from kneeling on the rock, if time would only stay still. But it never did and it didn't even drag like when one has nothing to do and one has to wait for something to happen and it takes such a long time before it does. He knew it because he got up, his arm held out slightly, stiff, the water dripping off his fingertips like tiny glass beads.

'Let's have a dip?' he said.

The water looked lovely as it was, but they were still in the shadow of the hill-top and being July it was cool, not very cool for the month but cool anyway. Benny wondered if he was serious.

'Do you mean it?'

'Yeh. The water's grand, just nice for a dip. Don't you believe me?' He looked again at the water as if for its reassurance, but the surface was quite still and only reflected back his upside-down image as he stood on the opposite side.

Staring through the reflection one could see the tiny black tadpoles on the bottom of the pool. 'I like this pool. Most of the time when the others go to the beach then I come up here. How would you like me to teach you to swim?'

Benny couldn't swim yet and he wasn't really friendly with the other boys so he never went to Long Beach with them when the weather was warm. The others could all swim fairly well and he didn't want to look silly scrabbling about in the sea and half-drowning when the waves got him. In a way it was also because he was afraid of the sea. He didn't like the noise it made when it smacked itself along the shore and once seeing somebody's baby nearly drown was enough for him.

The winter days passed and spring came and they spent many afternoons climbing and exploring along the hills. There was Augie's meadow. Sometimes, lying in the grass with his eyes closed, Benny remembered the meadow. It wasn't a meadow in the true sense of the word but the rich, milky grass grew so lush and thick there that they always thought of it as being a meadow. It was on the slope of a hill near the waterfall, so steep that one could feel the breezes feeling their way up from the valley away to the higher reaches of the kloof.

When he first went there, Augie said, 'This is my meadow.' He was proud of it, as proud as a king. Nobody else ever went there and he felt as if he owned it. It was his own little personal kingdom where the wind, the butterflies and himself were the only living things.

It was strange about the butterflies in Augie's meadow. That was the only place where one found them sleeping on the long, slender blades of dew-sprinkled grass, their tiny, fragile orange wings like the petals of many flowers. One could pick them up and they would sit contentedly on one's finger like sleepy kittens. Benny loved that meadow and he could have stayed there for ever and ever. But now he didn't go to that meadow anymore because Augie wasn't there and because of that absence it was silent and empty.

Even now he couldn't decide that Augie was really dead because he wasn't sure that he was. Everybody else said he was dead and he supposed that they felt they were right, but he still saw him in some of the old places. And yet he saw him die. It was strange and he couldn't help wondering about it.

It happened by the waterfall. They were going to cross the stream and the water was coming down fast because there had been lots of rain. It was all white and brown in places and bubbly along the banks and they could hardly hear their own voices above the noise because it was roaring like a train in a tunnel.

They meant to cross by swinging over on low branches. Augie went across first and then it was Benny's turn to follow. But he was so scared of falling into the water that he hesitated. Augie looked back, saw him waiting and Bennie could just make out the words he shouted, 'I'm coming back, I'm coming back. Hold the branch . . .'

He held the branch and Augie jumped. For a moment he seemed like a bird in flight as Benny waited for him to catch the branch, but suddenly Benny slipped in the thick mess of wet, rotten leaves along the bank. At the same time he felt his hands stinging as if they had been burned with a hot poker as the branch went flying out of reach and he saw Augie miss it and fall into the middle of the churning waters with a great splash. The memory of that moment sent a cold shiver through him as he remembered the frightened look on that face and the bent fingers of the hands clutching out to catch hold of the branch that wasn't there as the water swept him downstream until it reached the precipice and he went over the edge and was amazingly gone.

It seemed hours and hours before Benny could move and run for help, and when they came, there was nothing they could do but pull him out from between rocks in a pool at the bottom of the fall where he'd got wedged in. His body was all broken as if the bones in it had gone all soft and mushy.

Benny was screaming. He didn't know what to do because it was his only friend and he was quite, quite dead. Never again would he see the blades of grass swishing against Augie's legs as he walked through the mountain paths or see the stream of blood in the transparent body of a tiny fish he caught in the first waters of a mountain-pool in the springtime as he held it in the basin of his hands. He would never hear his voice alive and talking and laughing or see the gleam of his eyes watching the birds flying away on their long journeys before the long, cold months of winter set in. If only he hadn't let that branch slip he could still have had Augie alive instead of the lifeless way that he was always going to be from then on. His friend and everything that was part of him was dead and finished.

People tried to hold him back after he had looked at the wet body lying on the ground there. The grass around him was sprinkled with glistening drops of blood and water. It reminded him of jewels that he saw once in a jeweller's shop window downtown. Looking at it he couldn't decide if they looked more like costly gems than drops of blood and water. Somehow it really seemed to matter a great deal to know, and not being able to know worried him until he felt him struggling to free himself and they thought that he had suddenly become crazed with fright; and they held on tighter and tighter; but he struggled so hard that they had to let him go and he immediately ran up to the forest.

It was dark and cool between the trees in the forest and he couldn't hear anything except the hammering of his heart and the blood beating in his ears. Resting beneath the trees one could smell the sweet dampness of the leaves and earth in one's nostrils like the smell of an autumn that was never going to end.

There was somebody else in the forest. Benny could feel it even without lifting himself up to look. And even before looking he knew who that person was going to be. It was Augie.

He was standing higher up the slope of the forest by a tree. Looking hard, Benny could see the chips flying as he cut into the bark with a small knife. Calling to him, it seemed he couldn't hear Benny's voice. He turned away without even glancing in his direction and started up into the forest, silently disappearing among the trees. It seemed ghost-like the way he vanished with such suddenness. Benny couldn't even hear the crackle of the bushes that happens when one forces one's way through them. He should have heard it but there was nothing at all. It was silent.

Quickly running up the slope to the tree where Augie had stood, he looked for the fresh cut in the bark which would prove that he was there. There was the name spelt out in capital letters, A-U-G-I-E. But surprisingly, it had been carved out a long time ago because the letters were already brown and dry. It was strange. Had his friend really been there or did he just imagine it?

He was sure that he'd been there and looked around for traces to prove it. In places the sunlight fell between the thick foliage overhead and shone on the ground, bright glowing dabs of gold in the gloominess. Leaves shivered in a slight breeze and two coins of light glowed in the hollow of a fresh footprint where someone, a short while before, had just stepped deep into the softness of the mouldy, spongy earth.

[April 1955]

Black and Brown Song

RICHARD RIVE

Where the rainbow ends,
There's going to be a place brother,
Where the world can sing all sorts of songs,
And we're going to sing together, brother,
You and I,
Though you're white and I'm not.
It's going to be a sad song, brother,
'Cause we don't know the tune,
And it's a difficult tune to learn,
But we can learn it, brother,
You and I,
There's no such tune as a black tune,
There's no such tune as a white tune,
There's only music, brother,
And it's the music we're going to sing,
Where the rainbow ends.

Johnny-boy expected Amaai and Braim in the cinema foyer. It was usual to find them admiring the lurid posters of Hollywood stars until they decided to pay eightpence and enter the dirty Coloured bioscope. Johnny-boy spotted them as he sauntered along the pavement. Amaai was laughing raucously and rubbing his stomach, while Braim assumed an air of affronted dignity. Condescendingly he stared down at Amaai, pinching himself so that he would not laugh.

'Man, you're a crazy Hottentot,' said Braim rubbing his sore stomach.
'Gwan!'
'You're a crazy swine!!'
'Voetsak!!'
'As crazy as hell!!'
'Voetsak!!'
'Ought to ac' in a bioscope!'
'Voetsak again!' said Braim still holding his stomach.

'Hell they got a lot of money!'

'Who?'

'Actors man! You're as crazy as hell!!'

'Wish I could go to America!'

'They get over a million pound!'

'Phew!!' said Braim as he visualised the life of a Hollywood actor.

'Hell, I'll just sit on my backside and order thirty Kaffers to run around for me!'

'I'll buy the Metro and you can sit two-and-tuppence every day and smoke as much dagga as you like. I'd turn around and say, "Kaffer, roll me a pill!"' Both Amaai and Braim burst out laughing at the idea of Amaai sitting in the best seats at the local white cinema, ordering an African to roll him the intoxicating weed.

'Hoit Johnny-boy.'

'Hallo.'

'Got money?'

Johnny-boy narrowed his eyes and they could see the yellow skin stretching tightly over his high cheekbones.

'Hell no!!'

'Make a plan, it's nearly time for the serial. We just need one-and-six.'

'Take money from a Kaffer. They're bloody stupid. That bag round their belt always has money. Easy stuff.'

'Have you seen a Kaffer when he's wild?' Amaai said hesitantly.

'They can get bloody wild.' Braim agreed darting a quick glance at Johnny-boy.

'Christ, you afraid of a bloody Kaffer?'

'What'd you do if he had a knobkerrie?'

Johnny-boy flicked open his knife and looked knowingly at Braim and Amaai.

'God help any Kaffer that bothers with me.'

'And a white man? Johnny-boy?'

'That's different.'

'I'm not scared of a white man,' Braim said bravely.

'You are, you lousy bastard!' Johnny-boy's eyes twitched dangerously.

'I'm not,' Braim mumbled, watching Johnny-boy closely.

'Ag, let's go to bioscope!'

'Aint no money!'

'For Christ's sake, take some from someone!' Johnny-boy glared.

'From a Kaffer,' said Amaai.

'Or a white man,' Braim ventured.

'Who you're laying on with?' Johnny-boy's eyes again glinted.

'A Kaffer or anyone scared enough!'

'Let's get some money on a bus,' said Braim.

'There's plenty of pockets to pick.'

'Don't be bloody fools! Let's get the money from a Kaffer, or a kid or something! What the hell you want to go on a bus for with all the blooming Boere waiting to catch you and chuck you in gaol.'

Johnny-boy was angry.

A Hanover Street bus pulled to stop. People poured from it and jostled towards the bioscope entrance.

'Jesus! If I were rich I'd buy the buses and pick as many pockets as I like!' said Amaai laughing as he ran to the bus.

'I'd simply say, "Kaffer pick a pocket for your baas",' said Braim as he pulled a funny face and ran after Amaai.

> Fear!!
> A fear that is a deep fear.
> That creates the savage and destroys the man.
> A fear that is as false
> As the notes of a bad song.
> A black and brown song,
> Where the black is one tune
> And the brown another.
> And the melody harsh so that it grates the teeth.
> And creates a song that is not a good tune,
> And a fear that cannot be overcome.

Johnny-boy was conscious of a crowd. He was conscious that eyes were on him, but he knew that no-one would do anything. They would only stand and stare and not lift a hand. He well knew the peculiar way crowds reacted in District Six. They would only stand and stare while he drove the fear of hell into the African boy he had pushed against the wall of the cinema.

There was fear in the crowds, fear that they would be implicated, fear in Johnny-boy, fear that the crowd would notice the tenseness beneath his veneer of bravado, fear in the eyes of the African boy.

'Open your black mouth or I'll cut it open!'

The boy stared mutely at him.

'I said open your jaw!'

'Asseblief!'

'Asseblief baas, you black swine!'

'Asseblief, baas!'

There was a snigger in the crowd. Johnny-boy sensed the ludicrous situation of the African calling him baas. He, with his yellow skin and high cheekbones, his bare feet and three-quarter pants. The realization made him more tense and angry.

'What the hell are you doing in Coloured man's territory? You belong in the location,' said he, venting his angry feelings on the youth.

'Asseblief, baas.'

'Ja! I'm a baas, and don't forget it, Kaffer, or this knife will rip your guts!'

The black boy looked pleadingly at Johnny.

'How much money have you?'

'Nothing!'

'NOTHING, BAAS!!'

'Nothing, baas!!'

'You're lying, you swine!' Johnny-boy's hands went deftly through the boy's pockets and the realisation that the boy was speaking the truth made him more angry still. He had to show the crowd he was Johnny-boy.

'Get down on your knees, you pig!'

'Pleese, baas!'

'Come-on!'

'Oh, leave him alone!'

Johnny-boy swung around to meet this fresh challenge.

'Mind your own bloody business.'

'You're not white, so why must he call you baas?'

Johnny-boy looked threateningly into the crowd but failed to find the speaker.

'He's a Kaffer and I am a Coloured man!' And then again addressing the boy, 'You hear that, you swine! Down on your knees!'

Johnny-boy was now drunk with power. The boy either got to his knees or God help him. This was District Six and Johnny-boy's territory. Here he would show any man who he was. Even a white man . . . only that was different. After all a white man was a white man. This boy either got on his knees or he'd show him.

'On your knees, Kaffer!' Johnny-boy brought his knife up till the edge was just below the boy's eyes. 'Or else I'll pull this bloody knife across your black skin!' The boy shivered and stared as if hypnotised by the knife.

'Johnny-boy added a little pressure. The boy winced.

'It hurt, hey? You going to get a lot more hurt, if I pull this knife.' . . . The boy pulled. Blood spurted down the boy's face. Suddenly the tension was broken.

'Come-on Johnny-boy! Let's get inside the bioscope. We've got money!' Amaai pulled Johnny-boy away. The boy was terror-stricken and shivering, holding his bleeding face. Johnny-boy allowed himself to be led away.

'Let that be a lesson to Kaffers who meddle with me!' he said.

> Blood!!!
> The streets of the city are red,
> It seeps through the country
> And makes a redness through all the land.
> It mixes with the black and the white
> And the yellow and the brown,
> And holds a deep terror.
> For fear comes with blood,
> And fear awakens the brute
> that is within the man,
> And creates a different man,
> Who fears his brother because he is also different,
> And then makes the redness.

Johnny-boy had money, but was undecided whether to go to the bioscope at once or not. He still felt tense after the episode. He was unsure whether he had meant to stab the youth or not. In either case he had risen in prestige, if not with the crowd then with Amaai and Braim. He had shown them how to put a Kaffer in his place. He had proved the superiority of a Coloured man over an African boy.

'Jesus! but that Kaffer bled!' Amaai said.

'Hell man, you really mean to do things when you say it!'

'Suppose he gets help.'

'You'll get the whole bloody location on top of you!'

'A Kaffer's scared of a Coloured man!'

'Gwan!'

'That one was!'

'That was a pikkie!'

'He's still a Kaffer and Kaffers can get wild.'

'Suppose he goes to the police?'

'He's too bloody scared!'

'The police know how to work with Kaffers all right!'

'Knock the fear of hell out of them!'

'You're scared of the police yourself!'

'Who the hell aint?'

Johnny-boy avoided the conversation and stared at the vivid poster showing, 'Roy Kent in *Bandits of the Purple Sage*'.

'Johnny-boy aint!' Johnny-boy could feel the anger welling up in him.

'Let's get inside,' he said.

'CHRIST, LOOK OUT!!' Amaai suddenly yelled.

Johnny-boy ducked too late. A stunning blow, and his ears began to ring. He wiped the blood out of his eyes and was just in time to avoid another blow. He groped this way and that, trying to get to his feet and avoid the blows of an enormous African who towered over him. There was anger as of a roused giant, in the eyes of his assailant.

Johnny-boy shuffled to his knees and struggled drunkenly for possession of the knobkerrie. He was blinded by his own blood, and the hot smell almost stifled him. He managed to wrench himself free and make a run, but the African was upon him in a moment. He groped in his pocket for the knife but could not find it.

The grip on his throat suddenly relaxed and he saw the African topple over. Amaai was now hammering at the latter with a heavy buckle-belt. Braim also jumped into the fray, kicking at the African for all he was worth. Johnny-boy now got to his feet, and grabbing the belt from Amaai, continued to flay the insensible figure bleeding in the gutter.

'Bloody black swine! Bloody swine!' Johnny-boy panted between blows.

'Bloody swine! You're dealing with a Brown man!' He was now in a frenzy and beating monotonously. The watching crowd was as passive as ever. No-one thought of interfering while the three boys were beating up the African. This was a spectacle to relieve the monotony, a worthy prologue to the bioscope performance to follow.

The shrill blast of a police whistle awakened Johnny-boy to his senses. The crowd hesitated, then started to saunter away, not wishing openly to show its fear of the police. Johnny-boy strolled away as casually as he dared. Amaai and Braim were openly nervous.

'Let's get inside!'

'Ja, before the Boere start getting tough!'

'What's the hurry?' asked Johnny-boy, wiping the blood from his head as he strolled with affected nonchalance towards the foyer. A police van pulled to a stop and two burly white policemen jumped out. The African was still lying unconscious in the gutter.

'Here's one of them!'

'Come on, skittop! Get to your feet!' the policeman demanded.

The African was slowly regaining consciousness.

'Asseblief baas!'

'The Kaffer's drunk!'

'Komaan, get up!' The African made feeble attempts to get to his feet.

'As drunk as hell!'

'Where's your pass?'

'Asseblief baas!'

'*Komaan waar's jou pas?*'

'Asseblief baas!'

'Chuck him in the van, the Kaffer's drunk!' The African was lifted and thrown into the back of the police van.

'Right! The rest of you, break it up!' The crowd dispersed. Most flocked to the foyer of the cinema to buy tickets.

'Come on, let's get inside!' said Johnny-boy.

'Jesus! Don't Kaffers bleed!'

'Bleed like hell!'

'Let's get inside,' Johnny-boy repeated.

'Bleed like bloody hell!'

'If I were in Hollywood, I'd say "Kaffer, buy my tickets!"'

'Let's get inside!' said Johnny-boy.

'All right!'

'Okay!'

'Three eightpennies!' said Johnny-boy nonchalantly.

> This is a sad song, brother,
> Cause the tune ain't good,
> But there's going to be a time, brother,
> Where the white will not be one tune,
> Or the black another, or the brown another,
> But we'll all sing together, brother,
> At the end of the rainbow.

[May 1955]

Down the Quiet Street

BRUNO ESEKIE
[EZEKIEL MPHAHLELE]

Nadia Street was reputed to be the quietest street in Newclare. Not that it is any different from other streets. It has its own dirty water, its own flies; its own horse manure; its own pot-bellied children with traces of urine down the legs. The hawker's trolley still slogs along in Nadia Street, and the cloppity-clop from the hoofs of the over-fed mare is still part of the street.

Its rows of houses are no different, either. The roofs slant forward as if they were waiting for the next gale to rock them out of their complacency and complete the work it has already started.

Braziers still line the rocky pavement; their columns of smoke curling up and settling on everything around. And stray chickens can be seen pecking at the children's stools with mute relish. Nadia Street has its lean barking mongrels and its share of police beer-raids.

Yet the street still clung to the reputation of being the quietest. Things always went on in the *next* street.

Then something happened. When it did, some of the residents shook their heads dolefully and looked at one another as if they sensed a hundred years' plague around the corner.

Old Lebona down the street laughed and laughed until people feared that his chronic bronchitis was going to seize him by the throat and kill him. 'Look at it down the street or up the street,' he said, 'it's the same. People will always do the unexpected. Is it any wonder God's curse remains on the black man?' Then he laughed again.

'You'll see,' said Dikeledi, rubbing her breast with her forearm to ease the itching caused by the milk. She always said that, to arouse her listeners' curiosity. But she hardly ever showed them what they would see.

Manyeu, the widow, said to her audience: 'It reminds me of what happened once at Winburg, the Boer town down in the Free State.' She looked wistfully ahead of her. The other women looked at her and the new belly that pushed out from under the clean floral apron.

'I remember clearly because I was pregnant, expecting – who was it now? Yes, I was expecting Lusi, my fourth. The one you sent to the butcher yesterday, Kotu.'

Some people said that it happened when Constable Tefo first came to patrol Nadia Street on Sunday afternoons. But others said the Russians were threatening war. Of course, after it had happened Nadia Street went back to what its residents insisted on calling a quiet life.

If Constable Tefo ever thought that he could remain untainted by Nadia Street gossip, he was jolly well mistaken. The fact that he found it necessary to make up his mind about it indicated that he feared the possibility of being entangled in the people's private lives.

He was tall and rather good-looking. There was nothing officious about him, nothing police-looking except for the uniform. He was in many ways one of the rarest of the collection from the glass cage at Headquarters. His bosses suspected him. He looked to them too human to be a good protector of the law. Yes, that's all he was to the people, that's what his bosses had hired him for.

The news spread that Tefo was in love. 'I've seen the woman come here at the end of every month. He always kisses her. The other day I thought he was kissing her too long.' That was Manyeu's verdict.

It did not seem to occur to anyone that the woman who was seen kissing Tefo might be his wife. Perhaps it was just as well, because it so happened that he did not have a wife. At forty he was still unmarried.

Manyeu was struck almost silly when Constable Tefo entered her house to buy *maheu* (sour mealie-meal drink).

'You'll see,' said Dikeledi, who rubbed her breast up and down to relieve the burning itch of the milk.

Still Tefo remained at his post, almost like a mountain, like the Sphinx: at once defiant, reassuring, and menacing. He would not allow himself to be ruffled by the subtle suggestions he heard, the meaningful twitch of the face he saw, the burning gaze he felt behind him as he moved about on his beat.

One day Dikeledi passed him with a can of beer, holding it behind her apron. She chatted with him for a while and they both laughed. It was like that, often; mice playing hide-and-seek in the mane of the lion.

'How's business?' Tefo asked Sung Li's wife one Sunday on the stoep of their shop.

'Velly bad.'

'Why?'

'Times is bad.'

'Hm.'

'Velly beezee, you?'

'Yes, no rest, till we get over there, at Croesus Cemetery.' She laughed, thinking it very funny that a policeman should think of death. She told him so.

'How's China?'

'I'm not flom China, he, he, he. I'm born here, he, he, he. Funnee!' And she showed rusty rotted teeth when she laughed, the top front teeth overtaking the receding lower row.

Tefo laughed loud to think that he had always thought of the Sung Lis as people from China, which conjured weird pictures of man-eating people from what he had been told in his childhood.

When he laughed, Constable Tefo's stomach moved up and down while he held his belt in front and his shoulders fluttered about like the wings of a bird that is not meant to fly long distances.

When her husband within called her, Madam Sung Li turned to go. Tefo looked at her shuffling her small feet, slippers almost screaming with the pain of being dragged like that. From behind, the edge of the dress clung alternately to the woollen black stockings she had on. The bundle of hair at the back of her head looked as if all the woman's fibre were knotted up in it, and if it were undone Madam Sung Li might fall to pieces. Her body bent forward like a tree in the wind. Tefo observed to himself that there was no wind.

One Sunday afternoon Tefo entered Sung Li's shop to buy a bottle of lemonade. The heat was intense. The roofs of the houses seemed to strain under the merciless beating of the sun. All the available windows and doors were ajar and, owing to the general lack of verandahs and the total absence of trees, the residents puffed and sighed and groaned and stripped some of their garments.

Madam Sung Li leaned over the counter, her elbows planted on the top surface, her arms folded. She might have been the statue of some Oriental god in that position but for a lazy afternoon fly that tried to settle on her face. She had to throw her head about to keep the pestilent insect away.

Constable Tefo breathed hard after every gulp as he stood looking out through the shop window, facing Nadia Street.

One thing he had got used to was the countless funeral processions that trailed on week after week. They had to pass Newclare on the way to the cemetery. Short ones, long ones, hired double deckers, cars, lorries; poor insignificant ones; rich, snobbish ones. All black and inevitable.

The processions usually took the street next to Nadia. But so many people were dying that some units were beginning to spill over into Nadia.

Tefo went out to the stoep to have a little diversion; anything to get his mind off the heat. He was looking at one short procession as it turned into Nadia when a thought crossed his mind, like the shadow of a cloud that passes under the sun.

Seleke's cousin came staggering on to the stoep. His dress looked as if he had once crossed many rivers and drained at least one. He was always referred to as Seleke's cousin, and nobody ever cared to know his name.

Seleke lived in the next street. She was the tough sort with a lashing tongue. But even she could not whip her cousin out of his perennial stupor.

Dikeledi's comment was: 'You'll see, one day he'll hunt mice for food. The cats won't like it.' And she rubbed her breast. But Seleke's cousin absorbed it all without the twinge of a hair.

'Ho, chief!' Seleke's cousin hailed the constable, wobbling about like a puppet on the stage. 'Watching the coffins, eh? Too many people dying, eh? Yes, too many. Poor devils!'

Tefo nodded.

A lorry drove up the street and pulled up on the side, almost opposite the Chinaman's shop.

'Dead men don't shout,' said Seleke's cousin.

'You're drunk? Why don't you go home and sleep?'

'Me drunk? Yes, yes, I'm drunk. But don't you talk to me like these pig-headed people around here. Their pink tongues wag too much. Why don't they leave me alone?'

'There's no one in this bloody location who can read English like I do.'

'I'm sure there isn't.' Tefo smiled tolerantly.

'I like you, chief. You're going to be a great man one of these days. Now, you're looking at these people going to bury their dead. One of these days those coffins will tell their story. I don't know why they can't leave me alone. Why can't they let me be, the lousy lot?'

A small funeral party turned into Nadia Street on a horse-drawn trolley cart. There were three women and four men on the cart, excluding the driver. A man who looked like their religious leader sang lustily, his voice quivering above the others.

The leader had on a frayed, fading, purple surplice and an off-white cassock. He looked rather too young for such a mighty responsibility as trying to direct departed souls to heaven, Tefo thought. The constable also thought how many young men were being fired with religious feeling these days . . .

The trolley stopped in front of a house almost opposite Sung Li's. Tefo looked on. The group alighted and the four men lifted the coffin down.

Tefo noticed that the leader was trembling. By some miracle his hymn book stayed in the trembling hand. He wiped his forehead so many times that the constable thought the leader had a fever and could not lift the coffin further. They obviously wanted to enter the yard just behind them. He went to the spot and offered to help.

The leader's eyes were wide and they reflected a crowd of emotions. Tefo could not understand. And then he made a surprising gesture to stop Tefo from touching the coffin. In a second he nodded his head several times muttering something that made Tefo understand that his help would be appreciated. Whereupon the constable picked up the handle on his side, and the quartette took the corpse into the house. Soon Tefo was back on the Chinaman's stoep.

It must have been about fifteen minutes later when he heard voices bursting out in song as the party came out of the house with the coffin. Again Tefo noticed, the leader was sweating and trembling. The coffin was put on the ground outside the gate. The others of the party continued to sing lustily, the men's voices beating down the courageous sopranos.

Tefo sensed that they wanted to hoist it on to the lorry. Something told him he should not go and help. One of these religious sects with queer rules, he thought.

At the gate the leader of the funeral party bent forward and, with a jerky movement, he caught hold of the handle and tilted the coffin, shouting to the other men at the same time to hold their handles. Tefo turned sharply to look.

A strange sound came from the box. To break the downward tilt the other men had jerked the coffin up. But a cracking sound came from the bottom; a sound of cracking wood. They were going to hoist the coffin higher, when it happened.

A miniature avalanche of bottles came down to the ground. A man jumped into the lorry, reversed it a little and drove off. The trolley cart ground its way down Nadia Street. Tefo's eyes swallowed the whole scene. He descended from the stoep as if in a trance, and walked slowly to the spot. It was a scene of liquor bottles tumbling and tinkling and bumping into one another, some breaking, and others rolling down the street in a playful manner; like children who have been let out of the classroom at playtime. There was hissing and shouting among the funeral party.

'You frightened goat!'

'Messing up the whole business!'

'I knew this would happen!'

'You'll pay for this!'

'You should have stayed home, you clumsy pumpkin!'

'We're ruined this time!'

They had all disappeared by the time it had registered on Tefo's mind that an arrest must be made. More than that: a wild mob of people was scrambling over the bottles. In a moment they also had disappeared, with the bottles, the corpus delicti! A number of people gathered round the policeman.

The lousy crowd, he thought, glad that a policeman has failed to arrest! They nudged one another, and others indulged in mock pity.

Manyeu came forward. 'I want the box for fire, sir constable.' He indicated impatiently with the hand that she might have it. It did not escape Dikeledi's attention, and she said to her neighbour, rubbing her breast that was full of milk: 'You'll see. Wait.'

'Ho, chief! Trouble here?' Seleke's cousin elbowed his way to the centre of the crowd. He had been told what had happened.

'Funerals, funerals, funerals is my backside! Too bad I'm late for the party. Hard luck to you chief. Now listen. I trust these corpses like the lice on my shirt. But you're going to be a great man one day. Trust my word for that. I bet the lice on my body.'

Later that afternoon Constable Tefo sat in Manyeu's room, drinking *maheu*; Dikeledi, rubbing her breast, was sitting on the floor with two other women. Manyeu sat on a low bench, her new belly pushing out under her floral apron like a promising melon.

Somewhat detached from the women's continuous babble, Tefo was thinking about funerals and corpses and bottles of liquor. He wondered about funeral processions in general. He remembered what Seleke's cousin said the other day on the Chinaman's stoep. Was it an unwitting remark?

Just then another procession passed down the street. Tefo stood up abruptly and went to stand at the door. If only the gods could tell him what was in that brown glossy coffin, he thought. He went back to his bench, a figure of despair.

Dekeledi's prophetic 'You'll see' took on a serious meaning when Tefo one day married Manyeu after her sixth had arrived. Nadia Street gasped. But then it recovered quickly from the surprise, considering the reputation it had of being the quietest street in Newclare.

It added to Dikeledi's social stature to be able to say after the event: 'You see!' while she vigorously rubbed her breasts that itched from the milk.

[January 1956]

Let the People Drink!

D. CAN THEMBA

—THEY'RE DRINKING ANYWAY
Why not make it legal? If Parliament allows liquor rights for all, South Africa's crime rate will drop enormously. In this article D. Can Themba tells of the big rackets fostered by prohibition; he also tells of a thrilling stowaway ride he took on an illicit liquor run. If we repeal the 'prohibition' laws, we'll put the liquor gangs out of a job; and we'll give the police time to do their real work fighting to stop the present crime wave.

I went to a little one-room apartment in Good Street, Sophietown, Johannesburg. It is perched in the sky like a dovecote, and you have to go up a flight of rickety steps to get there. There was a door like a shed-door. I knocked on the door, and called: 'Ousie! Ousie!' A latch screeched back, and a broad face peered at me. Then the door opened, and I stepped into a shabby passage.

I was led to a second door beyond which a drone of voices flowed. I walked into a very well-furnished, brightly lit room. Modern jazz music of the hottest kind blared at me. And the room was crowded by African men and women sitting in clusters of threes and fours, enjoying – most of them – beer. The amber quart bottles stood all over, full, half-full, and empty. But here and there, a party was drinking brandy from tumblers measured accurately to the fourth finger.

This was the famous 'Little Heaven', Sophiatown's poshest shebeen.

'Hi, Can!' called the huge hostess, 'what evil plans bring you here?' Then she turned to the house at large, and announced: 'Say, folks, Can here is Mr DRUM. Maybe you'll soon find yourself in *Drum*.'

I grinned pointlessly. I had to, because I recognised a couple of fellows who belonged to Sophiatown's toughest gang. I didn't want them to think I was doing a story on them.

'Well, Can, what can we do for you?' asked the hostess.

'Beer,' I said.

'I got whisky, you know.'

'Yes, but beer,' I insisted.

I sat down on the studio couch, and looked around. In a corner on the bed I saw three very respectable people, two men and a woman sipping quietly from their glasses. The woman was a very well-known Staff Nurse. She caught my eye and smiled sweetly at me. The men turned round, and I recognised two teachers from one of Sophiatown's primary schools.

My drink came.

Half-way down my quart of beer, an African constable, cloaked in a heavy khaki-green overcoat, entered. Another one, without overcoat followed close upon his heels. They joined me on the studio couch, and I could see the sergeant's stripes on the arm of the one without overcoat.

Nobody turned a hair. The fellows at the table didn't even break their argument over the Freedom Charter. Our hostess waddled up to the 'cops'. They ordered 'Half-a-Jack' (half-a-bottle) of brandy. And they paid for it!

I rose quietly, and went to say good-bye to the hostess. I still had quite a few shebeens to visit that night, and many nights after.

In my ramblings round the shebeens of Johannesburg, I found that they were not all as comfortable and cheerful and 'safe' as 'Little Heaven'.

Those in the townships are of two kinds. There are the handsome, respectable ones like 'Little Heaven' and 'The Sanctuary' in Sophiatown, 'The Greenhouse' in Newclare, 'The Kind Lady' and 'The Gardens' in Western Township, 'The Basement' in Orlando, and 'Paradise' in George Goch. These make you feel at home, and the atmosphere is friendly and sociable. There are kids to go and buy for you soda water, ginger ale, or Indian tonic. There is often a private room where you could 'sleep it off' if you've had too many. These shebeens have obviously ploughed some of their profits into the 'business'.

But there are those that are just out to make money, and damn the customer. They are dirty, and crowded, and hostile. The shebeen queen is always hurrying you to drink quickly, and swearing at somebody or other. 'You b——s act as if you've licences to drink!' She sells everything, brandy, gin, beer and skokiaan, hops, hoenene, barberton, pineapple, and even more violent concoctions. It is in these that 'doping' takes place.

'Doping' is the weakening or fortifying of the strength of brandy and gin. These drinks are so precious, expensive, and difficult to come by that these shebeen queens often 'dope' it with water, or black tea, or even tobacco water, to increase the amount or to give it a quick kick.

The prices in the shebeens vary. A quart of beer may cost from 3/6 to 6/-. A 'straight' of brandy or gin, between 14/6 and 26/-. A bottle of whisky, between 30/- and 50/-. At one Syrian shebeen in Ferreirastown, you pay 14/6 for a bottle of brandy if you take it away and 20/- if you take it there. It is safer for the 'house' if you take it right away with you. Quite often you may get liquor below retail prices. This is because it has been stolen from a bottle store, and the whole price is sheer profit.

But I wanted to find out where all this liquor comes from. This was tough because nobody wants to talk. Not only from fear of the police, but because shebeens don't want to give away their 'holes' – the sources of their supplies.

My break came when a friend of mine arranged that I should be taken along when the 'boys' made a trip to go and fetch supplies for the weekend. We met in town at the corner of Diagonal and Sauer Streets. A grey van picked us up. I sat in front with the driver and my friend, and as I looked back over my shoulder, I saw two other chaps, unknown to me, sitting in the van. Beyond them covering the door of the van at the back was a lot of flowers placed so that you could not see into the van when the door was open.

Nobody would tell me exactly where we were going. We travelled through byways and back streets for about a half-hour, when we came to what appeared to be the outskirts of a town. From the registration numbers of the cars I saw, I knew that we were near Vereeniging.

Suddenly our driver swerved into the driveway of a house and stopped in front of another van. He ordered us to stay in the car while he slipped into the house through a side door. We waited there for about an hour until a white man came out, completely ignored us, and went to stand at the gateway of the driveway, looking up and down the street.

After a while the driver darted out of the side door, stood a moment alongside the vans, looking towards the gate. I felt that he was waiting for a signal. We were all tensely silent. Suddenly he made for the van in front of us, and opened the door at the back. The two fellows in our van clambered out through the flowers and joined him.

Then they carried out carefully packed cartons, about six of them, from the other van into ours.

'Is that the hooch?' I asked my friend.

'Mmm,' he replied.

And I could hear the faint tinkle of clinking bottles. Inside our van they arranged the flowers carefully to hide away the cartons in case the door has to be opened. The two chaps at the back put newspapers over the cartons and sat on two of them.

Our driver looked towards the gate, then got in the van, and backed slowly out. At the gate he dropped the key he had, and drove away.

'Surely that is not a bottle store?' I asked.

The driver laughed a little. 'No,' he said, 'that was not a bottle store. That man was just a contact.'

'Ever been caught before?' I wanted to know.

He laughed again. 'No. Only once the Flying Squad took a look at our flowers. That's where doing it in daylight helps.'

They dropped us at the same corner of Diagonal and Sauer Streets.

My friend who knew that I was doing a story for *Drum*, suddenly said: '*Ou Verwoerd notch skaars.*' (Verwoerd doesn't know a thing.) These boys think of Dr Verwoerd as the government.

Oddly enough, most of the liquor that flows into the illicit trade does not come from Johannesburg City. It comes from suburban bottle stores. One shebeen queen travels as far as Kimberley, in the Cape, to get her liquor.

A usual technique is for the bottle-store owner to drive through a white suburb and note down all the vacant lots. Sometimes he collects addresses of dead people or people in gaol. By spreading it out he can enter into his books sales that do not seem too large, and still he can keep his shebeens fully supplied. Most bottle stores do not deal with individual shebeens. They supply dealers, who in turn supply shebeens.

Another source is the 'big time' operators who break into bottle stores, usually with inside help, generally a white man, who gives them the layout of the 'joint'.

Several bottle stores have been hit by the 'Hole-in-the-wall Gang'. Their problem has every time been how to make all the noise they please in breaking through a roof or wall without attracting unwelcome attention. Someone has had to be silenced.

The wholesale merchant disposes of his liquor in one of two ways. He may either employ a runner who sells to the shebeen, or he may have his own shebeen where he sells the liquor.

Then there are small operators who employ white hoboes to procure the liquor for them. These democratic characters visit various bottle stores and make small purchases at each, and at the end of a day they are able to supply a runner with about six bottles of brandy. The police know about them but there are so many of them going that it is difficult to keep track on all.

Last year about five illicit stills manufacturing brandy and beer have been found on the Reef. Some of them were operated by Europeans, and some of them by Non-Europeans.

And last year, too, the cry has gone up: 'Let the Africans drink European Liquor!' On the whole, the police feel that their work would be considerably simplified if Africans were to be allowed light wines and beer. Many officials feel that crime would be reduced if Africans were allowed throughout the country to drink freely. The wine-growers are beginning to feel that the illicit trade in liquor cheats them of their fair share of the profits. And the Africans are increasingly showing their determination to get at European liquor.

The issue is no more whether Africans in general should be allowed to drink.

THEY DRINK IN ANY CASE. The issue is whether they may drink legally.

Prohibition has been proved impossible. There is too great a thirst for drink among the unentitled. And too great a thirst for money among the bottle-store keepers. And prohibition is asking for too much from the police.

According to the 1954 Report of the Bureau of Census and Statistics, there were in general 1 542 415 prosecutions of which 1 373 589 ended in convictions. Of the 1 542 415 prosecutions, 950 514 were for liquor and habit-forming drugs; and of the 1 373 589 convictions, 886 601 were for liquor and habit-forming drugs.

This means that 62 per cent of the 1954 prosecutions were for liquor and habit-forming drugs, and 65 per cent of the convictions were for liquor and habit-forming drugs. It also means that 93 per cent of the liquor and drugs prosecutions ended in convictions.

In other words if the illicit liquor trade were to be stopped, we could cut prosecutions and convictions very heavily. That could be cutting crime heavily!

The other day, in a shebeen, I was caught by members of the liquor squad with a nip of brandy (about a quarter bottle). At the police station I was told I could pay an admission of guilt that was £5 for a bottle of brandy or part thereof. The police were very friendly. They told me that a man of my standing ought to apply for a liquor licence, and not to be found drinking in shebeens.

I paid £5 like thousands of other men of my standing, caught in the same circumstances.

[March 1956]

Guts and Granite!
Lilian Ngoyi

'She's ambitious!' 'She's a remarkable orator!' 'She knows too little about political theory!' 'She has a brilliant intellect!' 'What kind of woman is this?' 'She almost rocks men out of their pants when she speaks!'

So say people about Mrs Lilian Ngoyi, now president of the African National Congress Women's League for the second term — the most talked-of woman in politics.

The roaring reception she got from a crowd of over a thousand men and women at Port Elizabeth last month showed how popular and well loved she is even outside the borders of her home-province. She was presented with a clock. This has been worked into a figure of a horse made of plastic. The horse is shown jumping over a boulder.

The Cape women told Mrs Ngoyi that in war a horse goes on ahead even after its rider has been thrown off. She, their leader, must move on, even if some of her followers fall by the roadside.

Revelry. Song. Dance. Laughter. War cries that recalled the passion, the heat, the blood and lust for life of a historic past. These were the ingredients of Mrs Ngoyi's reception in Natal, following on the Cape visit. The children of Chaka sweltered in hot and steamy Durban weather while they made merry at the Y.M.C.A. hall.

As Mrs Ngoyi sat in front of the crowd, a half-naked man came crouching forward like a panther, leading a black goat with Congress colours round its neck. The other people stepped aside to give him an aisle. Someone addressed the goat, called it soft names until the creature must have been half in love with death. He told the goat what a privilege it was to be chosen for the splendid sacrifice; it was not out of pure malice; through the ages African ancestors had offered it to the gods; so it has to be today; this time, as an honour to a great lady.

He said a few words to the women's president and ordered the goat to be taken away for slaughter. In a short time the 'high priest' came back with goat's meat and skin. He had the gall bladder in one hand. He took off Mrs Ngoyi's shoes, painted the big toes with the gall and poured drops of the green stuff on her head.

'A dumb goat has the sense to look for green pastures,' said the priest. 'How much worthier it is for human beings like us to seek freedom. The strength of the gods be in you always as you lead us.'

The woman of the moment cried silently. Not out of pity, or out of despair, but out of humility. She has never thought much of these traditional rituals, being town-born and bred. But she was moved by the symbol of dedication to the cause closest to her heart.

Who is Lilian Ngoyi? The woman factory worker who is tough granite on the outside, but soft and compassionate deep down in her. The woman who three years ago was hardly known in Non-European politics. The woman whose rise to fame has been phenomenal.

Hers is not a success story. Especially not the cheap popular success. It is the story of a personality fashioned in the crucible of a brutal past and present.

Born in 1911 in Pretoria of Bapedi parents, Mrs Ngoyi grew up in conditions of abject poverty. Her father, now dead, changed employment and the Matabane family moved to a mine in the eastern Transvaal. Her mother, still alive today, did washing for whites, and the father worked for £3 for six weeks. Little Lilian was noted to be the biggest crier in the neighbourhood. She would cry until she fainted.

She was sent to Kilnerton Training Institution while she was still in Standard II. She went up to first year of the teachers' course. The father couldn't afford the fees any longer, and so she had to quit school.

Lilian entered City Deep mine hospital as a probationer nurse. She then got married. But after a few years her husband, Mr Ngoyi, died.

Except for a short interlude of ballroom dancing in the competition ranks, her life slid into a quiet slow tempo.

In 1952, when the African National Congress launched its Defiance Campaign, Mrs Ngoyi left a critically sick daughter in hospital to join a batch that went to 'defy'. From this dates Mrs Ngoyi's hectic political career.

She went out with a batch to defy apartheid regulations at the General Post Office. She told inquiring officials and the police that she was writing a telegram to some Cabinet Ministers. They were later acquitted in court. Mrs Ngoyi then began to organise Orlando women for Congress.

As Vice-President of the South African Federation of Women, Mrs Ngoyi was chosen delegate to the Lausanne conference of women in Switzerland last year. Together with another African woman they were turned away from the boat in Cape Town as they had no passports bearing their names. Later they left the country by air, unknown to the officials and under dramatic circumstances.

They visited several European countries on both sides of the Iron Curtain.

They came back in the same quiet way in which they had left.

Mrs Ngoyi is the first African woman to be on the Transvaal Provincial Executive of the A.N.C. and on the National Executive.

In 1954 she became treasurer of the S.A. Non-European Council of Trade Unions. She is a member of the Women's Garment Workers' Union for the Reef, and is also Acting President of the S.A. Federation of Women.

Once in politics, Mrs Ngoyi knew that the nameless compulsion that had been working in her since childhood had become a reality. Those days she loved to read about pioneers who led their people to freedom. Not least was she thrilled by the activities of Hebrew leaders as in the Bible.

Another thing that made a lasting impact on her was the evil of migrant labour as men came and went between the Reserves and the mines.

Her father was bitterly anti-white. Strong passion expresses itself through her, too, but in the more meaningful form of anti-oppression – whether practised by whites or non-whites.

Mrs Ngoyi's weakness lies in being highly emotional. Her strength lies in the fact that she admits it and is always prepared to be disciplined. Her stubbornness is that of a centipede, which keeps the same direction in spite of any attempt to take it off its course. But again she admits it, and is always prepared to submit to cold logic.

She also admits her weak educational background. She is therefore not much of a political thinker, but she gets down to a job in a manner that shames many a political theorist. For this woman has bundles and bundles of energy. Granite reinforced with wire.

She will often begin her family washing at 10 in the night – home cleanliness and sewing are a religious passion with her.

Mrs Ngoyi is a brilliant orator. She can toss an audience on her little finger, get men grunting with shame and a feeling of smallness and infuse everyone with renewed courage.

Her speech always teems with vivid figures of speech. Mrs Ngoyi will say: 'We don't want men who wear skirts under their trousers. If they don't want to act, let us women exchange garments with them.' Or she will say: 'We women are like hens that lay eggs for somebody to take away. That's the effect of Bantu Education.'

Again, Mrs Ngoyi will say: 'A day will come when Congressmen will feel cold in their bowels and want to sit by the fire like Peter before he denied Christ. They will be asked, "Do you know this man called Congress?" I wonder whether they will slink away.'

At a recent anti-pass meeting one masculine fire-eater advocated violence as a solution to the African's problems. Mrs Ngoyi replied: 'Shed your own blood first and let's see what stuff it's made of.' She denounced the theory of violence as stupid and unpractical. This seemed to act as a hosepipe, because the firebrand spluttered, flickered and sat down to smoulder, feeling embarrassed.

Mrs Lilian Ngoyi has several critics. Some say she has rocketed to premature fame. Some, that she hob-nobs with whites who groom her in their political kindergarten. Others, again, that she works too hard because she is ambitious.

But these critics seldom say these things to her. She has an uncanny way of inviting criticism in order to test her own beliefs. And then they are left confounded.

Mrs Ngoyi is still a political question mark. One thing is clear though; it has required guts and granite to lead and inspire thousands of women who have now come to the front line in African politics. The heat and pressure of the times have provided a Lilian Ngoyi to perform that function.

Masterpiece in Bronze
[March 1956]

'BABY COME DUZE'

THERE'S A NEW LINGO IN THE TOWNSHIPS, BRIGHT AS THE BRIGHT-BOYS, MADE OF AFRIKAANS, ZULU, SOTHO, ENGLISH AND BRAND-NEW WORDS. HERE'S A STORY IN LINGO – AND EXPLANATIONS.

Story by 'bra' D. Can Themba.
Pictures by 'bra' Gopal S. Naransamy.

Prettyboy: 'Globe daar, man, Snooky man. Daai's nou eintlik die real goete. Jy notch?'
Snooky: 'Jy val babies bo. Daai's die Casbah Baos se rubberneck, en sy vat nie moegoes kop-toe nie.'

Prettyboy: 'Get a load of that one, Snooky. That's the genuine article. Get it?'
Snooky: 'You go for every skirt. That girl belongs to the Casbah Boys, and won't go for suckers.'

'Say, baby, you got me crazy!'

Prettyboy: 'Ek sê, baby, 'n man pitch cruel vir jou. Pun-yuka ek net, dan hol ons die toun toe.'
Ellen: 'Jy's babies verskrik, hê! Wat gaan vir wat en wie gaan vir wie? Ou Bull van die Casbahs maak jou hinty, finish en klaar, Daak!'

Prettyboy: 'I say, baby, I'm nuts about you. Give me a break, and you and I will paint the town red.'
Ellen: 'You're girl-crazy, eh! What's cooking? Bull of the Casbah Boys will kill you off, finish and flat, Scoot!'

Ellen: 'Toe was ek mix-zup van die out-tie, maar ek nyekeza. Ek was gestoot. Ou Bull is coward met 'n gounie, en hy neinen net vir molle. My Mma hoor my, is Jozi die!'

Ellen: 'But I fell hard for the bright-boy. Still I played angel. I was cornered. Bull is cruel with a knife, and goes to jail just through dames. Goodness, this is Joburg!'

'Lay-off that doll, small-fry!'

Bull: 'Jy deal met my moll, spy. Pazama weer by daai cherry, dan quip ek you vuil.'

Bull: *'You string with my girl, small-fry. Just dare go near that dame and I'll beat you up bad.'*

''n Shot maak jou nie wild as jy Judo notch nie, man. Ga hom voor hom hele laaities . . .'

'A bigshot can't scare you if you know Judo. Grab him in front of all his boys . . .'

'Spin hom; hy moet brul soos 'n os as hy vlie ant hulle is almal sissies as jy pluck hou.'

'Throw him; he must roar like an ox when he flies for they're all cowards when you show courage.'

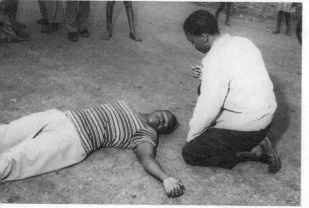

'Die Here weet, die dikker die vark die harder val hy.'

'God knows, the bigger the pig the harder it drops.'

Prettboy: 'Toe kom Easter – mdlalos, nice-times, piekniet! Maar waar! Ons los die bricados in die shashi, ek en my mama, two-out. Jy gaan dit vat ek gee, maar ons dlala tot die beeste romantic word.'

Prettyboy: 'Then came Easter – fun parties, picnic! But what! we dodged the boys, my dame and I, all by ourselves. You'll think I'm pulling a fast one, but we spooned till even the cattle became romantic.'

'Night and day, you are the one I love.'

Prettyboy: 'En daai aand mova ons titch-toe cruel ge-clip. Die toun was mca, hinty man. Die baby ga my, is shandies kalykit crackets sgoer-sgoer in my koukie. Ek was weg, man, weg man . . .'

Prettyboy: 'And that night we went home, in close embrace. The town was beautiful. Silent. My girl pressed me, things exploded as if crackers burst in my head. I was gone, man, gone, man . . .'

Loving, and laughter, forever after . . .

Ellen: 'Moet dit 'n laaitie is, dan maak hy nyakanyaka onder die cherrekies net soos hom ganbini. Dan squeal hy die mamzan globe hom weg met 'n evil while hy nog boeke oopmaak.'

Prettyboy: 'Yefies! Yefies! Dan lê hy die baby by die mong, dan rwa hy haar met die ou spead: "Baby, come duze!" Yefies! Yefies!'

Ellen: 'If it's a boy, he'll cause trouble among the little girls just like his father. And he'll grumble that her mother stares him off whilst he's still making love.'

Prettyboy: 'Geewhiz! Geewhiz! Then he waylays her at the chinaman's shop, and then he deceives her with the old flattery: "Baby, come closer!" Geewhiz! Geewhiz!'

[April 1956]

THE END

African Song

RICHARD RIVE

Muti knew when he felt angry. There would be something hard in his throat, and he would clench his hands tightly so that the veins stood out. But this time he knew that he was not angry but afraid. His mouth felt dry and there was a clamminess in the palms of his hands. Somehow Muti could feel, or rather sense, that they were going to meet the police. Yet when the blue uniforms entered the dilapidated meeting-place he was as surprised as if he had not expected them. He stared as if bewitched as they marched in and covered all entrances. And Muti knew it was not an anger he felt but a deep fear which he could not understand. He was far more afraid of the blue uniforms and glistening buttons than of the fact that he had no pass. These were useless regrets now that he had come to the meeting, useless regrets that he had not first learnt the ways of the Big City and got a pass. He only felt a numbness and a terror. His tongue felt enormous and his mouth felt dry. Muti eyed Mpisa and noticed how calmly he took it. But his uncle had a pass and Muti had none. Muti could almost feel Mpisa imploring him to keep calm. But how could one keep calm when there were policemen at the door, and policemen at the window? Some his own colour and some who were white.

And then everyone was standing and Muti watched fascinated as the people sang; but still he sat because he had no pass. And what Muti knew must happen was happening because the blue uniforms were coming nearer, as this one shuffled in his pocket for a pass; and that one had terror in his eyes because he knew he had not one; and still another was calm like Mpisa. And still the people sang. And Muti felt a great calm come over him like a warrior feels before battle, and he clambered clumsily to his feet.

And already this one was led away because he had no pass and that one lifted the hand in protest. But one must not lift the hand in protest. And still the people sang. And Muti was filled with the wonder of it all and was not afraid of the prison walls and the blue uniforms. And then in a hoarse voice Muti also began singing the song of Africa, and not one Muti sang but a hundred Mutis, ten thousand Mutis, and they all sang the song that was Africa.

And as they sang there was a deep calm.

And this is what they sang:

Nkosi Sikelel' iAfrika . . .

which means God bless Africa. God bless the sun-scorched Karoo and the green of the Valley of a Thousand Hills. God bless the mountain streams that chatter impudently when they are high in the hills and are young, but roll lazily from side to side like old women in the Great Plains. And the dry pans which twist their tortured bosoms to the hot skies. And the mighty waters that hurl themselves against her shores and mockingly retreat only to come again with a new energy as if to engulf the mielies and the land and the villages and the towns, even great Africa itself. God bless the cataracts that taunt the solemn rocks, and the African sky that spits blood in the evening. And the timeless hills where the shy roebuck rears its tragic eyes and the dassie sips in silent pools. And the blue krantzes where man has still to breathe. God bless this Africa of heat and cold, and laughter and tears, and deep joy and bitter sorrow. God bless this Africa of blue skies and brown veld, and black and white and love and hatred, and friend and enemy.

For where there was rich laughter there is now sorrow and indifference. And where the eyes were shot with joy for the richness of the soil, there is now a gloom, for the mielies are no longer thick on the stalk. And before the milk lapped the sides of the calabashes, but now they are dry and the milk does not spill over the sides. And even those in the Great Cities who had laughter in their eyes and remembered their ancestors, and the land and the people, now speak in whispers and no longer remember their ancestors, and the land and the people. For now the land is without joy.

There is a heavy mist over all the land, and the mist is thick so that the eye can hardly see through, but where it does lift one can see sorrow and weariness which only Africa can understand. For the ancient koppies are weary, and the veld is no longer gay, and the people are tired, and the mielies bend their heads and weep.

God bless this Africa, this Africa which is part of us. God protect this Africa. God have mercy upon Africa.

And still they sang:

Maluphakonyisw' Upshondo Lwayo . . .

which is lift up our descendants. And Muti thought of himself and wondered if he were a better man than his father, and his father's father and the many before him. For he felt like the Great Bird that flies higher and higher till it is a brother to the sun and can see the land even before the white man came. And then Muti climbed higher like the Bird and saw the land even before the white man came.

But Muti did not understand. Where were the cities and the towns and the villages? And the buildings and the shops? And where were the ones who lived in the cities and the towns? And the white ones and the black ones? For Muti saw nothing but the burning veld and the flat koppies and the hardy renosterbos. And when he searched even further for his own people, he found them at last, and then his heart burst with pride. For he saw proud warriors with plumes of ostrich feathers and shaking armlets which clicked as they raised the hands. And these warriors were huge ones and proud, and lifted high the legs and stamped upon the earth so that the ground shook. For they danced the dance of the young men and it was a vigorous dance and required much strength. And they were fearsome to behold.

And Muti also saw the small ones that hide in the sand and the bushes. But these one must not look upon for they hunt the crab and the shellfish and eat the flesh of the dassie. And Muti felt no man should look upon them and so he turned away his head as if he did not see, and gazed upon the warriors. And he heard them roar out, 'He is one who sees everything. No he is a lion for he hunts alone and kills many!' And that is what Muti heard them shout and it pleased him.

And then like the Great Bird, Muti saw the workers in the field, and the huts and the women threading the beads. And the beads were of many colours like the stones which the sun splits, red and yellow and orange. And Muti admired their hair which was stiff with the clay of the river, and he saw they were buxom and pleasant to behold. And there were cows and fat-tailed sheep. And there was much beer and much laughter and plenty to eat.

But Muti also saw the days that were lean, when the gourds were empty and the animals panted heavily. And then there was much throwing of bones and this one was sacrificed and that maiden must spill her blood for the gods were angry.

And Muti was filled with a shame lest those warriors should see him. And he wanted to hide his face lest the tillers of the soil might see him, or the crab-hunters laugh derisively. What if they saw how frightened he was because he had no pass. But they could not feel frightened because they did not know the ways of the white ones. And then Muti did not feel so ashamed.

And still the people sang.

Yiwa Nemithandazo Yayo Nyi Sikelele . . .

And this means hear our prayers and bless them. And now Muti again saw the look on the face of the Old-one and felt the sadness in her heart. And like one in a dream he saw from afar and heard from afar.

'I am going away, my Mother.'

And she has said nothing but only stared at him with ageless eyes.

'I have decided to go away, my Mother.'

And she had stared and said nothing.

'I will find work and make much money, for there is not much money in the soil. And when I find work I will have much money in my hands so that you will laugh, my Mother. And then,' and he had winked slyly, 'then there will be a wife.'

And then she had sighed as if from a great distance and said, 'It is well.'

But he felt it was not well and he wanted to ask why it was not well, why he left the land of the fathers, and the fields and the cow, but she only said, 'It is well.'

'But I shall not go to Johannesburg, my Mother, for that place is not good. I shall go to some other place.'

And she said, 'I have a brother in Cape Town, he will be good to you.'

And then he said, 'It is good, I will not go to Johannesburg.' For he was filled with a great anger and said aloud, 'And am I a mole that I must climb into the ground and dig the earth?'

But she said, 'No you are not a mole, you are a man.'

And then he laughed and slapped his thighs and was pleased that she had said that, and he said, 'Ho, Mother, you are indeed a good one.'

But when he went for the pass he was not a man, for the white one in the office was angry and his face was red so that one could count the wrinkles. And at first Muti felt that the white man was angry because he was leaving the land of his fathers, and the fields and the cow. But when the white man asked him to go to the Great City, Muti did not want to, for there one becomes a mole.

But there are ways to get a pass if one has money, and so Muti sold the cow, and then Muti came to Cape Town.

Ho, but this is a beautiful place, and the Great Water is bigger than many dams. And there are people who travel far on the Great Waters. And if one works well and has a pass one can also go on the Great Water to the land of the white ones. And there is a big mountain that is flat like a Karoo koppie but higher than many kraals.

And Muti remembered the bull-necked white man and was afraid because he still had no pass. But there are ways to get a pass if one has money, and at the meeting would be his own people, and Mpisa would be there who knew the ways of the City and could speak the language of the white ones.

But Mpisa told him to be careful until he had a pass, especially of those in the blue uniforms, and that was why there was a clamminess in his throat when they entered the meeting.

And still the people sang.

Yiza Moya, Yiza Moya, Oyingcwele . . .

And still Muti sang these words which mean, forward spirit, forward spirit which art holy. And as he sang he felt as if he could burst with pride and love. For he felt proud of this Africa, but his pride was tinged with a shame, and his love was not a true love. And as he sang he had a wonderful vision of the Africa of years hence, maybe ten years, maybe a hundred, though his vision was of two kinds, and this was the first vision.

He saw the face of a black man and the face was grinning so that he could count the teeth. And the black man was laughing in the face of another and this other man was a white man. But there was no malice in the laughter and the white one nodded and grinned back. And there was much merriment and slapping of backs. And then the vision changed to the Great Cities. And there were houses of plenty and shops laden with the produce of the earth, and there were many people passing up and down without any fear in their faces. And Muti almost laughed for the wonder of it when he saw how they did the work that men and women always do, only this time black men and women were also doing such work, and white men and women also, and brown men and women. And they ate and drank and cooked the foods and made merry, and everyone was full of laughter, and Muti himself laughed with the sheer wonder of it that the black and the white and the brown could so laugh together.

And then Muti saw the fields, and the maize was thick and the grapes hung in clusters on the vine, and there stood a black man with a hoe in his hand straightening his back, and he spoke to a white man, who lifted his work-soiled hands to scan the horizon. And there was much more than laughter, an understanding of the soul, of the land. And this was the first vision.

But there was a second vision. And now Muti saw a black face that was filled with smouldering anger, and there were tiny wrinkles around the eyes and mouth which were not good. And this time the mouth was clenched tightly and one could not count the teeth. For this time it looked into a white face that turned away. And then Muti had a vision of the Great Cities. But this cannot be, for everywhere there were black faces, and the policemen were black, and the people were black, and the one who takes your money was black, and the women who were hurrying, and the men. But where were the others? The white ones and the brown ones? And Muti was filled with a great disbelief. And a great sorrow overcame him when he saw that they were hardly there, but the few who remained were doing the things that black men used to do. And on the land there were no white ones, and in the Great Cities there were no white ones, and Muti was still filled with the disbelief.

And this was the second vision of Muti.

Nkosi Sikelele Thina Lusapho Lwakho . . .

And still the people sang these words which mean, God bless us Thy children. God bless the children of Africa, for Africa is old but still a child; for she is old in sorrow and suffering but young in laughter and merriment. For the world does not understand Africa, even as a mother that flings the child from her breast. And the land suffers, and the people suffer and the children. God bless the children of Africa whose eyes are not so bright and in whose voices there is not much laughter, for the children are part of Africa, the children are Africa.

Go and see the child in the fields where the maize bends its head. Can you not see that the eye is dimmer and the mouth that of an old man? Can you not see that the soul is wizened and that the laughter is full of sad meaning? For Africa is old in its youth, and grey in its childhood. For even the baby is old in suffering and knows when the breast is dry and the calabash is empty, and the dust is thick on the bed of the river. And the father grunts and turns away the head. And the children have seen the tears in the eyes of the mother and they have also wept silently although they still do not understand. And these are the children of Africa, who are old men and women, but laugh with the voice of youth.

God bless the children in the Great Cities, for they have no beards but are as men. And there is sadness in Africa for the children who no longer play in the streams but follow the ways of the Great Cities. And the laughter of the veld is lost in the sorrow of the towns, and the little ones swagger and laugh insolently. And there is a knife in the hand and hatred in the eye, and mistrust, for the ways of the Great Cities are not good.

God bless us Thy children, make us also ageless but make us part of Africa. God bless our descendants who will be the people of Africa. God bless the cities, and the towns, and the villages. God make us to see a great light so that the ways of man may become better ways. God bless the people and the children, and the veld, and the koppies and the krantzes. God bless Africa.

And still the people sang and the blue uniforms came nearer and Muti knew that he had no pass. But still as they sang Muti's face was lit up with a great light.

God bless Africa . . .

And another man who had no pass was led silently away.

Maluphakonyisw' Upshondo Lwayo . . .

And Muti felt as if he could burst with all the pride and love.

Hear our prayers and bless them . . .

And still the uniforms came nearer and the brass buttons glowed as the lamps caught them.

Yiza Moya, Yiza Moya, Oyingcwele . . .

Forward spirit, Forward spirit, which art holy.

Nkosi Sikelele . . .

And Muti could hardly contain himself for the love he felt for his people.

Thina Lusapho Lwakho . . .

God bless us Thy children, with a hoarse voice and a body that trembled all over. And then, as the blue uniforms stood before him, the last triumphant note.

Nkosi Sikelel' iAfrika!

[June 1956]

Marta

D. CAN THEMBA

The people in the queue stood drearily with an air of defeat waiting over them. Sophiatown on Monday mornings is like that. An anti-climax after Sunday's excesses.

Then Marta came along, still drunk. Her baby was hanging dangerously on her back as she staggered up Victoria Road. Somebody in the queue remarked drily, 'S'funny how a drunk woman's chile never falls.'

'Shet-up!' said Marta in the one vulgar word she knew.

She stood, swaying a moment on her heels, and watched the people in the queue bitterly. A bus swung round the Gibson Street corner and narrowly missed hitting her. Three or four women in the queue screamed, 'Oooo!' But Marta just turned and staggered off into Gibson Street, the child carelessly hanging on her back.

There was no gate to the yard in Gibson Street, because there was no fence to make a gate into. So Marta just walked up to the house. She toed the door open, and just then, feeling that she was going to be sick, dived for the unmade bed. The child nearly shot out of the pocket on Marta's back. It started crying, but Marta just said, 'Shet-up.'

A tall African whose complexion was five minutes to midnight turned round from the mirror, his hand arrested around a half-made tie-knot. He had a shock of hair on his head which made him look like a tall golliwog.

In his eyes an anger crept like the back-splash of the tide. His upper lip curled, showing a flash of the whitest teeth. When he spoke it was in a sort of a snarl.

'S'true's God, Marta,' he growled with that abrupt accent of the Rhodesian, 'one of these days I go to chock you tille you die. I'll teash you to stop drinking and for to start looking after your house – ' And just as if to make his point, he stepped into a plate with dry morsels of food that crunched under his weight. 'Agh, sies!' he hissed.

'Aw, shet-up, man!'

For a moment he stood there and stared at her in stark, stupid fury. Then suddenly he was galvanized into action. He leapt at her and grabbed her by the throat, squeezing, squeezing . . .

What's the use of fretting? Life is too large for that. And life must be lived – sweetly or bitterly – but always intensely. It is like a burning log that crackles at every knot and explodes in little bursting pellets of fire. The pain or the slow-creeping sorrow. The sudden fear of dark location alleys. The shifting aside to avoid the attention of young hooligans who sit and swear on the street corners. Then the wild, fire-mad midnight parties. Getting drunk. It comes on you in fumes, thick folds of smoke that trap you and cloud you. And suddenly, illogically, the police! The police! The police! What's the use? You carry a dangerous weapon, the police get you. You go without one, the tsotsis get you. But it is nice to have a woman, your woman, made yours by the long moment of fierce love and the close embrace, tighter, tighter, tighter . . .

Until a child cries in sudden panic!

Jackson realised with a shock what he was doing. Had he killed Marta? O God! What had he done? He saw all the tawdry, vulgar, violent recklessness of their lives. Something just keeps coming off wrong in this hit and run mislife. And it's not so much Marta's drinking or his adulteries . . . It's – it's – it's, well, dammitall!

Marta stirred and coughed. She tried to rise but found that she could not. Hoarsely she said to Jackson, 'The child, the child.' He saw where she had pinned him down with her body. He lifted her and pulled out the child. Then he stood there looking at Marta and the child anxiously. He felt they needed care . . . but then a man's got to go to work.

You do anything, but you go to work. The police arrest you by mistake; you do your all to get out, because you got to go to work. You pay Admission of Guilt. You admit to anything, anything! So long as you go to work. But sometimes you got to go to jail. Then you go. It does not matter. Almost everybody you know has been to jail.

But then that long queue of men you had seen at your place of work, looking for work . . .

Outside in the street Jackson saw two little girls suddenly breaking into a dance. For the sheer swing of it! He thought of how well Marta could do it.

Marta lay quietly for some time. Her throat was smarting, but her head was whirling less dizzzily now. Then she reached out for the child and dragged it across her body. It felt like trying to hoist oneself by tugging at your socks. But she made it in the end.

She examined the child carefully. It looked all right. It was gurgling now. She put it down on the bed again. Sleep came jaggedly.

She woke up to what sounded like wild yelling. Then she saw them, shouting at her to come on and get up. Sophia was there, Emily and Boet Mike. They were nice. But Marta's head was still clanging. Drink does that to you when it rushes out.

'Come-ahn,' said Emily, 'Boet Mike's ship is in and Sophia stands all right. He-e-e, Boet Mike say, a bottle of straight! Sophia says, straight! Boet Mike says, straight. We said, no, let's get Marta first! Come-ahn, Marta!'

Marta hesitates. 'Jackson will kill me.'

Sophia looked as if she had never heard anything quite so funny. 'Since when have you been scared of Jackson?'

'All right,' Marta yielded, 'but let me first find Pulani to look after the child.'

Sophia insisted that they go to her favourite shebeen in Gerty Street, because her husband who had got the 'shakes' does not go there. Not ever. Of course, Marta did not like the woman of the house in Gerty Street. She puts on such airs since she's got her new radiogram. But it's not every day that Boet Mike's ship is in and that Sophia stands right.

The house in Gerty Street was made up of a veranda, then a room, then another room, then a back-veranda. The first room was a combined sitting-room and bedroom. The second one a combined dining-room and kitchen. They went into the sitting-room bedroom.

Somebody in the dining-room kitchen was practising jazz solos on a set of drums. But Marta and company did not mind.

Boet Mike said, 'Straight.' And they brought a bottle of brandy that looked like guilty blood. The drank from the bottle first, slowly, Emily serving into all sorts of glasses. She managed to serve an equal shot each time, because she measured the drink by her fingers into one glass which she in turn poured into all the others.

And the drum was raving on relentlessly. It was as if the drummer himself was getting drunk ahead of them.

The bottle went down slowly, but before it reached its ankles, Sophia who stood right said, 'Straight!'

Suddenly Marta sprang up and jived to the rhythms of the rumbling drums. The others chanted out for her. Marta's arms went out before her, her legs spread, her knees sagged, her eyes drooped, her mouth opened a little, and she moved forward in a shuffle like a creature drawn irresistibly, half-consciously, to its doom. She shuffled towards the dining-room kitchen.

The others followed her. In the other room the furniture had been moved aside and in one corner a young man surely not eighteen yet was beating the drums as though he wanted to work something evil out of him.

He suddenly broke into a rapid roll of raw rhythm. His arms were flailing in and out, so fast that they blurred. Marta was caught in the wild burst like a loose fish and chips wrapping churned up in a sudden gust of wind. She leapt up, and when she landed again her feet sprinkled about in an intricate tracery. Then just as suddenly her feet stopped, so suddenly that the shock still shivered through the rest of her body. Infinitely minute tremblings.

The drummer was watching her now. Their positions were reversed. It was she who was giving him direction now. She was transmitting the wild energy, with clenched teeth and open hands, creeping towards him. Her every movement tore a roar from the drums.

Then abruptly she stopped, and the cymbals clanged!

Marta sank tiredly into a chair. She felt that she had come back from somewhere, had committed something before which her spirit had often quailed. She didn't want to dance again, or drink any more. She looked at the boy behind the drums. He seemed very shy, very young. Could he, could he really be that innocent even after this thing he and she had done together?

He rose and started to go out, but Sophia, quite drunk now, would have none of it.

'Uh-uh, man, brother,' she drawled. 'Don't go yet. Come with us, man. We stand right.'

He hesitated, looked at Marta shyly. She looked at Sophia. She knew Sophia wanted him for herself, but then she knew Sophia and didn't like it. Somehow she felt this boy should not be dragged into their company. There was something about him that, she felt with stupid stubbornness, should be left intact.

'Come here, man, brother, come to Sophia.'

'No!' Marta was surprised at the violence of her own voice.

Sophia giggled. 'So, you want him. Well, I don't carre damn. You're a friend of mine, see?'

Marta caught the boy by the sleeve of his floral shirt. 'Let's get away from here! Quick!' The urgency in her voice impelled him.

Boet Mike said how about finishing off another straight, but she didn't wait to reply.

Outside Marta realised that she was drunker than she had thought. She looked up into the young man's face and tried to smile. 'Looks like you've got to take me home,' she said.

He gave her a look of sheerest adoration. It stung her to the softest centre. 'Look here, kid, I want you to promise me one thing. Promise me that you will never drink.'

'But I don't drink,' he protested.

'Still promise me that you will never drink.'

A flash of anger showed in his face. 'You think I'm a kid, eh?'

'Nnnnnnooooo,' she said thoughtfully. 'I don't mean just drinking. I mean don't go rough.'

He was shy again. So she said: 'O.K. Take me home. I'll try to explain there.'

'Honestly, Sophia, I didn't think that the explanation would take that long . . . all day. I didn't know that we were at my place so long. All I know is that Jackson just suddenly returned home. It was hopeless . . . I could see from his eyes that he thought I was revenging for what had happened that morning. But I couldn't do it! I couldn't do it with that boy!

'Maybe it's true I was fed-up with Jackson. Maybe I did want in my heart to make Jackson feel that other men could like me. But not with that boy, Sophia. Not with that boy.

'Now the people say, "No case at all". No case at all because he was in my own house. In Jackson's own house, and Jackson had a right to kill him. But there's nothing that he did.'

Sophia felt for a moment like laughing lecherously. But somehow she just couldn't. She just couldn't.

Softly she asked, 'But you loved that boy, didn't you?'

Marta looked up through her tears. She looked at Sophia long before she decided that Sophia might understand.

Then just: 'Yes. The drunk woman's child has fallen.'

[July 1956]

Man of Africa

JORDAN K. NGUBANE

Nobody could mistake the omens. Trouble was in the air. The shrill voice of a woman in distress tore through the stillness of the night like a streak of lightning through massed banks of clouds in a storm. Something exploded and shook the neighbourhood. Amber tongues of fire leapt to the sky and lit the hills for miles around . . . A moment later another voice pierced the midnight air . . . also a woman's. The explosion followed, then the flames. The pattern was the same always: the woman, the explosion and the fire. It went on like that, right through the night, from hill to hill until Cato Manor looked like a veritable hell in which the flames roared with demoniacal fury from every side.

Earth's ugliest things lurked in the night. Nobody could unravel the mystery of the Indian women screaming in the dark. The explosions gave little more than clues. Only the flames told the whole story . . . the Zulus were on the warpath. The Zulu was terrible when his fighting instincts were roused. He asked for no quarter and gave none. He had been brought up in the tradition that he was beneath contempt who could ask mercy of his enemy. In that mood danger, pain or death ceased altogether to have any meaning for him.

At the historic battle of Ncome, for example, the Boers had surrounded themselves with their wagons . . . a laager, they called it. The Zulus came down the hills from every side, wave after wave of the bravest in the land. The Boer fire was accurate and deadly. It mowed them down in their thousands. Word came from the battlefront to the great King Dingane's capital: 'The King's warriors perish at Ncome; the white man's stick breathes fire!' From every mountain pass, from every hill and valley came spontaneous song:

> Come, noble sons of Zulu!
> The Boer's guns spit fire;
> The dead from Ncome call;
> Sing and march and follow,
> Yea, into Ncome's crimsoned mud!
>
> A bridge of corpses fling,
> Pile upon pile from bank to bank,

Till yon Boer's beard is singed
The fight undaunted we shall wage,

Today, tomorrow, forever.
While one Zulu lives
In battle's glory shall we join
Till yon Boer's beard is singed
For who shall say
He's conquered a Zulu?

Come ye lads of the King!
The dead from Ncome call;
Sing and march and follow,
Yea into Ncome's crimsoned mud!

The warriors polished their spears and poured into Dingane's Umgungu-
ndlovu Kraal and thence to the front. They fought as the finest of the human
race have fought down the ages for the things they loved and considered
precious in life.

The terror of the night had gone and the voice of the Indian women was stilled.
The charred petrol drums and the ruins gaping to heaven told a terrible story.

The story was in the tension which filled the atmosphere. Danger could be
sensed in the air men breathed. The streets of Durban were like the streets of a
city of the dead. The great factories in the industrial areas were all quiet. So
quiet indeed that from the centre of the town could be heard the distant hum of a
thousand voices in song. It sounded ominous in the midday air. The music could
not be mistaken . . . it was martial music; the Zulus from the Point were
coming. They sang and marched and followed as their ancestors had done at
Ncome:

Come, noble sons of Zulu . . . !

They were a community by themselves, these Zulus. They were cut off from
the rest of their fellowmen in the city by miles and miles of white hotels on the
beachfront and, farther afield, by the white man's main trading centre.
Elsewhere they were surrounded by the sea. They were picked men at the peak
of their strength. The great ships from the Americas, Europe and Asia rushed in
and out of Durban's harbour as if they had conspired to drain the last bit of the
African's strength from which came the gold and the uranium the nations
wanted.

Work continued without ceasing at the Point – by day and by night. Men whose wives and children starved in the Reserves worked like demons when offered a few shillings more that what men of their race earned elsewhere. That is how things were at the Point. You had to work like a demon and live like a demon and think like a demon to earn bread for your children.

The men sang and marched up Point Road, through Milne Street, into Old Fort Road. Nobody stopped them. Only death could. They marched on and on, up Berea Road, through Toll Gate and finally into Booth Road. From there they spilled into Cato Manor and surrounding Indian settlements to reinforce the terror which had vanished with the coming of the dawn. Human passions, wounded and frustrated over the years, had suddenly burst out in wild excesses of rioting.

One section turned off Booth Road, crossed a stream and marched up the side of a hill to a group of Indian cottages. They surrounded the first they came to. Their leader went to the front door and kicked it with his boot. Nobody replied. The door was locked. They smashed a window and set the curtain on fire. They went to another, and the next, until the whole house was in flames.

An Indian woman from a banana plantation nearby saw the smoke and shouted across towards the hill. A moment later a figure in a pink saree sped down the hill. A group of Indian men tried to stop her, half-way down the hill.

'You can't go there,' they shouted, 'They'll kill you.'

'My children . . . ,' she cried.

'Where are they?'

'In the house . . .' The woman was still running.

'Don't go, we tell you.'

'Is that all you can do for me?'

'Those fellows come from the Point, if you don't know.'

Fear gripped her. She stopped running. She remembered the ugly stories she had heard about the men from the Point. They lived in barracks like soldiers. No woman visited them in the compounds except by special permission. Their dogs had almost lost their barking instincts – but they barked viciously when they saw a woman.

In the soft wind which blew, her ear caught the wail of her two daughters. She tore past the men trying to stop her, dashed down Booth Road, crossed the stream and ran up the hill. By that time she could hear the voices of her children very clearly . . . What else could a mother do? Her arms and legs trembled. She tried to pull herself together. Her foot caught in a fold of her saree. She stumbled and fell. But to fall that day was to invite trouble . . . serious trouble. Danger lurked among the bananas and in the grass between the plantations.

She was struggling to rise to her feet when she heard heavy footsteps behind her. She turned her head. A man of Africa was coming towards her . . . a stranger. She screamed and tried to run but strength was gone from her legs. She stood, waiting for the worst.

'Brother . . .' Her voice was like a whisper from another world. She tried to say more . . . in vain. He had heard. The hardness from his face began to melt. Her heart beat faster, half in fear and half in hope. A helpless and beautiful woman had to fear when a man who could kill her started showing a kind face. Besides, his clothes were in tatters. He stood to gain by looting Indian homes. He was barefooted and could, merely by joining the mob, get himself a new pair of shoes.

There was something remarkable in his looks. Poverty and the strains of suffering in the white man's world had carved massive wrinkles all over his face. His lips were anaemic. But between the wrinkles on his rough face she deciphered a language she understood; the language of mercy and compassion. It made her no longer feel in the company of a stranger, an enemy. She felt in the company of a fellow human being, and with that came hope.

His first impulse had been to walk past her. His people and hers were at war; at least that is how he saw it. She was an Indian and he an African. The fashion in South Africa was to evaluate vice and virtue in terms of race. Virtue was always on your people's side and vice everywhere else. He resisted a temptation to take offence when an Indian called him brother. Besides, if he stood much longer by her side there was always the danger that the menfolk of her race, probably hiding among the bananas, might shoot him.

On the other hand, the conflict between his people and the Indians did not make any sense to him. Why should people, both of them in shackles, kill each other? But, he told himself, it was none of his business to right the wrongs of a lunatic country. He had his own wife at Mahlabatini, right in the heart of Zululand, and his two little girls to look after. He did not want his wife widowed or his daughters orphaned. He had left the road to keep away from danger, he reminded himself. He turned to walk away.

'Brother . . .' The woman whispered again. Something swelled up within him and made him stop; something he could not suppress . . . Her helplessness; he could not be indifferent to. It was against the traditions of his people to do that, he told himself.

The men who perished at Ncome had died because they believed he was beneath contempt who could regard his fellow man as his inferior.

It aroused his anger, all his fighting instincts, to see his own kin, the descendants of the heroes of Ncome, find joy in the murder of men, women and children, just because they were Indian.

'What do you want me to do, Makoti?'

'Save my children, brother . . . from that burning house . . .'

He looked at the flames. It was death to go anywhere near them.

'I am not a hero, you know!'

'Don't you have children?' He did not answer.

The flames had enveloped the whole house and gushed lustily out of the windows. Amid the roar of the fire he heard young frightened voices like those of his own little girls at Mahlabatini. He could not be deaf.

'Come, Makoti, let us go to the children.' She almost ran over the last few yards between herself and her children. The men from the Point laughed and jeered when they saw her.

'Good luck to you, son of Zulu! She'll be yours for life.'

He did not look at them; nor did he reply.

'Where are the little ones?' the man from Mahlabatini enquired.

'This side . . .' She led him to a window. The wall had collapsed on it and made entry through it to the children impossible. Everywhere else was fire. He smashed another window on the same side. A burst of smoke hit his face, then a ball of fire. He coughed. The flames subsided. He held the sill of the window with both his hands and jumped into the house.

'Are you mad,' the men shouted outside, 'to risk your life for an Indian?'

He did not hear this. His mind was on the fire and the children. He brushed the flames off the tattered ends of his clothes with his hands until he got to the children's door. He pushed it; it jammed. Part of the ceiling in the children's room had fallen and barred the way. It burnt fiercely on the wooden floor between the door and the children. He pushed again, this time more forcefully . . . the door fell from its burning frame. The children had cried themselves hoarse with fright. When they saw him they clapped their hands.

His coat was in flames and his right arm burnt. The girls stretched out their arms. He flung himself through the flames, straight on to their cots. He took them both in his arms, tucked their heads under his armpits and with one supreme effort hurled himself at the raging inferno between him and the door. He fell into a hole in the burning floor boards.

A pointed piece of flaming wood pierced his left eye and destroyed it. His face was scorched. He pulled himself out, groped into the next room and saw the woman at the window.

He shoved the child he held by the left arm through the window. The mother took her. He strained the burnt right arm as he did this. The second girl slipped from his grip to the floor. She was too terrified to wait for him to pick her up. She screamed and started running hither and thither in the dense smoke. He followed her voice. He was covered in flames and exhausted when he caught her. He felt his way along the wall to the window where he gave her to her mother.

The men outside had stopped talking. The fire had driven them a distance from the house. Amid the crackling of the burnt wood, the man from Mahlabatini heard the mother pacify her children . . . He felt rewarded . . . He gripped the burning sill of the window and tried to jump out. The sill collapsed and with it the entire wall. He fell back into the flames. He heard the woman shout in broken Zulu: 'Hold on to this! Do you see the bamboo? Hold on to it and I'll pull you out.' He could not see anything. He groped about from one burst of flame to another.

The men who had burnt the house started running away. They were among the banana trees when they heard a powerful voice above the noise of falling iron cry: 'Tell my wife, O sons of Zulu, not to mourn. I did my duty!' They ran faster into the plantation, like men in flight from something deadly in the skies.

The walls of the house cracked and then fell. The roof collapsed with a deafening crash. The woman sat down and wept . . .

[August 1956]

Lesane
[The Lesanes of Nadia Street]

EZEKIEL MPHAHLELE

Midday. Nadia Street was bright and gay. *Lu-lu-lu-lu-li-li-li-li!* the women shouted. Crowds of people converged on Lesane's place as his son was approaching together with his bride and their party. Women shouted and stamped on the street. Spectators nudged and jostled one another. The crown was lovely; the bride's face might have been a little shorter; the bride seemed much younger than her husband; the groom's dress had a rustic flavour about it; the bridesmaids were perfect. Shame, how pathetically beautiful they looked. So said the spectators. And the bridal party slowly approached the groom's house. They stopped at the entrance. A tiny man stood like a sentinel at the door, forbidding them to enter. Custom. He had to be there. And it didn't look funny to the spectators that the forbidding majesty of custom should be personified in such a tiny man.

'Why don't they go in?' someone asked. 'Who knows?' The information spread round and was relayed from tongue to tongue. Custom was in the way. The groom's people must pay a goat to the bride's people before she entered the house of her future keeper. 'How much is a goat?' asked Seleke, the shebeen queen. 'Two pounds and five shillings,' Ma-Sibiya, the litttle woman said. 'It was one pound five shillings before meat control, wasn't it?' The question was beyond Ma-Sibiya. The money was paid, and the bridal party entered the room. A new shawl was also brought for Ma-Lesane by the bride's mother. The previous day it had been the bride's mother's first turn to get a new shawl from the Lesanes. 'Custom, didn't you know, stupid?' Ma-Sibiya said. 'But it's the Xhosa way. The bride is Xhosa.' 'Where I come from we don't do such things,' said someone. 'Nor do we,' another said. 'You're Basotho, I see,' was Ma-Sibiya's remark. 'And so's Lesane, you see.'

The guests went to the back quadrangle where a tent had been pitched for the wedding dinner; the main item. 'What's a wedding without food?' as people always say. News had gone round that two oxen had been slaughtered; both had been presented by an uncle of Diketso's – not the bald-headed one who was a lawyer's clerk: he had boycotted the wedding. It was the one who lived somewhere in Eastern Transvaal. Many people said he was a rich man, and pointed him out as he walked with all the dignity becoming a feeder of multitudes. He knew that people don't wait to be invited to a wedding. They just attend.

Ma-Lesane's chubby face was radiant with pride and ecstasy. Yes, a beautiful and remarkable thing, to decide to marry, and to get married. Since Diketso's eldest brother had announced to his father that he wanted to get married, the news had shot up and down Nadia Street like electric current. Along the rows of dilapidated houses that stood cheek-by-jowl as if to support one another in the event of disaster. It had no fences to jump because there are no fences in Newclare. The flies hovering over the dirty water in the street seemed to buzz it around without being involved in the joy of it. The news had percolated through wooden and cardboard paper windows, lashed about from tongue to tongue in the greasy, sticky darkness of Newclare rooms. It took a turn up and then down the next cross-street, and then got out of hand so that it banged insistently on the eardrums of Lesane's enemies and drove them frantic with envy. Diketso's brother was going to get married.

'Diketso's brother! At last!' Ma-Mafate had said, turning her washtub in front of her room to face Ma-Ntoi, also doing the white people's washing in front of her room. 'He's marrying,' people always say in the continuous tense; which implies a long, long process. 'Which one?' Ntoi had asked. 'The one who looks like his father.' 'Wasn't he going to be a minister one day?' 'Can't a man do both at the same time?' 'I don't know. Just thought he was getting too old to want a woman on his hands. He he he!' 'A man is never too old to marry, or to have children, you know that.' 'Our old man thinks the man is too proud and that he'll want another to rear his family for him and to know his bedroom secrets.' It was always 'our man' when a husband was referred to. 'Our man says Lesane is too hard on his children and his son has always been a roadside pole with girls chasing one another round it and laughing and breaking away.'

Every day Ma-Lesane had slung her shawl over her shoulders and gone to the rooms of those she knew, to invite them formally. As usual invitation cards had been sent to the younger set and to far-away people. The grown-ups had to be told in person. If someone else had been sent or an invitation card received, the stock complaint would have been: 'She lives nearby and she sends someone as if she didn't know me'; or, 'I just hear from the air his son is marrying . . .' So both Lesane and his wife had to be careful and nurse the feelings of even the eccentrics. At the wedding there were, for instance, Old Mbata from up Nadia Street, who was living with his only son after he had been 'spat' out by his son-in-law, as he put it; Ma-Ntoi, who came from a new mining town in the Free State from which she had been expelled because she couldn't own a house as she was a widow; Ma-Sibiya, the little woman who sold monkey-nuts and fruit at the Westbury bridge nearby; Shigumbu, the soft-hearted but dried-up bachelor from Nyasaland, who was trying desperately hard not to annoy the authorities lest he be sent back to his homeland; Seleke, the shebeen proprietress who had just moved over to Nadia Street with her eternal appendage, her cousin; Ma-Mafete, the shoemaker's wife. This one had just recently quarrelled with Seleke. But Ma-Lesane pretended she didn't know.

In the front room the bride and groom sat like statues, listening to long speeches by their next-of-kin, advising them on married life. Custom. Uncle after uncle, aunt after aunt, all the available ones, took his and her rightful position in the speechifying. 'You've now left you mother's house,' they kept hammering on and tugging at the heartstrings of the bride. She had to cry, and cry she did. Custom. The groom sat still, like a windswept tree that is determined to stay evergreen. 'Go forth, my children,'·said one aunt, the one from Pretoria. 'Remember, a man is a man because of other men. See this woman (pointing at Ma-Lesane). She wants a grandchild to hold on her lap. That's your first duty.' The groom took it in solemnly, looking steadfastly at the opposite wall. His seated posture suggested that he might jump up suddenly and cry: 'A child! My wedding suit for a child!' like a warrior. Outside there in the street the young folk were dancing. Dancing as if yesterday they didn't have a riotous beer-spilling raid; as if tomorrow they might not have a pass and tax raid. For them today was just a chunk of sweetened and flavoured Time. And in all this there was a spirit of permanence which they felt, without thinking about it.

A hired turn-table blared away in its fashion on a rickety table where normally there would be a sidewalk. The August dust and whirlwinds didn't mar the wedding spirit. Diketso, the groom's younger sister, also abandoned herself to the aching sweetness of the jive in-between serving in the tent. She danced with half-shut eyes, her partner with a hanging lower lip, lapping the rhythm all up, the rhythm of the earth, the heavens, the ages. 'You shouldn't have come here!' she hissed to her lover as they danced. 'Do you want him to murder you?' He smiled. They kept well inside the crowd. There was an ecstasy between them that would have dared the most ascetic matron of a nunnery. A few moments later a little brat caught hold of Diketso's dress. 'Some more cake,' said the boy. It was her little brother. 'No, you've had too much already.' 'I'll tell.' 'Tell what?'

'I saw him dance with you.' Diketso furiously cut a piece for the brat and sent him away. Ordinarily she was quick with her hand on the brats and with a clap she would send them out of the room squawking and shrieking. The very next day the newly-married brother left the Lesane house and settled down to making a home in a hired room somewhere outside Newclare. 'That's right.

That's what a man should do,' said old Mbata, wrenching his pipe from between his teeth. 'If you can rear your own cow, why let others do it for you?'

The old man was a regular visitor of the Lesanes. He came down and sat with Lesane on a bench against the front wall – two men coughing and sneezing out the last years of their lives. He smoked a very small pipe, filling it and refilling it. They sighed and ho-hummed and o-yaed and muttered and grunted and gurgled and sneezed, seeming all the time to be immune to suffering, appearing to be above the broken purposes of human lives that littered the street. Now and again they looked at each other as if only they understood the scheme of things. And yet, although they looked so weary and sick at heart, they knew, secretly, that beyond these broken purposes there must be a bigger purpose of living weaving itself somewhere with the passage of years.

'Your boys are growing up well, Lesane,' Old Mbata said, looking at the smallest two who were dragging each other in turns on the stoep of Lai Tong's shop. 'I'm proud of the little rascals. Taken after their mother, that's what! Especially the one who's seven. Can't cheat him. If their little friends visit them just before meal-time, he leaves his brother with the guests and comes in and gobbles his food and returns to them. Then the little brother leaves him with them and gobbles his food. They learned many a bitter lesson before they planned it this way.'

After the newly-married son had left, the Lesanes didn't know whether to rejoice that there was one person less to fit into the front room or weep because there was one pay-packet less. Fanyan jumped on the bed in the brother's place and slept with the other brother opposite Diketso's bed. The little brats continued to sleep in the parents' room.

'Why don't you send your younger son – what's his name? – Fanyan, to school?' Old Mbata suggested. 'The lad from the country, I mean. He can get a school pass and then go out to work like any other boy who's born in town. Strange boy you have there.'

Lesane rested his chin on his hand and planted his elbow on his thigh. 'No, it's dishonest.' He pulled mucous through the nose passage into his mouth and spat and then grunted.

'In town here your honesty can only carry you to the end of Nadia Street,' said Old Mbata.

After casting his mind this way and that Lesane decided. Fanyan must go to high school. Lesane spat a few times and said, 'Yes, he'll go to school. Of course he will.'

Lesane and his family are eating supper in their room at Rose Street. There is nothing extraordinary in this: many other families in Newclare – everywhere else – are eating their supper just about this time. But perhaps there is only one Diketso in Newclare – anywhere else – who is not eating her supper; who is watching others eat. She is not allowed to eat tonight. She has made her father very angry and her mother sad. Bad behaviour, they call it.

She is now sitting on her bed which is in the front room. Here the family also cooks and eats. Opposite Diketso's bed is another, on which three of her brothers slept, two facing one way, the third facing the opposite end.

Diketso, nearly twenty-one now, is a big, lovely girl. As the family is eating, her father keeps looking her way between bites, wondering what kind of child he has brought into the world.

Her eyes rove about the small room. From the antheap of porridge which her father is mowing down from all sides to Lesane's distended jaw-veins; his wilting shoulders and greying hair; her mother's broadness and chubby face; her two bigger brothers sitting on their bed on the opposite side, with their plates on their laps. Her eyes rove to the monstrous shadows of these people on the walls, cast by the flickering candlelight and then to the three little brats, the smallest of the brood, sitting on the floor. She can barely make out their faces, but she is sure they are making faces at one another, as they often do when they reserve their bits of meat to tantalise one another with.

Then she thinks about her lover, the lad from the nearby municipal location. They met a few moments ago at Reno Square, at the tin-and-sack shanties of the squatters. Her father has often flayed her for this lover, the reason being that he does not like his parents.

The meal is about to finish, and Diketso knows it is coming: the sjambokking she has so often received from her father. The thought of it seems to make her heart flicker like the candle when a slight breeze comes in. An impulse seizes her: to run out to Old Mbata up the street. She has often done that. He is such a kind old man, the man who fled from his son-in-law's tyranny the other side of the railway, the part of Newclare called Setikitiking, where the sun never seems to shine. And then a certain stubbornness overwhelms her. She continues to sit.

Her father leaves her to collect the dishes. The three children are packed off to bed in the parents' room, the only other the family has rented. The dishes are washed on the dining table. As Diketso goes back to her bed her father comes out of his bedroom, bending a sjambok this way and that. He goes to her, catches her by the wrist and brings down the sjambok on her back and shoulders with purple fury.

'If I see you with that boy again I'm going to kill you,' says the father. 'I'll kill you, I tell you. As sure as the heavens see me, I'll chop you with an axe. Into pieces, pieces, pieces, get me?' No answer.

More whipping. The daughter does not easily cry aloud. It makes Lesane think that she is defying him and daring him to more beating. So he lashes out more furiously, until Ma-Lesane rises from a corner where she has been sitting stolidly, and tells her husband to stop. 'The girl has had enough,' she says, as she holds his trembling hand. Diketso's younger brother intervenes.

The elder brother continues to sit on a bench, chewing insolently and somewhat sadistically. He considers it a judicial punishment. She has no ears, he thinks; whipping will give her a good live pair. The three small brats have been rudely aroused from their own drowsy reveries and are leaning on their elbows. But they go down again: just the usual thrashing, they think; nothing dramatic – yet.

The father having stopped, pants with a wheezing sound, his eyes looking murderous. He is full of angry steam, and it looks as if any moment it will make his small wilting frame take off into space.

'You see,' he says, to nobody in particular, 'she won't even cry. How do I know the devil feels it?'

'She's such a wilful child, I don't know,' Ma-Lesane says, with a deep sigh.

'She could poison all our food, if she had a mind to it,' Lesane says. 'This wilful, desperate little ruffian! You'd burn us all out of here, wouldn't you, little witch? You would, that's what.'

'Give her a few more years,' Ma-Lesane sums up, 'and you'll see she'll be straight as my finger, straight, I tell you. Taken after her aunt, that's what. Looking at her today you wouldn't say she once bit my father in the arm. She's straight as this finger.'

It always gave Lesane a sense of triumph over his wife to see her lift her perpetually crooked forefinger to illustrate the idea of straightness. He was the grim, tight-jawed, snuff-taking, spitting, church-going type. Never missed a morning service on Sunday unless his kidneys and his feet 'refused', as he put it. His religion made him behave like a man who has bet heavily on a horse he doesn't know, working on the blind faith that the other people must be right. He also realised that location conditions made religion necessary but difficult.

He was a timid little man who lived in fear of his large, authoritative but obedient wife. So he liked to justify his manliness by pouncing upon Diketso with his sjambok. His wife, Ma-Lesane, had more laughter in her. When the children clung all over her, she looked like a merry-go-round swing unit.

The whole of Lesane's family lived in two rooms they had hired. Like most Newclare houses, this one had no verandah. It was a rusty old iron-and-timber structure. Ma-Lesane had very clean habits, and she heaved and puffed and sighed about the house to give the rooms a respectable appearance, but in vain.

There were other tenants behind them, whose rooms formed a small quadrangle in the centre.

'What a pity we couldn't keep Diketso in high school,' Ma-Lesane said. 'She loves schooling so, poor girl, and since she left it she's like a door on one hinge.'

'If these children give me more pain than my kidneys and sore feet,' her husband muttered, 'the winter will pass with me, that's what.'

'The government is a strange person, I don't know, Elisha,' Ma-Lesane sighed. 'He won't give you sick pension or whatever you call it, and then our Fanyan cannot get a permit to live with us and work here, and the family pot is big. Strange person, the government is.'

Lesane had been discharged from the mines owing to his kidney trouble. Fanyan, the 18-year-old son coming next after Diketso, had just come to the city. He had grown up in the country with his grandparents, although he had been born in Newclare. 'He's from outside the area, and he's not allowed to seek work here,' the Influx Control people said.

'Even so,' said Lesane, 'what can we do, Rabina?'

In the meantime Diketso continued to meet her lover. They were like refugees, meeting there on Reno Square, at the squatters' camp. The squatters themselves were refugees from Setikitiking, where the Russians had recently run riot. Refugees. Violence. The lovers' lives emerged in the heat and blood of this all. Two lovers seeking refuge among other refugees, from the wrath of parents who, like most townfolk, were also refugees from somewhere outside Johannesburg.

Sometimes her father got to know about it and whipped her, until her mother's tough heart sagged a little, too; until her father's also lost a beat or two in primitive sympathy. Diketso was lost in the rapture of every moment of that nocturnal hazard.

But on every meeting with her lover, Diketso knew she was hurting herself; hurting her father and her whole family! hurting everything and everybody for the loneliness, the deserts of inadequacy she felt in herself because of the need to work when she wanted to be in school. Perhaps one day she would go back; perhaps land in some hospital as a nurse. How she liked to picture herself in white, attending an operation or injecting medicine into a patient. Perhaps . . . A patient, gnawing perhaps . . . But before that day came, it would have to be this, and heaven, too; and hell, too.

'Father beat me again yesterday,' Diketso said to her lover.

'Your eldest brother warned me again last night at the bioscope against meeting you.'

'And then?'

'I said seeing you're big enough to make up your mind about this he should talk to you.'

'U-huh?'

'Said you're but a child, he said, and the whole lot are there to think for you. Told me I mustn't think you're a lost bitch I picked up rooting on the rubbish heap, and you've brothers, and you were born decently, and your family know my parents, and quite a long sermon besides.'

'The savages!' Diketso hissed.

'Savages or no savages, I can't bear your being whipped like this.'

'They'll give birth to another Diketso before they make me leave you.'

'Lovely little devil! Your body can't always take it.'

'I know.'

'That all you can say?' He felt the nodding motion of her head. 'Tomorrow's your birthday. Twenty-one, remember?'

'Yes,' she said automatically. 'Forgot about it. One spends so much time running and dying and running and dying.'

'See here.' He gave her a parcel. She opened the wrapper and found a chiffon and a set of handkerchiefs and a beret. Diketso felt a current of something warm sweep through her and soothe her aching self. She lay her head on his chest and cried, a thing she would not do out of physical pain.

'One of these days one of us is going to get hurt,' he said. 'Your brothers, or you or me.'

'Don't talk about hurts,' she begged. 'Now, the old people will soon be coming from church, and I must get back.'

Somebody did get hurt, in a way Diketso's lover had not dreamt of. It took place against the violent background of the squatters' camp, now shivering and chattering and buzzing in a pall of smoke. Tonight, as always, the lovers' parting kiss was a trembling, foreboding kiss.

[December 1956]

Lesane
[Fanyan]

EZEKIEL MPHAHLELE

Fanyan felt awkward and clumsy being in Form 1 at the age of 18. 'Hey, you goat!' the arithmetic master said. 'You, there, don't be such a clumsy owl!' shouted the English mistress. 'No, no, no, we don't construct a triangle like that. Where were you born?' the mathematics master said. Fanyan felt a wild storm rage inside him, especially when the girls of his class said: 'Shame!' and clicked their tongues with pity. They made him feel as if he were soft.

He knew he couldn't do high school work fast enough. His schooling had been retarded in the country, where there was so much hoeing and harvesting to do in between school terms. They hadn't told him at home why they had suddenly changed their decision to let him work. In order that his conscience should sit easy Lesane ordered Fanyan to stay at school for about a year. 'It will add to his country education. I went to country school myself. Did me no good.'

'Wai, Elisha, you used to write to me when you were courting,' said his wife.

'Yes, yes, but nothing more.'

Fanyan's going to school was part of the little reorganisation in the Lesane home. Ma-Lesane started to do white people's washing. The eldest of the three brats, a nine-year old boy, was sent to the Anglican nursery school two streets down. Fanyan had to carry the washing to the suburbs after school, the mother fetched it on Mondays.

He had just delivered washing at a suburban house one afternoon when somebody called him from the other side of the road. It was a policeman. Fanyan stopped. He sensed that the policeman wanted him to cross over to him.

'Where's your pass?' the constable said sharply.

The lad searched all his pockets. Then it suddenly flashed into his head that he had left it at home. He gaped at the constable. He tried to plead. Just then the pick-up van swerved maliciously round the corner and came up to them like a dog that had been sniffing for something and suddenly located it.

'Bung him in!' said the driver, a white policeman.

'Please, please, my pass is at home. Please, please, we can go and fetch it.'

The constables laughed heartily. 'Bung him in! Throw him in!' one shouted. Fanyan was thrown in.

Inside there was a crowd of others. It took time for his eyes to adjust themselves to the dark. When he could see the faces he couldn't recognise any one. He was in a fright. He wanted to jump out, but there was a strong gauze-wire barrier at the entrance.

The night in the cells was enough to give Fanyan a foretaste of the wrath of the law in all its frowning terror. A man from another batch was taken to the charge office at the end of the passage. He came out puffed, with purple eyes. Ripping laughter. Prayerful stuttering lips. Agonising thuds. Gasping, knee-buckling fright. Cheeky passive snorting. He saw and heard them all within those greasy walls that looked like the devil's own spitting ground.

The policeman who stood next to Fanyan's batch and kept prodding one here and another there in the ribs smiled when he saw how terrified the youngster was. Poor fellow, how green he is still, the policeman was thinking.

Out in the country Fanyan had actually stood five yards away from a mounted policeman. He remembered how frightened he had been of the law that stood erect on four large hoofs and great lumps of animal muscle and stirrups and shining spurs. But he also remembered that it was not nearly as terrifying as the law on four wheels; the law that darted from one place to another with lightning effect on screeching tyres; the law that stretched out a large paw and caught you by the scruff of the neck; the law that often gave a long weird whining but sharp sound with a siren.

The next day Lesane paid ten shillings to have his son released. The police would not even look at the pass the old man brought. The fine, they said, was for failing to take out a pass when asked to.

A week later Fanyan was at Seleke's. There was something mysteriously charming about Seleke, Fanyan thought, even in the light of a candle and she often showed a sisterly affection for him. He got used to calling on her. Seleke and her cousin had moved over from Nadia Street. 'Good for business,' as Seleke explained it. Like all other shebeen queens she was believed to have powerful contacts with the police. Fanyan reflected that perhaps it was just that kind of boldness Seleke had which he lacked that charmed him.

Her cousin, known simply as 'Seleke's cousin' – nobody cared to find out his real name - drank as much as ever. 'He simply can't help himself, poor chap,' said old Mbata with the usual shock-absorbing piety. 'Kiss your elbow if he doesn't wet his blankets at night,' Ma-Sibiya said. Lesane pointed to the skies and said, 'A cow will give birth to a pig if that cousin of Seleke's doesn't end up in a mental hospital.'

Seleke's cousin had ceased trying to help himself. He became more and more stubborn against criticism. He didn't work in town. He just did odd jobs at home for his keep, like digging holes for his cousin's beer, running errands and keeping their two rooms clean. He had long stopped trying to keep clean himself. His trousers were always either too small or too big for him. Often one of the constables who drank at Seleke's gave him articles from old police uniforms. 'The uncle with the government trousers,' boys would say.

'You think I'm drunk, eh?' he said to Fanyan who sat opposite him in the front room. He turned to lower the volume of the radiogram music at the corner. 'Right, I'm drunk – hic. But I can speak English better than any of them – hic. The bloody cheap swanks! Why the – hic – hell can't they leave me alone? I live my own – hic – life, not theirs.'

Fanyan later understood that 'they' were the people who were supposed to be talking of Seleke's cousin as an incorrigible drunk – just a useless 'hole-digger'. There was a tribe of such men in Newclare backyards who were prepared to drift from one house to another as long as the people were prepared to keep them while they dug holes for beer and kept watch against the police. When people labelled a man 'hole-digger' they had given him up. And then they looked at one another smugly, with the obvious satisfaction that they had found a solution to an intricate puzzle.

Seleke came in from the back room. She gave her cousin a leg of chicken and one to Fanyan. 'You're going to be a great man one day,' her cousin said, pointing at Fanyan with the leg of chicken. He had no top front teeth, and his tongue kept flicking out between the two fang-like canines. He tore the meat with one fang and, with a sinew hanging down mischievously as far as the chin, Seleke's cousin went over to Fanyan and leaned against him.

'Oh, leave the boy alone. Never!' Seleke said. Even when she was not disputing anything she said, 'Never!' Fanyan noticed that she was a little drunk. 'Don't mind him, Fanyan.'

One of the things Seleke's cousin had stopped trying to do was to argue with her. He removed himself timidly, but not before he issued the final warning to Fanyan: 'You'll be a great man one day.'

'Scared of the police, aren't you?' she said to Fanyan. He nodded.

'Never! You'll get used to it, don't worry. Just hold your heart in two hands. A police badge used to make my toes sweat. It's like looking at King George's medal now.' Then she told a frightening experience she had with the police when she was a girl. She got up to demonstrate with her arms that were shaped like a constable's baton. She had a heavy bust, and when she leaned over the table to support herself while laughing, Fanyan observed the division of her breasts. They parted where they united. At once bashfully, delicately and boldly. As she laughed the breasts seemed about to spill over the bodice of her

frock, and Fanyan suppressed an instinctive urge to hold out ι.
prevent them from falling.

'Never!' she said without provocation.

'What gives you such a strong heart with the police coming in and out of ϒ
rooms?' Fanyan wanted to know. He marvelled a this 35-year-old round bundlᴄ
of vitality that had a streak of ruthlessness as well.

'When you want to live, then you've got to have a tough heart. Never!'

'How did you begin?'

'Like most of us in the townships. School, no money, school, no money, out,
factory, out, no money, marriage, out, lie, cheat, bribe, live. Nothing more.
Never!'

Fanyan made to go. 'Heavens! Do something good for me, Fanyan. Do. You
know Shigumbu, four houses down? Of course you do. Run down there and tell
him to give you a small packet. Bring it here. Do. Almost forgot. Never!'

Fanyan left. A few minutes later he was knocking at a room in a backyard
four houses down. Backyards, he observed, had their own peculiar life, with a
continuous buzzing noise. Shigumbu opened the door. He was the dried-up
bachelor from Nyasaland. After three years of city life he had decided that
Johannesburg was 'rittel bit better than Nyasaland, bludder,' quite aware that he
was comparing a city with a country.

'From Seleke, are you not?' Fanyan nodded. Shigumbu looked groggy. He
put a paper-wrapped packet into a glass jar, and gave it to Fanyan. He went
about the room like a cat. 'Give her this.' The set of false teeth he had gave him
an evil, snarling appearance when they touched the empty gums of the lower
jaw.

Fanyan got out into the street. He was going to swerve in towards the row of
houses when he saw a policeman standing not far from Seleke's room. His heart
seemed to fall on a concrete base in the pit of his stomach. He made a visible
movement to change his course and walked back into the street.

'Hey! Come here!' the policeman said, going towards Fanyan. The lad
bolted, and the policeman followed. He passed his home and made for the
cross-street. He jumped on to the stoep of Lai Tong's shop. Another policeman
turned the corner from the opposite direction. Fanyan stopped. Fear choked him
and seemed to spin him round like a top.

The policeman who saw him first wrenched the jar from his hand and took
out the packet. He unwrapped it, put his nose to it and nodded several times.
Dagga, as he thought.

'Whose is this?' the constable asked, as if he was bored.

'My sister's – Seleke's,' Fanyan managed to whisper.

'U-huh. Where's your home?' The lad pointed down the street.

'Come. We go there first.' He felt the policeman's grip tighten round his wrist. 'Thank you brother,' the constable addressed his colleague.

Immediately the two entered the front room, Lesane stood up. Then Diketso and then Ma-Lesane stood up, her hands dovetailed together and lifted up to the chin.

'That boy is not my son! He's not my son, do you hear me?' As if he had spent the last atom of his energy saying those words, Lesane collapsed, unconscious.

Ma-Mafate turned her washtub round to face Ma-Ntoi.

'Didn't I tell you?' said Ma-Mafate, adjusting the petticoat string which kept slipping down the shoulders.

'What?' enquired Ma-Ntoi.

'That woman Seleke. A hundred Sodoms and Gomorrahs put together in the woman's rooms.'

'I still don't understand, she wasn't arrested.'

'See what I mean?'

'What?'

'She's in love with the policeman who caught that Lesane boy.'

'Oh, no.'

'What was he doing in front of her rooms?'

'Now I see.'

'My cousin in Nadia Street tells me these things. He knows all about her and the police.' She had tried so often to keep the petticoat string in place and she simply left it to hang.

'But are we to say every woman loves a policeman if he does not arrest her?'

'What else?'

'She can buy him over to keep his mouth shut?'

'But I hear they were two policemen?'

'Buy both. She's got the money.' But Ma-Ntoi knew that this sort of defence would merely whet her friend's appetite for more talk and speculation.

'My cousin says it must have been her lover standing in front of her place.'

'No one has so far told us he saw the policeman. Only Lesane's family saw him.'

'They wouldn't talk about it in any case, surely. Somebody else must have seen the policeman.'

Ma-Ntoi shrugged her shoulders.

'Else how did we get the news that Fanyan was caught by a policeman and that dagga was found in the jar he had and that he said it was Seleke's?'

Ma-Ntoi looked around as if to locate the source of the rumour. She didn't know, but these things travelled mysteriously, she said.

'Here's Old Mbata. We'll ask him,' Ma-Mafate whispered. They waited.

'Greetings, mothers.'

'Come over, let's hear something.' Old Mbata stepped over to the women.

'Give us a bite on the tip of the ear. We hear there's a bit of trouble in Lesane's house.'

'No trouble, woman. But Lesane's not well. You know he has had bad kidneys for a long time.'

Being cautious, eh? they both thought.

'This thing that happened last night?'

'Oh, that? Nothing much. Lesane's lad is dead scared of the police. He had a bottle of herbs and the young fool dug his toes into the ground when he saw a policeman. Well, they caught up with him. But they found it was only herbs. Seleke's. One of these days that boy's going to scream in front of a policeman like a goat about to give birth.'

He shuffled off, thinking to himself: the babbling female creatures!

'The sly old man!' Ma-Ntoi said. 'He thinks we were born yesterday.'

As the news travelled the story of Fanyan and the police changed in plot as often as in the style of telling it. Some were sure it was nothing more than herbs. 'That boy's going to be the death of his father,' others said. Shigumbu, the dried-up old bachelor, made sure that, in Rosa Street at least, the story should revolve round herbs.

'I bought the herbs at Mai Mai myself, bludder. For a cough. Well, if people want to think it's dagga let them, my bludder. Look at the moon and say it's a woman's breast, you can fly up and kiss it if you want it, bludder. I can't help it if the moon is not a breast, can I now? I didn't make the moon what it is. Solly, bludder.' He felt secure. Nobody could retrieve that dagga from the drain.

To Seleke, Shigumbu said: 'How could you send a rabbit-hearted fellow like that, sister?'

'Don't get excited, man,' said Seleke.

'Just think if the fellow wasn't the type whose tongue you can cut off with £20 —whew! I can't think of eighteen months in gaol, no fine, sister.'

Lesane took the better of an hour to come round. The sight of a son of his in the hands of the police was too much for him. Seleke came over the same night and then in the morning and got him to cool down. But the picture of a policeman and his son! He knew he couldn't easily forget it.

'I'm sorry it came to this, old father,' Seleke had said. 'Don't be hard on the lad. If only he doesn't lose his head when he sees a constable.'

'Why should he get used to seeing a policeman – to be the devil's messenger?'

'No, old father, because he'll see many more.'

'Look here, woman –' Lesane couldn't finish the sentence. He knew how true it was, and felt the pain of it. He dismissed Seleke.

'Next week you must go out and look for work.' That was an instruction to Fanyan. 'No more school for you.' Fanyan was not displeased. He was only a little annoyed that it had to be announced with such tight-jawed gravity as if it were important. But he soon realised how important it was – in more ways than one.

[January 1957]

Lesane
[The Indian Hawker]

EZEKIEL MPHAHLELE

Fanyan left school and went to look for work. He didn't know exactly what kind of work he wanted to do. But on the fourth day of tramping the streets of Johannesburg he realised that there wasn't any choice of employment to talk about.

He was beginning to see city life in clearer perspective. Certain mental habits were forming in him: suspicion, for instance, and a timid alertness. Often, without reason, he imagined a number of policemen converging on him from all directions, like a swarm of birds over a cornfield. Without reason he dodged about or his muscles gave a violent twitch at the sight of a police badge or a Flying Squad car. Fanyan felt plagued by a new sense of insecurity.

First he had to go to the pass office to have himself registered for employment and to have his pass 'fixed', which, after long red tape, amounted to the affixing of a rubber stamp.

A young white clerk with large ears and a sharp nose took his reference book at the registration office and paged through it.

'Where did you attend school?'

'It's in the book,' Fanyan said, meaning to be helpful.

'I know, but where?' The lad gave him the name of the school.

'Born here?'

'It's in the book.'

'The hell it is! Can't you say yes or no?'

'Yes.'

'*Were you born here?*'

'Yes.'

'Where?'

'Here.'

'Don't fool. We're busy here.'

'Yes,' Fanyan said, not wanting to waste the white man's time. The clerk was in a rage.

'I know you were born in Johannesburg, but where the hell about?'

'Sophiatown.'

'Which way does Annadale Street run?' Fanyan faced north and swung his arms to indicate the direction.

'What street is the Coloured school?'

Fanyan looked at him.

'How many schools are in Sophiatown?' It came like a thunderclap. Caught, Fanyan thought.

'There are many,' he said. The clerk smiled tauntingly.

'How many streets?'

Blank.

'How many churches?'

Blank. By this time Fanyan was thoroughly upset and bewildered. The clerk smiled and said, 'We can't give you a permit. You weren't born here.' Fanyan knew he was being dismissed.

The next day he went to the registration office with his former headmaster. He was given a permit without further difficulty.

It took him a month before he could get a job. He became a delivery-man in a dry cleaner's shop.

'I don't know, I wish he wasn't such a coward,' Lesane said.

'But Elisha,' was Ma-Lesane's remark, 'you told us your great-grandfather used to sleep in a pond full of water the whole night instead of joining his army against an invading enemy.' Lesane gave a dry cough.

'Well,' he said, 'we can't go digging up graves to find out who's to answer for Fanyan's ways, can we?'

'No, we can't,' she said, as if she had been thinking seriously of doing so. 'But he'll learn in his own good time, now he's working. I don't know, but he must buy a shirt and trousers with his first money. My poor boy will soon be in rags – his things are giving in so.' Her husband looked at his own trousers and fingered bashfully the acres of strong cotton reinforcement over the knee. 'Look here, old man,' Ma-Lesane said with a genuine feeling of concern, 'you must also get a pair. But, wait, I've been putting a little aside from my washing money. Lesane snorted and gurgled with satisfaction. At such moments he always felt like a soldier who has been discharged against his will.

'Hm-m-m. He'll learn and come straight as my finger,' she summed up, pointing her crooked finger up to the ceiling.

Yes, Fanyan was learning. Lots of things. The ways of white folks and black folks working in the city and black foremen and white liftmen who looked to him like a tribe of eternally disgruntled, deformed people. 'No lift!' 'Catch your lift in the basement, John!' 'Your lift starts on the first floor, boy!' 'Go to the other baas over there, boy; he'll tell you!' And invariably when he went to the basement, Fanyan found a goods lift which climbed up like a fat woman and came down with the greatest care and consideration. Whenever he found himself in an unattended lift with whites he felt guilty. Some of them glowered at him as the birds are said to have done when they attacked the owl and exiled him for good. Another thing, they hardly talked to one another. Just like in their trains and trams and buses. They just looked ahead of them; unfriendly, uncompromising, self-possessed, mysterious, just dumb.

Now you wouldn't find Africans sitting or standing together without a word to say to one another, without something to laugh about, would you? he thought.

Beneath all this, Fanyan sensed the power of the white people – power in the most deformed of white folks – more power still where black folks were weakest and most helpless.

'D'you want the baas to give me the sack?' a foreman might say, reprimanding a worker.

'Leave him alone,' another would say. 'I'll none of him, I'm here to work for my children, not to keep complaining to the white people!'

'You see, my lad,' a worker drew Fanyan aside, 'see that foreman. He's heavy. You can't do him a thing.'

'What thing?' Fanyan said naively.

'He's heavy, I tell you. He always boasts he has a strong witchdoctor and he'll never lose his job. Every year he takes a holiday and goes to the high mountains of Zulu. He's heavy, I tell you. He'll tell you that some day.' And Fanyan saw a grave look on the man's face. 'Watch your tummy, boy, otherwise you'll go – out of this job, out of this life. Show him you fear him, and you'll stay here until you're fifty. He's been here thirty years and he's never wrong.'

On a Saturday Fanyan came home dragging his feet heavily. He stopped to talk to his father on the bench outside. A short while later Lesane entered the house spitting blue fire.

'Do you hear your son?' he bellowed to his wife. 'Do you hear him? He's gone and lost his job. Lost his job. Think of it! After two months!'

'Trouble with you's that you sleep on a job, on your feet, in your shoes. Always looking bewildered. You handle the white man's tools as if you were ploughing. Wake up! Lost his job, do you hear him? The white man keeps time and he still wants to watch the sun, that's what. I mean to say do you hear what the boy's saying?' He talked to the boy, to the mother and to both at the same time. 'You haven't all eternity to yourself. Everyone must bite his share of it and move along to the next stop. Keep moving, lad, and don't stand chewing your cud. By the spirits, you should have been with me down in the mines.' (He pointed to the floor as if one might sink a shaft just there.) 'You'd sweat and spit and just about urinate blood. There's too much sweat in you that wants squeezing out. You'd grow four eyes, four ears, four nostrils, four lips, double everything, down in the mines, that's what. You've lost a job. He's lost his job, do you hear what he says! He's lost his job!'

There was a moment of silence.

'How did it happen?' Ma-Lesane asked.

'Do I know? Let him tell you,' her husband said.

'I had a quarrel with the foreman. He wanted me to pick up heavy bundles of clothing, and I said I can't, and –'

'Listen to him,' his father cut in. 'Just listen to him – he had words with a white man. Have you ever heard such a thing. Haven't they ever told you you can't answer a white man back? Just listen to him. Spirits of my great-grandfathers, come and bear witness to a miracle! How many more have I to see in my tottering years? Do you know the might of the white man? Don't you feel the might of his many arms flapping over you like the wings of giant birds? Oh, spirits, where was this boy when brains were being rationed?'

'But father –'

'You hear him! he doesn't even know he's not to answer back when grown-ups talk to him! Have you been living in baboon society in Pietersburg?'

'But the foreman is a black man, father.'

'A black man, was it? Green or brown, any foreman thinks white.'

Fanyan moved towards the door. 'Wait a minute,' his father said, suddenly remembering something. 'Why didn't you go to church yesterday evening?'

Silence.

'Don't you know people must go to church?'

'Yes.'

'And so?'

'I'm tired of going to church.'

'What! Listen to him. Just listen to him. Do you hear your son? How can't he lose a job when the devil has been building a nest in him? So you don't want to go to church, eh? Now get this: as long as you're under my roof you're going to do what I tell you. Else I'll break you into pieces, pieces, pieces.' Lesane lifted his hand to bring it down upon Fanyan. The lad held it by the wrist. His father tried to wrench it from his grip, but couldn't. Later he gave up and slumped into a chair, looking very old.

'Get out of my house, you heathen!' he burst out, throwing his head up.

'No, Elisha, let him stay,' Ma-Lesane pleaded. Diketso sat like a clay model on her bed during this scene. The elder brother sat in a corner.

'I don't know what's gone wrong with these children. Do you and Diketso want another father? Next thing you're going to kill me, that's what.'

'Elisha, you're not well. Don't work yourself up so. You wait, he'll grow up straight as my finger.'

A moment of thick silence followed.

'And now he's going to have trouble again having his name in the pass office books,' Lesane sighed.

'I don't know what kind of man the government is,' his wife remarked.

'It is not a man, Ma,' Diketso said.

'Whoever it is, the government is a strange person.' And Ma-Lesane's word on the matter was final.

'Stop outside and look out for Chipile, Diketso,' she said, 'and buy vegetables for tomorrow when he comes past. Pay him last week's money, too, child.'

'Hei chipile! Hei chipile! Hei chipile! They're cheap, they're cheap!' Ahmed Moosa, the Indian hawker, could be heard shouting a few streets up. His cry always shot up high above the buzzing noise of Saturday afternoon. The people called him 'Chipile', and he didn't mind it.

Saturday. The weekend was around again to bottle up the people's weariness, their anxieties, their pains. They would pick up the bottled mixture the next Monday; a mixture pickled for them to eat up again before they ran for the train on Monday. And so the cycle went on. And when black masses poured out of the trains a strange buzzing noise would begin.

As they plodded to their homes with hunched backs and disappeared into the townships the noise rose to a wicked pitch, and later the darkness would muffle it.

Men and women came out of the trains like the live vomit of some monster in a folk tale. They came out the trains in the morning: savagely without heed to woman or weakling; through windows as well as through doors. Inside there it had been hell, and the workers were glad to be walking in the streets without pushing and tugging and chafing in the crowded trains.

'Forced to live like beasts,' Old Mbata often said. And then 'Savages!' as if to correct himself.

The masses continued to pour through platform barriers into Newclare streets like lava. Your tough nerves ached and the flesh longed to hurt itself; to bleed the heat out of itself; to sweat it out in some orgy, or to collide with flesh for the excruciating pain it got out of mingling fires.

And then – panting exhaustion, and the desire to sprawl and stretch your body out so as to feel something palpable settling down in you, or something ooze out of you, and you felt the conflicts that raged in you during the week resolved.

It was Saturday. The white man's work was suspended.

And then someone beat his wife and children. A boy dug his knife into human flesh. A boy twisted the arm of a girl. The Zionists sang their half-pagan, half-Christian songs. All so brutally.

'Hei chipile! Hei chipile! Bananas, potatoes, tomatoes, gabbish, beetrootis, carrotis – holl presh!' The Indian hawker approached singing his daily song. 'They're cheap – all fresh!' He kept on chanting. Looking at him stop just past his home, Fanyan wondered what there was to sing about when a few hours before he had lost a job.

Ahmed Moosa was a darkish, benign, middle-aged man. A small 10-year-old girl – his daughter – travelled with him to serve those who did not come out of their holes at the sound of the hawker's voice. They were a lovable pair, and Moosa never seemed to be able to get annoyed. He joked with women and children and they also teased him often.

'See my hoss?' he was fond of saying to women. 'My hoss and all its pleas (fleas) and plies (flies) on it love you, love you, love you!' And they'd go off in peals of laughter.

Seleke's cousin, who always did Seleke's buying, found some kind of delight in talking to Moosa. 'Tell me Moosa's story again, my prend,' Moosa would say to Seleke's cousin. Seleke's cousin had told it to him so often, but Moosa could never suppress his laughter; and he had chestfuls and bellyfuls of it, although the hero of the story was his namesake.

'Well, chief,' Seleke's cousin would say, as if he were telling a new story altogether. 'There's this Moosa – you say you don't know him – well, this Moosa is giving evidence in the magistrate's court. African boy run over by car, you know. Moosa goes: "Car come, Hafrica boy come. Car go pi-peep! Hafrica don't hear. Car and Hafrica go boom! Hafrica under car, car on top of Hafrica." "What's your name?" they ask Moosa, and he tells them, and also spells it: "M, one O, another O, S, A."'

Moosa and Seleke's cousin held their aching stomachs, exhausted by laughing. The hawker gave his entertainer an apple, not fresh, but not gone bad. He always wondered how Seleke's cousin lived, looking as he did like a man who had gone through three rivers and drained at least one. He didn't know that Seleke's cousin never worried his precious head about living. He just wanted to be left alone to manage his own affairs, which centred on drinking.

But Seleke's cousin must hurry off with the vegetables now, lest his cousin and keeper should get cross. And Seleke shouldn't get cross on a Saturday and stinge him drinks. He left.

A man coming up from the station stopped at the trolley. He asked to buy an apple. Moosa gave him one and took sixpence from him. He walked off, biting the fruit. He took an instinctive look at the apple after a bite and noticed that he had bitten off half a worm. He spat furiously, and cursed, and wished desperately he could vomit. An elderly man standing next to his two-wheeled pushcart full of sacks and bottles looked at the man and was shocked by the foul language he was using.

The man walked back to Moosa. 'Is this what a man pays for?' showing him the apple. Moosa saw what was wrong, and held out another apple to the fellow, laughing light-heartedly.

'What if this has a worm too?' the customer said. 'Just like you bloody coolies. Always bleeding us poor blacks and giving us rotten things.'

'Sorry, sorry, sorry, my prend. Take this one.'

'To hell with sorry, sorry, prend, prend!' And he flung the rotten apple which caught Moosa on the chin. Two other men came up. They laughed. And then they caught the fever once they sensed vaguely what the complaint was about. They shook their fists at Moosa, still laughing. Moosa was rattling off many 'sorry's'. Soon there were many people about. The hawker's daughter cried out and ran home to report.

Moosa took out an iron lever which he always kept for such emergencies, but not with the intention to attack.

'Heu! Heu' the people shouted and laughed. Nadia Street was in for some sport and it sounded as if it was going to crack from a fit of laughter. Several people took vegetables and fruit from the trolley and flung them at Moosa, laughing all the time. He raised his arms in despair. Soon the trolley was empty, while the horse, bewildered, stamped skittishly as if the tar were too hot under its hooves. Some people picked up the fruit to eat. They looked grotesque, chewing and laughing like that. Others caught hold of Moosa, and in a few moments he was all blood. He broke loose and ran. Fanyan ran deeper into the crowd, caught Moosa by the arm and pulled him out and led him to his home – Lesane's.

Someone beat the horse, which started off in a gallop. It barely missed the old sack-and-bottle man by the breadth of a hair. The trolley knocked his cart over, sending one wheel flying off and careering in a circle. The horse, spurred on by the people's riotous laughter, turned up the cross-street and made for the location gate. As it went through, one end of the cart hit an iron pole, and the horse could not move further. A wooden bar had got jammed in the gate railings.

The wooden part of the trolley was badly damaged. One wheel was curved and the spokes broken. The front axle was badly bent. The horse swung his head this way and that to ease the pressure of the bit in his mouth.

Moosa came later, crying. His daughter, walking beside him, was also crying. For a long time he stood, looking at the wreckage, not decided what to do next.

The sun was sinking lower and lower, and Nadia Street seemed to be panting, tired after the jolly good laugh.

[February 1957]

Lesane
[Neighbours]

EZEKIEL MPHAHLELE

After its mad Saturday abandon which ruined Moosa the Indian hawker, Nadia Street assumed once more its weekday look of innocence. Ma-Lesane tried to urge a group of women to collect money to buy a trolley or stock of vegetables and fruit, or anything to show Moosa how sorry the people were. She got Ma-Ntoi, Ma-Mafate, Ma-Sibiya to agree. But the bulk of Nadia Street people were either not interested or too busy thinking about things that concerned them personally. The plan failed. The matter blew up into verbal bubbles.

'A fine, decent idea,' some left it at that.

'Now why would people go and destroy another man like that?' Old Mbata said.

'Don't worry, God will deal with them. He's not foolish,' another prophesied.

Some were just outright rude to Ma-Lesane. 'And like as not she has not a grain of sugar at home,' a man said to others. 'But she worried her head over Indians.'

'What is an Indian?'

'And her husband out of work and sick with the kidneys and not able to walk, I don't know she's not doing right by Lesane.'

The Lesanes all agreed that Moosa had been a victim of a big, ugly cruel joke.

Fanyan and his sister Diketso talked about it one afternoon. One of the very few times they ever found something to say to each other. But it soon became clear that Diketso wanted to prepare the ground for another matter.

'What were you talking with Pitsi?' Diketso asked.

'Nothing.'

'You know he's the Russian chief?'

Fanyan nodded.

'Want to join him?' He merely fixed his eyes on her and then looked down.

'He'll chop you with an axe if he has a mind to it.'

'Why?'

'Because it's Pitsi. He has power to destroy and it's gone up to his head. Bellyful of it, too.'

'What's wrong with that – with power?'

'Everything.'

Silence.

'Keep clear of such killers,' she warned him. For a moment Fanyan was bewildered. The minute he sensed Diketso was blaming him he felt it like a thin razor-edged slash. Quick and deep.

'I don't want to kill anybody,' he said sulkily.

'Who said you wanted to?'

'That's what you're thinking.'

'Maybe I am, maybe I'm not.' She was parrying, looking for a chance to dig in further and find out more.

'Just saying these Russians are killers and they may get you to kill. Don't be stupid.'

'Where do you think they get all the power against so many people?' He felt his curiosity sharpened.

'Any donkey could tell you there's big money behind them and a strong arm supporting them. They've the damned cheek to cross sticks under the nose of the police.'

'How come you know so much?'

'Just putting two and two together, that's all. The point I'm making is you must shake off Pitsi.'

'Supposing I don't?'

'You can't last the pace. You're scared of the police, aren't you?' Another swift and deep gash.

'Since you're being so offensive, well, be careful of your soft little lover, too. The way I hear my brothers talk there'll be real trouble for the two of you.'

'What do you know about it?'

'Plenty. I see you many times – more than you know.' He noticed how she stiffened up. She knew if she dared tell her father about Fanyan's movements and associations . . . Not that she had ever thought of doing so before. She liked to be of sisterly help to Fanyan. But the lad kept out of reach, silently and yet provocatively.

They heard the creaking of a bed in the next room. Their mother wanted them to know she was within earshot. When they heard her cough a sense of shame crept in between them. Ma-Lesane came out into the front room.

'Ma, why do people suddenly run wild like they did and want to kill Chipile?' Diketso asked.

'This is how, my children: if you put your foot hard on a heap of pebbles, you'll hear them grate and you'll feel them push one another outward. It's like that with us. There's something big on our shoulders, and so we stab and curse and beat one another.'

Her children understood. She didn't show that she had been weeping silently in the room while they were talking. She was thinking about them – about all her children. The little innocent brats; Fanyan and Diketso, who seemed to be for ever looking for something they hadn't lost; their elder brother, who never seemed to want anything more than he had; their eldest brother – now that was a model of obedience (how gravely responsible he could look – the spit of his father). She loved them so. She prayed hard that they survive the brutal alley that was Newclare life. She had thought of Chipile and her heart went out to the hawker without any bitterness against Nadia Street people.

'Has Ma seen the new couple in the backyard?' Fanyan said.

'Good you reminded me, my son. I'll go and see them now.'

A few people had arrived in Nadia Street to settle. Yes, people are unstable and insecure in Newclare. They move restlessly from one landlord to another. Or to another township like restless winds that blow today here, tomorrow there: perpetual pilgrims, eternal emigrants, constant refugees. Tonight a smelling, tattered waste of a man will slouch to a backyard, or a wall that is sheltered from the wind, to sleep. Tomorrow he'll move, for ever going, never coming, never arriving.

So it was no unusual thing to see new faces in Nadia Street. First there was the Coloured man Comingo. He was always spoken of as 'Mr Comingo' – the 'Mr' was never translated. He had a daughter and a wife. He had bought the house of Cassim, the Indian, down the street. He had no tenants and he said to his wife, 'Thank the Almighty, Hettie, tenants are like ants, they'll eat you raw.' Mr Comingo drove a big biscuit-coloured car. Ma-Mafate and Ma-Ntoi soon found out that he was well-to-do, had only one child – shame! And his first-born son was lost – shame! And that the boy disappeared at the age of six, three years before. He had never been traced – shame! But Comingo carried himself with an air of distinction, although they had only a vague idea of what he was distinguished for. It was his habit to drive the length of the street. His daughter was a pretty girl of nineteen – shame! Ma-Ntoi had heard say she was proud as a nanny-goat. Two young African women worked for the Comingos and called them 'Missus', 'Baas' and 'Nonnie'.

And so Mr Comingo became something apart from Nadia Street, except as a term of reference. 'He thinks he's Mr Comingo,' people might say. Or 'He's a boss of himself, like Mr Comingo.' Or 'A dance frock! Who d'you think you are – Mr. Comingo's daughter?' And Mr Comingo occupied the position Nadia Street assigned him without resisting or acquiescing.

Reverend Anton Katsane arrived. It was a dramatic entry. Two rooms, not one. Now there was somebody you could leave a pyjama leg unpegged on the washing line to talk about; someone you could shoot your spit into the soap suds over your washing for the sheer delight of talking about. He had a broad body; a large head; a short neck; a smooth black face; a modest stoop; quick, short strides that made him look as if he were corseted. Moruti (pastor), as he was addressed, had broken off from the Presbyterian Church after a quarrel about some church moneys or some such thing. Some said he had resigned, others that he had been expelled by the white superiors. Moruti, in a non-committal way, boasted he had left the church. He had tried forming his own, but having a restless and insatiable something in him, he could never manage a congregation. He wanted to get about. He did. Pietersburg received him as a teacher in one of the schools. Always when he arrived in or departed from a rural or semi-rural area, Moruti all but organised a reception and a farewell function for himself. He had a soft and painless way of thrusting himself and his demonstrative manner upon people. And they found themselves believing him when they knew they oughtn't to.

But Reef town dwellers knew him too well. They annoyed him that way. He came back to them. He set up some vague practice in a city office as a social worker and employment agent. He organised a domestic workers' union. He always looked forward to Thursday when the young women and the girls were off duty and would come to his office for a meeting. They were well dressed. One thing the church hadn't deprived Moruti of was his sense of beauty. He patted them on the back in a paternal manner after he had appointed himself paid chaplain to the union. Nobody ever asked exactly what he was to do as chaplain. But as they vaguely sensed that the position has something to do with religion, what doubts they had thawed. It had honourable associations.

The women danced in a borrowed dilapidated hall in the city – African House, Diagonal Street, and played indoor games. Whenever the Reverend Katsane supervised their games, standing with arms folded in shirt sleeves and a spotlessly clean shirt and palm-beach trousers, and arms lighter in complexion than the face, Moruti felt pleased with himself; and looking at them gathered in one place he couldn't help thinking of ripe corn.

He had tried at one time to organise a strike among domestic workers. It was a fiasco. Few people, if any, knew how Moruti's Domestic Workers' Union died – a beautiful and graceful death. There was talk of misuse of moneys, but it evaporated.

Moruti, robust and unrelenting as ever, had his dog-collar starched and collected moneys from white people for a fund he declared was to go into the building of a church house under the name of 'Independent Bantu Presbyterian

Church'. Nothing was heard of again about the matter. But Moruti was not the man to show a drooping face.

When he came to Nadia Street, it was not known precisely what his job was except that he baptised all comers, buried every comer, married all comers as a freelance minister, and collected his fees without a tremor. Many unattached Christians went to him only in times of need. Again when he came to Nadia Street, the Reverend Anton Katsane had just lost his wife and had sent their two children to his only sister in the Free State. And still, physically at any rate, he was not the worse for it. He would carry his inevitable walking-stick, which dangled from his arm, and a black bowler hat. Every morning he took strides down the steps at Westbury station, his face invariably ashen with a thin layer of cream, and entered a third-class coach so as to walk about two-thirds of the length of the train towards the small second-class compartment right in front. Hat in hand, and a clean handkerchief jutting out impertinently from his shirtsleeve, Moruti bowed left and right all along the aisle from one coach to another, greeting the passengers aloud.

The ritual annoyed the sophisticated and amused the simpler folk, who often hailed him aloud.

'That Moruti,' said Ma-Mafate to Ma-Ntoi, 'one day we shall know more about him. Here, I'll bite my elbow if he lasts long in this street.'

'I don't understand him somehow. Wish I could,' Ma-Ntoi said.

Moruti was a good mixer. It didn't take long before he got used to the Lesanes. Although he was not of their church, they accommodated him, without even thinking of the distinction between the pastor and themselves.

'Diketso, my child,' her mother said, 'do go and clean Moruti's rooms this Saturday.'

'Yes, Mamma.' She did. Several subsequent Saturdays, too. It wasn't hard work, Moruti being a very tidy man. Often on such days Diketso cooked lunch for Moruti. And then he always insisted she should sit at table with him. She was shy at first, but got used to it. This was only a temporary arrangement – until Moruti should get a reliable woman to do regular cleaning and cooking for him.

'Why does Ma-Lesane do this now?' Ma-Mafate said to Ma-Ntoi as soon as the two women had settled down to their washing.

'I mean about Diketso,' when Ma-Ntoi affected ignorance. 'She's too young for that kind of thing.'

'That's why it shouldn't matter. Moruti must be forty now.'

'Wai, have you ever seen his kind getting too old for anything?'

'In our grand old days,' said Ma-Ntoi with slight impatience, 'it wouldn't have mattered because we were human beings. And nothing would have happened, because we were clean.'

To her man, the shoemaker, Ma-Mafate said: 'Do you see what I see?' Her husband, who had a long drooping neck, was rather slow to register impressions.

'What?' he said.

'Moruti Katsane and Diketso.'

'What have they gone and done?'

'That's what I'm itching to find out. Ma-Lesane's such a good woman she sends Diketso to clean and cook for a man who doesn't have a wife.'

'Now doesn't he?'

'Agh, father of Nosi, you know his woman died and his children are in the Free State.'

'You know a lot of things, eh?'

'Agh, it's common knowledge.'

'Well, Moruti must hurry up and marry.'

'Not if he goes on like this.'

'Well, then, that's his affair.'

'Naturally.' She knew it was hopeless trying to pursue such a subject, and she thought: these shoemakers – all they know is shoes, shoes, shoes.

Ma-Mafate found Ma-Sibiya, the little woman, sitting at her usual place at Westbury station, with her monkey-nuts and fruit spread before her.

'Ma-Lesane is a very good woman. I don't know, but I think she's doing wrong sending Diketso to work for Moruti. Now tell me if I'm right or wrong, tell me.'

'It's not as bad as you think, you know,' Ma-Sibiya said, 'Ma-Lesane would want to mother the whole of Newclare if she could. We'll see. It's only stripes that'll tell you you're looking at a zebra.'

But there were others who were enchanted by the idea of a dog-collar romance and so they passed it round, often as if it were fact.

The Reverend Katsane and Diketso had just finished a Saturday lunch.

'Haleluiah! anything worrying you, my child?' Moruti asked.

'No, Moruti.'

'Oh yes, there is. Haleluiah, I can see it in those eyes.'

She didn't answer. And then tears gathered in her eyes. Moruti came over to her. 'Now tell me, child, if it's a secret, it's safe with me, Haleluiah!'

'My father beats me. He beat me last night. He treats me like a child. I know what's right and what's wrong, Moruti. I wanted to finish school, they didn't let me. I don't just want to be a factory girl, and . . .' She burst into sobs.

'Have you ever told your parents about all this?'

'Mother understands, perhaps. Father wouldn't.'

'All right, I'll speak to them. Haleluiah, that's bad.' Then Moruti drew

Diketso closer to him and gave her a huge paternal hug. It made the young woman feel a current of warmth and flow of comfort in her damp and clammy soul.

For a time she forgot how worldly Moruti was. She was only sensible of these crowded moments of deep consolation. Here was an optimistic, cheerful, humorous pastor who had ceased trying to be an example to thousands of people; who had interpreted the Bible to his flock, dishing out hunks of mouldy moral lessons to hungry people who hoped God would throw them down a slice of bread – even after taking out their church dues; the pastor who couldn't reconcile his own self-acknowledged weaknesses with the pretentious righteousness of his white superiors . . .

The Reverend Katsane felt a strange intuition creep into him – a sense of being spied upon. He moved towards his front door. Even as he did so, he heard a woman's laughter resounding: 'Oo-ha-ha! Oo-ha-ha! No wonder church-bells have stopped ringing!' He stood on the threshold. There she was going down the street. Ma-Mafate. Looking at those beefy buttocks shift up and down made Moruti feel anger bubbling with effervescent sharpness up his throat; because the woman's broad back seemed to say to him: I've heard, I've seen, cut out all the explanations, if you try to explain, I'm not listening.

Later that afternoon Ma-Mafate saw Diketso walk down the street. As she passed, the older woman called her.

'Child, your Ma is such a good woman and my heart would break to see a knife pierce her heart because of your behaviour. Be careful of Moruti, child! People are talking – about your boy and Moruti.'

She didn't finish the sentence. Diketso bit her bottom lip and smacked Ma-Mafate hard on the fat cheek. Some people in the street saw the incident. What, a mere girl hit a woman! Unheard of! Diketso? Unthinkable! Ah, but you don't know Diketso, cheeky, devilish, that's what. People mixed up what Ma-Mafate told them about Moruti and Diketso's fury and her lover.

'Fixes Ma-Mafate,' someone said. 'Talks too much!'

'We all talk. Everybody talks,' another said.

'Good as hitting her own mother, I say.'

When Lesane and Old Mbata heard what Diketso had done to Ma-Mafate, they looked at each other and Old Mbata said: 'The world is coming to an end, brother!'

[March 1957]

Battle for Honour

ALEX LA GUMA

We parked the transport lorry on one side of the little square and climbed down from the driving cabin.

Arthur peeled off his driving gloves. We strolled over towards the Buckingham on the other side of the square. A bunch of sharks hung around the Non-European entrance, and watched us as we went in.

We moved up to the bar and stood there, elbows on the smooth, grained teak, until Bruisky, the barman, came in from the European side. He was short and stout and clay-faced.

'Vell! Vell! You boys just get in?'

'South-West,' Arthur told him. 'Dry as hell.'

'South-West Africa? But it's nice ven you've got company.' He smiled at me. 'How you keeping, sonny boy?'

'I'm fine. How you, Mister Bruisky?'

'Company,' Arthur said and grinned sourly. 'You call this sonofabitch company? Him and his books.'

I winked at Bruisky. 'This ignorant joker. Got no culture. Even if I got to talking to him, all he wants to talk about is women, women, women.'

Arthur said, 'Gimme a double and a ginger ale.'

I asked for lager-beer and we stood there.

The swing-doors opened and a young man came in. We knew him a little from coming to this pub now and then. He was tall and good-looking, except for the battered nose. He had been a welter some time back and there had been pictures of him in the papers. Right then, I didn't know how he earned a living, but he always had money. He wore flashy suits. I guess that was why everybody called him Fancy.

He said, 'Hoit, boys,' and came around, bellying up next to Arthur.

'Howzit,' Arthur returned.

'You johns going to have a drink?'

Bruisky filled up for us and went away. Arthur asked, 'What you doing these days, Fancy?'

'I don't have to work. Horses work, *mos*.'

'You're a lucky rooker.'

'Got me a goose up in Walmer. Nice piece. Her old man don't know about it either.'

The swing-doors opened again and it was one of the sharks. He was wide and flabby, with his belly hanging over his belt, and he had a soft, shiny, booze-bloated face covered with greyish stubble. He slouched up beside me and leaned on the bar.

Then Bruisky moved up from the other end of the bar, looking first at the shark and then at me. 'This bloody rubbish bothering you?'

'No, he's okay,' I said, feeling a little awkward.

'Vat d'you vant?' Bruisky asked the shark.

'Hell, give him a drink,' I suddenly found myself saying.

'You sure?'

'Go on! Give him a drink.' I didn't look at the shark, not wanting him to find any sympathy. Bruisky glared at him and reached for a wine bottle.

On the other side of me Arthur said, 'What the hell you messing your chink on a blerry shark for?'

'Never mind,' I told him. 'Take it easy. It's my money, isn't it?'

He glowered at the shark for a moment, and then turned back to his conversation with Fancy. In the mirror I saw the shark look at me and grin crookedly, his eyes screwing up inside the folds of greyish flesh.

Fancy was saying, '. . . should have seen the goose I had before this one. Left her man for me.'

'Had me a goose on the Port Elizabeth run,' Arthur said, trying to hold his own. 'Knobs like pineapples.'

'Man,' Fancy said. 'That one was really awake. But I got tired of her and so I took a stroll. She walked out on her old man for me, and I walked out on her. He was a no-good barstid, anyway, accor'ing her. She told old Fancy he was always on the bottle. Have another roun'?'

He signalled to Bruisky and waited while the drinks were poured.

'She go back to her *ou*?' Arthur asked.

'Hell, no. Scared, I reckon. Maybe too much pride, too. Last time I heard she was in one of those houses. Those goosies can make money easy.' He chuckled. 'Real nice goose. Name of Lilly McDaniels.'

'You're a real lucky *juba*,' Arthur said, grinning.

Then from beside me the shark said suddenly and thickly: 'Fancy, you're a . . .'

I looked at the shark. He had his thick hands on the top of the bar, and had turned, looking past me at Fancy. Arthur put his glass down and looked at him. Fancy was looking at him too, a pink flush rising under the tan of his face.

'Talking with me, pal?' he asked, a hard look in his eyes.

'Who, then?' the shark said. 'You're a . . .' he repeated. 'And you can go to hell on a broomstick, you dirty, little wise barstid.'

Fancy reached out, taking the front of his greasy shirt in a fist, and said: 'You old . . . ! You want to get flogged?'

'Leave him alone, Fancy,' I said.

'Listen,' Fancy said. 'This old barstid insulted me. It's a matter of honour.'

Then the shark seemed to lose his temper and took a wild swing at Fancy's face. Fancy danced away, pulling the flabby man with him so that he stumbled awkwardly, tearing his shirt. Fancy turned him about, shoving him towards the door, releasing him at the same time, so that he staggered out, scattering the men gathered on the pavement at the entrance.

We all went outside after Fancy. I said to Arthur, 'You better stop him. He'll murder that old boy.'

'Hell,' Arthur said. 'He asked for it, didn't he?'

Fancy stepped off the pavement towards the shark, squaring off as if he was in the ring. He danced in, feinting and laughing softly, and the old boy watched him come, backing away. The crowd jeered and yelled at him to go in and fight, but he kept on retreating further into the square. Then somebody got behind him and gave him a push that sent him right into Fancy.

Fancy hit him low. The flabby man was down on his knees. The crowd hooted.

He climbed back to his feet, shaking his head to get his long, matted hair out of his face. Fancy grinned and said, 'Come on, *Oupa!*'

The shark stood there. Then he charged.

Fancy swung again and again, catching the thick, wine-ruined body in the midriff and face, but the sheer weight of the onrush drove him back. He broke the wide, drooling mouth before the big arms encircled him in a clumsy bear-hug and tightened.

I could see the savage look in the shark's face, and the look of pain and terror coming into Fancy's eyes. The crowd was on the shark's side now, yelling, eager to see somebody get hurt. Then the shark gave a sudden wrench sideways, and Fancy staggered away crazily, making muling sounds with his pain-twisted mouth.

The shark went after him. He had his hands clasped together into one big double fist, and raised above his head as if he was lifting a sledge-hammer. He reached Fancy and brought the joined hands down in a clubbing swing. There was a sound of snapping bone and tearing cartilage as Fancy's nose went.

Fancy sat down on the kerb-side holding his face, and the shark came after him again, saying, 'You barstid! You barstid!' lifting him by the front of his coat and clubbing him, until the rage was out of him. Then he let Fancy drop back on to the pavement.

'Come on, let's blow,' I said.

'I don't get it,' Arthur said as we walked towards the lorry. 'How come did that old man want to start the fight? Fancy wasn't bothering him. We was just standing there talking about some goosies. I don't get it.'

We climbed up into the driving cabin and Arthur started her up. The diesel hummed and thundered, then settled down into its steady roar. The shark came around the back of the truck and past the cabin, still breathing hard.

Arthur stuck his head out of the window and called down: 'Hey, old dad, how come did you do that to that john?'

The shark looked up, grinning a little painfully with his split lips. He said above the sound of the diesel: 'Well, it was a matter of honour. You see, pally, my name is Joseph Henry McDaniels.'

[November 1958]

The Life and Death of King Kong

NAT NAKASA

Ezekiel 'King Kong' Dhlamini – that rugged, ever-unkempt giant with the iron muscles of a Durban rickshaw puller – is back in the limelight. Within two years a legend has emerged round the man who threw himself into a dam rather than face the grey sameness of prison life.

That is as he would have wished. That the whole land should remember his death. That the whole land should remember the strange, fabulous incidents that crowded the 32-year life of 'Lightning Marshal'.

Right this moment, here in Johannesburg, King Kong's gorilla face is on red posters pasted on to walls, his name splashed in the papers and pasted on to car windows. A musical elephant-size job with over fifty men and women on the stage is being made on King's life. The estimated cost of the opera's production is £6 000.

The 'Spice Smasher', the 'King Marshal' – Mandlenkosi Dhlamini if you want to be official – met his first boyhood days in the district of Vryheid, Natal, around the year 1925. After showing up, fairly regularly, in a Roman Catholic school for two years, King Marshal turned his back for the last time on a classroom.

Only about fourteen then, according to his brother Elliot, King Kong went to work in Vryheid, herding a white family's milk-cow and keeping their little garden in lookable condition. There wasn't much in the way of pay. But what a pleasure to be away from his father's whip in the family fields!

Only a few months hurried by and King Kong was gone. Nobody had any idea where he was. The next to be heard of him was when he wrote – at least supervised the writing of a letter to his mother – reporting that he was in Durban. But Durban was too quiet for this tall Tarzan-youth.

So without much waste of time, King Kong took his exit from Durban. Off to the wild, stabbing, over-populated Johannesburg. Much, much further away from his parents. He also left behind his three brothers and two sisters, all his junior.

Not bothered for one moment about getting himself a job and a boss, King Kong tried his big hands at gambling with cards and shooting dice – just to knock together some kind of a living. It was a gambling argument that landed the King in jail after a man had been battered to death. King was acquitted, and swaggered straight back into his old life.

In those days he used to visit places like training gyms and singing or dancing hangouts since he had tons of time on his hands – which 'won't work' hasn't? He found his way to the sparring rooms at the Bantu Men's Social Centre – a den with hard-hitting boys under the famous hand of William 'Baby Batter' Mbatha.

Those who tell the story of King's first day in the gym have now turned it into a joke for entertaining guests at the township parties. He is said to have laughed himself sick at the sight of people fighting with 'cushions' round their fists.

'Why don't they use bare fists, these chaps?' King is said to have asked.

To King Kong the whole thing looked silly. He told the boys he could lick them all in a row, gloves or no gloves on. What's more, when he was shown the trainer, he repeated his words: 'I can lick your boys any time all in a row, including you their boss.'

The trainer laughed it off and went his way. But when King insisted, getting more insulting and aggressive, trainer Mbatha got into a pair of gloves and flung two to King Kong. In two or three rounds Mbatha sent this Goliath to the ground, proving his point.

But this didn't stop the King from being stubborn. In fact, the defeat made him angry as a wild beast. Yet some sense had been knocked into his head. The defeat made him want to take lessons from Mbatha. After some time, results began to pop out. In many a tournament King was awarded a walk-over win since there were no opponents in his division – the heavyweights. Promoters told the black giant: 'Your trouble is that you are too heavy. Try to reduce.'

King listened to the advice, and the trick seemed to work. In 1946 King was matched against Joe Maseko, then a seasoned amateur boxer in the middle-weight shelf. King lost on points to Joe, just like everybody had expected. This, of course, meant a serious grudge against Joe Maseko. For King Kong always had a grudge against anyone who got one up on him.

Then came a big moment for the King, when he was matched against Gilbert 'Kwembu' Moloi, a respected and thoroughly feared boxer from Jo'burg's Sophiatown. King Kong was fresh throughout the night, and put Kwembu down every round, to win the fight on points.

King Kong showed plenty of his unorthodoxy that night. Every time he dropped the humiliated Moloi, he would refuse to go to his neutral corner. He stood over Moloi with his fists clenched, ready to pummel him to the ground should he get up.

In a South African Amateur Championship Tournament down in Durban that same year came King's next tussle in the ring. The opponent was Durban's sleepy-eyed heavyweight, Nat Mngoma. When the King lost this fight, it only meant one more creature's name in the long list of those he was going to 'fix up one day'. Mngoma should have counted himself among the lucky guys because King Kong did not run after him in the streets, challenging him to a return fight. And King could have done this without any persuasion.

The story has been told time and again how King Kong once cornered one of his challengers at the Durban railway yards. Here's how it goes: A light-heavyweight in Durban, Sam Langford, said something which sounded like he was keen to face King Kong. The King heard of this, so he took a single ticket to Durban – 400 odd miles from Johannesburg – just to see this boxer who dared challenge him. The poor fellow was busy sweating away a day's work when King Kong confronted him at the railway.

'Are you the chap who wants to fight me?' King inquired impatiently. 'Let's get going now.'

'But how can we fight here in the yard at work?' Sam protested. 'These things are done through promoters and managers and trainers. And it must be in a ring.'

'Listen, boy,' King cut in. 'You said you can beat me any time, any day of the week and twice on a weekend. Now what are you scared of?'

King Kong was already weaving and bobbing in the yard when a third party – a fellow worker of Sam's – intervened. Some sense was spoken into the King's head, and he walked off satisfied that Sam was a damn yellow guy.

Round about September 1951, King got a fight for the Transvaal heavy-weight title against John Sullivan – roundly hailed as a tough in the boxing game. The BMSC hall in Jo'burg was packed to the roof that night.

Famous for his unfailing stamina, King chased poor Sullivan round the ring from corner to canvas, piling face-tearing punches with the speed of a flyweight. King would stand hands up or rubbing his tummy while Sullivan landed feeble punches all over the giant's front. After a few rounds King got to work again, giving Sullivan the powder that brought the fight to a sudden end.

The next step in the King's programme was to become the South African champion – to beat every heavyweight in the game here. And he got what he wanted. That's when he beat Joe Mtambo in Cape Town.

But then again King Kong found himself without opponents. It got so bad, this lack of opposition, that the King landed up doing barefist fighting on Sunday afternoons. The boxing bug was in him. He had to exchange blows with some willing victim.

For weeks on end he would travel long distances to Pretoria and the mine dumps of the Reef. Pedi tribesmen would pay his fare and offer him stakes if he came to their open-air, barefist fights. The lonely champ would line them all up and knock them out one by one. Even at these fights the South African champion wore his maroon and blue 'King Marshal', 'Spice Smasher' gown.

Not satisfied with these barefist foes, King Marshal would occasionally show up in Johannesburg's busiest streets – all gowned up for exercise. Stunned shopping crowds on hot summer days would watch this oversized six-footer shadow-boxing on the pavements and on street corners.

It was during these eccentric times that King Kong's last fight – against Simon Greb Mthimkhulu – was clinched. Greb was a real good and tough boxing man. But nobody really expected to see him beat King.

There was big confusion when the King failed to show up on time. But still the crowds waited on him. In the meantime the King was trotting the two-mile distance from Jeppe Hostel, the usual big crowds running behind and around him. When he ultimately made the ring and flew over the ropes in his characteristic boastful style, he was soaked in his own sweat.

With a 14-pound advantage over Simon Greb, King Kong toyed around with his opponent. Two friendly jabs and a slap on the face sent Greb breathless on to the canvas for a short count. It became a foregone thing the King was going to crush Greb any time. But then King Kong started dancing about, swinging his arms like a policeman during a drill session. What's more, he left himself open for any attack.

It happened in the third round. Greb rushed in with a stinging right to the tummy and pressed home a butchering left on the King's jaw, sending the champion to an immediate, peaceful sleep. The King lay flat on his back, his fans shocked.

This was to be a turning point in King Kong's life. From then the great King Kong lost some of his glamour. He wouldn't have anyone look or laugh at him. 'What are you looking at me for?' he would ask. 'What's so funny about me?'

Yes, his reputation had been injured. But his strength and skill remained with him. He could have easily beaten Greb had he not done those ballet gimmicks in the ring. But his end in boxing was near. It came in a secret sparring session in Johannesburg with the white man-mountain, Ewart Potgieter.

Potgieter sent the black giant twice over the ropes. The King got so hurt that doctors urged him not to fight again for some time. King Kong himself felt he was getting weaker and weaker each day, but still he had one more fight.

'He used to grumble a lot to me,' says Elliot, his brother, who is in Johannesburg. 'He used to tell me that some doctor had given him an injection that reduced his strength. He always said wildly that he would kill that doctor if he found out who he was.'

That was the end of the King's ring career. But even a King must live, so the man with the strength of ten began operating as a bouncer in gangster-infested dance halls. With his change of occupation came new kinds of trouble – with the law. While bouncing one night he stabbed a troublesome knifeman to death. He pleaded self-defence, and was let off.

But the big conflict – with the law and with himself – was still ahead. It is a night in 1956 at the Polly Centre Hall. The King was out with his only known girl, Maria Miya. King suspected that the girl had been unfaithful to him for some time. So when a misunderstanding came up between them, King stabbed her to death. While a shocked crowd muttered around, King himself ordered them to 'Call the police.'

The police came, to find the giant standing in the hall, a knife in his hand. 'Drop that knife,' the police ordered. King refused. They warned that they would take action if he did not drop the knife. King still said 'No.'

With the hall all tensed up, the police opened fire on King Marshal. Three bullets went through his body and hit two policemen behind him. Everybody thought his end had come – but the King lived on. He was taken to hospital, where he stayed only a short while. Before he had recovered, he was taken to The Fort jail at his own request. A rather strange choice. But he was granted his wish.

The peak of the drama in his life was now near. After a few months he was in the Supreme Court, tried and sentenced to twelve years in jail. Even the trial of King Kong was not to be without its touch of the fantastic: he begged the judge to give him a death sentence instead of jail.

A reporter who spoke to him before he was locked up says King Kong had this to say: 'I have nothing to say. I'm not bothered at all about my girl's death. My only worry is that by the time I come out of jail I will be too old to fight.'

If there's one thing King Kong never feared, it was jail. Those with him tell that he had a royal time in the cells. Neither the guards nor the fellow convicts wished to be involved in a brawl with him.

It was the dull disciplined life of jail he must have hated. In the outside world he was constantly surrounded by crowds of people. People who talked about his fame and his might. This admiration was a part of his life. Not the grim-faced crowds, like the bunch of hard-labour convicts who saw him hurl his life away; saw him drown himself in a dam at the Leeuwkop Farm Jail on April 3, 1957.

The King had himself granted his death plea to the judge.

[February 1959]

If Bugs Were Men

It was the year 1758. Two bugs were sitting and chatting in a nook of a wall in the House of Discussion. One bug yawned and confessed that it was feeling sleepy. But it dared not sleep. It always enjoyed listening.

A leading Official had just remarked that half the members of the Opposition were asses, whereupon someone asked him to withdraw. He withdrew by saying that half the members of the Opposition were NOT asses, whereupon he was roundly congratulated for being the first person to withdraw a remark instead of stamping out of the house like a bull.

'Do you believe in evolution?' the yawning bug asked its friend.

'Yes. Why do you ask?'

The first bug scratched its head and said: 'Well, I was just thinking. Last night I bugged that chap who calls himself President. His blood is flowing in my veins, so I'm his blood relation in a way. Maybe some centuries to come I might evolve into a human being, and who knows I might be elected President too!'

'What will you do when you're a President?'

'I will make laws. Humane and human laws. Nothing but laws.'

'That means you will forget your bug brothers, even me?'

'Nix, chum. I will appoint a Minister of Squalor, whose sole business would be to see to it that every human being stays dirty. I will ban all disinfectants; encourage bug immigration; and tighten up on emigration. Anybody who disagrees with me, even on such a small matter as the weather, will be named a bugomist and banished to a concentration camp for an indefinite period.

'By bugs, I'll make such laws bugs will build me a monument after I'm dead for being the one bug who fought relentlessly to uphold Bug supremacy.'

'You wouldn't escape criticism from other democratic countries if you carried on like that.'

'Woe unto those who dared point a finger at me. I would of necessity have to be tough. After all, my problems would be unique. What with a President who was once a bug.'

But the other bug was bored with all this kind of rambling. It stifled a yawn and said: 'Stop talking like a human being and let's sleep. Wake me up at midnight.'

The two bugs fell asleep immediately, and dreamed of human beings.

[February 1958]

Johburg Jailbugs

CASEY MOTSISI

It was just a few minutes after dusk and the two bugs sat silently in a nook of the prison cell No. 13 in Section D of The Fort. Their eyes were bloodshot. (Bloodshot eyes are as much part of a well-sucking bug as a paunch is of a wealthy rural Zulu.) The first bug sighed and turned to the other. The second bug sighed too for lack of something to say. Silence. The minutes fattened into hours. 'I can't understand human beings,' the First Bug barked and looked into the wrinkled face of the Second Bug. The Second Bug nodded its ageless head in a manner which said: 'You're telling me.'

'Whenever they talk of the old days they refer to them as The Good Old Days,' the First Bug continued.

'But to us bugs,' the Second Bug fell in with the conversation, 'the old days were lean days. Jolly lean, I say. Couldn't find enough prisoners to bug. We were practically forced to practise birth control, so lean were the old days.' The First Bug coughed a little and spat out blood. No matter, it thought to itself, I'll refill tonight. 'I remember the Seven Lean Years way back in 1887 – this prison was not built yet, only trees where it now stands - there were only two prisoners. I mean black prisoners, you know. I love black prisoners. They're so full of blood and so harmless. White prisoners scratch a lot. Insomnia, I guess. But as I was saying, there were these two prisoners here and a whole swarm of us to bug them. We bugged them dry, man, dry, and all most of us got was just a droplet. Then we decided to crawl over to the cells of the white prisoners.' The Second Bug was shocked. 'Did you actually take such a risk? Why you might have been squashed! The things hunger can drive a bug to!'

'We crawled over, all right. Lost a bucketful of bugs because of the disinfectants they use in the white cells, but some of us managed to get back just before dawn. I lay sick for a week. Then human beings talk of the old days as the Good Old Days. They complain now that Times are Bad. To us bugs these are Good Young Days. More black prisoners coming in to be bugged by the pick-up load every day. Permit raids, beer raids, pass raids, pickpockets, payroll snatchers, foreign Natives, immorality, night specials, slogan writers, political agitators - why they all come in to be bugged ever so regularly. These, indeed, are the Good Young Days.'

'Shush,' cautioned the First Bug. 'Here come the boys from their hard labouring. And they look comfortably tired for us. The minute their heads touch the cement floor they'll fall asleep and we can go and have our fill. Shall we make it a small drink or a blow up?'

'Let's make it a blow up, I'm thirsty tonight.'

The way you like drinking, blood will be your undoing one night,' the First Bug teased. 'Say, there's a new one tonight. That fat one over there. Do you see him?'

'I know about him,' the other bug said importantly. 'He's a reporter. The Ghost Squad roped him in with two other men while they were drinking gin in a shebeen in Malay Camp – you know the one just opposite Marshall Square Police Station? We must bug him solid tonight because his Editor might come for him tomorrow. You know what Editors are.'

'Poor boy, we'll bug him so good he'll learn to leave the white man's liquor alone and develop along his own lines.'

[September 1957]

On the Beat
[Kid Hangover]

CASEY MOTSISI

One of my pet hates is going to a midnite party – you know those riotous money-making affairs which begin on Friday and follow through right up to the impossible hours on Sunday.

But I guess I'll have to go to this here midnite party 'cause the bizaro who's throwing it happens to be my pal with the name of Kid Hangover. And besides I reckon he'll need the boodle he charges guests since he's been out of a job for a mile of a time and spending the better part of it in the jailhouse on account he didn't square up with the maintenance of his two bambinos – not that he's wedded.

It's about eight bells, and the bright Saturday moon makes me feel somewhat romantic and adventurous. I leave my Sophiatown shanty and head for Western, which is the place where this here midnite party is participating.

When I reach Western I find the place spilling over with humans, and I reckon Kid Hangover is going to make himself a good screw. There's enough booze to keep Mr Khruschev blotto for weeks on end. I go to the back of the house, where there's a tent pitched for 'rockagers' who now and again want to shake a leg.

Benches are supplied for those who are tired or can't get partners, and those – like myself – who want to battle with the bottles.

A busty young girl in jeans slides a disc on the battered gramophone, and some rockagers begin to dance while the Elvis of Presley accuses each and everyone of being 'Nothing but a Hound Dog'.

Kid Hangover walks in and pats me on the back, then asks if I have been attended to. I put on my best midnite party manners and howl: 'Waddya mean attended to. You crazy? Shake a leg boy and give me half-a-dozen beers. I'm thirsty!' I pay him 35 bob of hard-earned pennies. As it is I don't need all those beers but there are janes around, and a guy's got to make an impression.

In fact, I don't need beer at all – sissy stuff – and I could do with some hooch. But I know that midnite party hooch is always 'doctored' with methylated spirits calculated to knock the hair off your chest, after which the boys can get at your pockets undisturbed, to say nothing of the five-day long hangover.

I can see that I've made an impression all right 'cause no sooner had I opened the first bottle – without spilling a drop thank you – when I'm being surrounded by a batch of gum-chewing cherries all breathing down my neck and telling me that if there were more guys like me life wouldn't be the touch and go affair it is.

The girls howl for some more, and I oblige. This time we switch over to vodka.

In the wee small hours of the morning I find myself under one of the benches. Needless to say my boodle is all gone – whole week's pay. All I have between me and starvation is my hangover. That vodka must have been over-doctored. I brush myself and criss-cross home.

Three weeks later Kid Hangover corners me at a bus stop and tells me that he went and lost all his money at the races and it's about time he paid some more maintenance for his bambinos. Can't I loan him five quid?

This, I tell myself, is moral blackmail since he knows I have money on account it's payday. I give him three begrudgingly, and remind him that I'm not his father.

Now here I am twiddling my thumbs and wondering when Kid Hangover is going to throw another midnite party – which I won't attend – so's he can pay me back the three quid I loaned him so's I can pay Aunt Peggy for the 'straights' I got on tick the month before.

[May 1958]

On the Beat
[Kid Playboy]

CASEY MOTSISI

Everytime a hick job comes around in the office I get saddled with it. Now the Editor pushes this folded white card at me and says to find out what I can get out of this here invite. I walk out of the office and read the card once more. According to the goldlettered words a certain Kid Mabothobotho stays out Dube is getting hitched to an Alexandra cherrie.

On Saturday the wedding will take place at the cherrie's place in Alex. I decide I'd rather wait for it to come around to Dube on Sunday because I'm somewhat scared of hopping off to Alex, especially on weekends on account the bright boys over there have turned the place into a gunsmoke and knife-happy township.

On Sunday I haul out my top hat and tails to make ready to go to Dube. I expect it to be one of those high society shindigs, as you know how hoity-toity these Dubeheimers can get when they want to. I get a good look at myself in my landlord's son's wardrobe mirror as I put on the tie he lent me, and I see that my eyes are unusually clear – sure sign among the boozing fraternity that I've been keeping shebeen queens, especially Aunt Peggy, waiting.

I get to Dube and don't have any difficulty spotting the place where this wedding is taking place on account of the half-a-dozen beribboned convertible cars parked in front of the house. A guy who meets me at the door looks scornfully at my not-too-well pressed trousers, whereupon he gives me the V.I.P. treatment. Only he reckons the 'I' in V.I.P. stands for 'Inconsequential'. He tells me to go and sit in the tent at the back of the house. I tell him who I am, whereupon he smiles and ushers me into the room.

This girl this guy's getting married to is so beautiful that I can't take my eyes off her for a pretty long time. After a while I manage to pull my eyes away from her to look at the groom. Cripes! It's none other than Kid Playboy. I feel the blood revolting in my veins. This is the same Kid Playboy who took away from me some time back the only girl I ever loved. He promised this girl of mine everything in the world and crowned the long list of promises by telling her that he would build a fire under the ocean just so's she can swim in winter.

And like all starry-eyed girls, this girl of mine went and believed every word he told her. Maybe if she hadn't been so gullible she would still have been alive today. As it turns out, Kid Playboy gives her the bird after stringing her for a month on account another foolish cherrie falls for his sweet talk. So what does she do, but commit suicide!

Kid Playboy's eyes meet mine and I pull out my tongue at him. He turns coal black and his adam's apple starts moving up and down like someone who's seen a ghost. The guy looks real scared, and I am just beginning to hate myself for having scared the boy by sticking out my tongue at him when I realise that it's not me who's the cause of his sudden jitters. There's a girl who's sitting a few feet behind me who is proving to be the why for Kid's jaded nerves.

I turn around and look at this girl to see what it is about her that can cause so much panic in a satanic soul. But all I can see is that she's an ordinary homely girl, and the small sleeping child she's holding in her arms is the sweetest thing I ever did see.

I'm still busily occupied at looking at this fear-instilling girl and hoping that she's not a ghost, when a voice that sounds like a constipated ostrich's booms: 'Ladies and gentlemen, all those who have presents for the bridal couple may now see the "mabalane" (the M.C. of the wedding).' The 'mabalane' stands up, breaks into a toothless grin, bows and sits down again.

I thought they had invited us to a wedding; now they want to fleece presents out of us! But seeing as the announcer man said 'ladies and gentlemen', I reckon he has left me out on account nobody ever accused me of being a gentleman, let alone a lady. So I happily ignore him.

A few folk get away from their eats and drinks with parcels of varying sizes beneath their armpits. They stand in line before the 'mabalane', who jots down the name and address of each and everyone who dumps a parcel on the table. Some guys who had decided beforehand that it would be much better to save the few pennies they have for paying their rent instead of buying presents for Kid Playboy and his spouse – and perhaps a few others who have a needle against him, like yours truly – suddenly discover that the room is too hot and march out.

After some time the last name and address is written down, and I can see the 'mabalane' hinting at the groom's people for his payment for services duly rendered – a nip of hooch. But he doesn't get the hooch. Instead, the girl with the baby, who had so disorganised Kid Playboy a short while ago, stands up and walks to the 'mabalane'. She dumps the child, who is now awake and bawling his young head off, on the table and says, 'Here's my present to the bride and groom. My name is Maisie.' She gives a Mapetla address somewhere in Site and Service. She winds up by saying Kid Playboy's the pop of the child.

All of a sudden, there's a bang of a hulabaloo going on. Kid Playboy is making a hurried exit out of the house, and the bride is tearing at her bridal dress and hurling all sorts of names at Kid Playboy and his family, including the late ones. After every burst of unprintable words she keeps chorusing that she's got a lawyer that's going to show them what makes the grass green.

Up to today nobody ever hears a word about Kid Playboy. But Mr Rumour goes around the townships telling all and sundry that Kid Playboy is in his hometown somewhere in the Tanganyika Territory, although the folks from there pronounce it 'Tananika Torrotoro'.

I reckon the next time the Editor tells me to go and cover a wedding, I'm gonna take an advance on my salary and hightail it to Aunt Peggy's joint and cover a bottle of hooch with Kid Playboy's ex-bride on my lap, as she now frequents this place ever since her lawyer proved not to be as hot as she had thought him to be.

[February 1959]

On the Beat
[Kid Newspapers]

Cross my heart, I'm not trying to give a free puff to advertising agencies, but believe me, advertising brings quick results. At least, that's what Kid Newspapers tells me. Now it's not difficult to find out why they call this guy Kid Newspapers. You can always find him breathing down a newspaper at Aunt Peggy's joint. But Kid Newspapers only reads adverts in the 'smalls', nothing else.

One day I ask him what fun he gets out of reading adverts when everybody seems to be interested only in keeping abreast with the latest score concerning Jane Mansfield's controversial bust measurements. This Kid Newspapers tells me that it pays to read the adverts. It takes me some to get proof of this statement, and this is the how.

I snoop down to Aunt Peggy's after telling my Editor that I want to get around the shebeens and make an on-the-spot investigation of how the potato boycott is affecting shebeen queens, seeing as some of the concoctions they brew call for potato jackets boiled with horse lungs.

I go through the backyard, which is the place where Aunt Peggy accommodates her 'Both Hands' drinkers. These are the customers who go for her homemade concoction called 'Joe Louis' on account it packs the same wallop the Brown Bomber used to dish out with his mitts during his salad days. Now Aunt Peggy decided to baptise these customers 'Both Hands' seeing as they have to use both their hands to lift up the painted tin scales to their mouths each time they take a swig.

The backyard is as crowded as an ant heap and I reckon that Aunt Peggy, who has apparently sworn on a mountain of Bibles that nothing will come between her and the blackest penny, has not thrown in her lot with the potato boycotters. I reckon she's what is known in political lingo as a sell-out. Or could be that she hasn't heard that there's this potato boycott going on, although I've been under the impression that what Aunt Peggy doesn't know about this man's burg is not worth knowing.

I run up the stairs to go and tell Aunt Peggy what I think of her, and also that I won't put my foot any more in her house, and I almost slip on a banana peel.

When I get into the room I find Aunt Peggy testing her Joe Louis brew for kicks in one of the test tubes I asked one of my university pals to lift for me and ultimately for Aunt Peggy at their lab. I ask her to give me a nip on the cuff and the smile of welcome on her face turns into a snarl as she hears me call her a potato-pedlar.

She tells me that she's a true daughter of Africa and wouldn't touch a potato even to throw at a cop batoning her. But seeing as she has to satisfy her customers' thirst, she decided to use banana peels instead of potato jackets when brewing her Joe Louis.

I'm still arguing with Aunt Peggy to give me a nip of brandy until my ship comes in, with her refusing and saying my account is running too high, when Kid Newspapers walks in with a paper on his arm. Also on one of his arms is a cherrie with lips like two bananas, dressed in a fur coat that even a Rockefeller would buy on the 'pay while the moths get at it' plan.

Obviously Kid Newspapers must have overheard me trying to convince Aunt Peggy that account or no account I've got to have the pep-up liquid, 'cause he tells Aunt Peggy to pull out her very best bottles for his old pal, Casey. Aunt Peggy gives us a bottle of imported whisky, and it is while we are charging up that Kid Newspapers intros me to Miss Fur Coat and I ask him to give me the low-down on how he got scented with the sweet smell of boodle.

To answer me, he pulls out a newspaper and points at it. There's a ring around a little advert for a night watchman. Kid Newspapers tells me that on the same night that the advert appeared in the newspapers, he went around to the firm, and he and the boys had the easiest time removing the safe and bolting away with it as there was no watchman. The safe was loaded with dough, he tells, and that's why he could afford to buy Miss Fur Coat's love with the fur coat. He even pays Aunt Peggy the money I owe her and I reckon he's a regular guy.

I'm still on my potato boycott investigation a week later when I run into Kid Newspapers' cherrie, Miss Fur Coat, in a Sip and Fly joint in the boiler room of a posh building in one of the European suburbs. But for her banana-shaped lips I wouldn't have recognised her on account she isn't wearing a fur coat.

I pitch myself next to her and ask her where on God's earth is Kid Newspapers. The story she tells me convinces me all the more that it is much safer – and exciting – to read about beauty queens than bother with reading adverts. She tells me that Kid Newspapers' roving eyes spot another cherrie one day and he decides to string along with her. But this new lover has one weakness: she drinks like a whale. So Kid Newspapers has to dig deep into his pockets to make sure this new lover doesn't lack a stagger as she gave him fair warning that the minute such an unforgivability happens, she's going to give him the bird.

It so happens that after a while Kid Newspapers runs out of mazuma. He decides to go to Miss Fur Coat and tells her that they should sell the fur coat and get married on the takings, which will go to pay the lobola. Like a woman, she falls for the idea.

They sell the coat and Kid Newspapers sprints back to spend it on his new lover. It is while they are on one of their drinking sprees that Miss Fur Coat walks in on them, whereupon she straight-away pulls out Kid Newspapers' new lover's hair. Kid Newspapers fades out before Miss Fur Coat can give him her undivided attention. For days she looks for him so as to get settled with him, but she draws a blank. The guy's just nowhere to be seen.

But hell hath no fury like a woman shorn of her fur coat and Miss Fur Coat does not prove an exception. One day she hits upon the one thing that will bring Kid Newspapers into her itching clutches. An advert. So she adverts in the newspapers that a jewellery shop in town is in need of a watchman to start work immediately. The same night, Kid Newspapers and two of his boys turn up at this ice shop to do business. But the cops, who had earlier received a tip from an anonymous caller, rope these guys up and run them down to the cooler. She tells me that Kid Newspapers gets three months for attempted burglary.

I'm no end fed up with what this cherrie has done, but then I guess it does prove that Kid Newspapers was right on the ball when he said advertising brings quick results . . .

[September 1959]

More Than Telling a Story
Drum and its Significance
in Black South African Writing

MICHAEL CHAPMAN

The stories in *Drum* of the 1950s mark the substantial beginning, in South Africa, of the modern black short story. Prior to the appearance between 1951 and 1958 of over 90 stories, only a few by black South Africans existed outside the 'anonymous' oral tradition of folk-tale: around 1930 R. R. R. Dhlomo in the Johannesburg-based magazine *The Sjambok* had published several 'moral' sketches involving situations on the gold mines;[1] Peter Abrahams's collection *Dark Testament* (1942)[2] included a few urban evocations; and Ezekiel (now Es'kia) Mphahlele's first volume of stories *Man Must Live* had appeared in 1946. What distinguished the *Drum* stories most expressively was their style. As Mphahlele puts it, the style of the fifties was

> racy, agitated, impressionistic, it quivered with a nervous energy, a caustic wit. Impressionistic because our writers feel life at the basic levels of sheer survival, because blacks are so close to physical pain, hunger, overcrowded public transport, in which bodies chafe and push and pull . . .[3]

Most of the writers were concerned with more than just telling a story. They were concerned with what was happening to their people and, in consequence, with moral and social questions. It is this which distinguishes the *Drum* writers from purveyors of pulp fiction.[4]

Protest against the retribalizing policies of apartheid could take unexpected forms, as in Todd Matshikiza's music reviews which celebrate the 'international' experience. In 'Dam-dam!' (December 1953) Matshikiza's idiomatic style, dubbed Matshikeze, is heard at its most undiluted, as English, the language of international acceptance, bends to the culture of township jazz:

> I said to Dam-dam [Nathan Dambuza Mdedle, leader of the Manhattan Brothers] yesterday: 'Dam-dam, I bet you my last shirt you're the biggest playboy going on.'

He said: 'Blow you, Toddie-boy, I'm still looking for my dream girl!'

I said: 'What happened to the juicy berries I've seen hanging on you?' For Dam-dam knows a nice dame when he sees one.

He said: 'Skip them. You wouldn't bet your dough on a donkey on the racecourse, would you? I dream at the pace of a racehorse. They dream at the pace of a lame donkey . . .'

As Mphahlele's remarks above betray, however, such 'vitality' was often a desperate defence against the forces of politics and economics, which cared little for the quality of township life and saw the primary need to secure a convenient and docile labour force. Mphahlele indicts *Drum* itself as part of an oppressive socio-economic structure; while the proprietor, Jim Bailey, describes the magazine as a 'great popular educator'.[5] From their own perspectives both are correct, and Lewis Nkosi's impressions in his article 'The Fabulous Decade' are thoroughly paradoxical: the fifties was a time of 'infinite hope and possibilities . . . It was a time when it seemed that the sound of police gunfire and jackboot would ultimately become ineffectual against resolute opposition and defiance from the new "fringe" society'. But: 'Alas, we didn't realise how small and powerless we were.'[6]

In the context of the 1950s – the character of which I want to chart in the first part of this essay – the stories of *Drum* extend beyond their own communicative immediacy to release an extra-textual dimension of significance. For one thing, the impact of racial discrimination in South Africa changed both quantitively and qualitatively after the coming to power in 1948 of Dr Malan's Nationalist Party. Determined to refashion South African society according to Afrikaner ideals of racial purity, Malan and his followers set out to end once and for all any possibility that the country might move toward an extension of economic and political rights for blacks in 'white' South Africa. During the office of the first Nationalist government, 1948–53, the rhetoric of trusteeship, as had been advocated by Smuts, fell by the way as one repressive measure after another was advanced in parliament and passed into law. The list of apartheid legislation (described by Brian Bunting as South Africa's Nuremberg Laws)[7] makes depressing reading. Between 1948 and 1960 the government legislated against mixed marriages and interracial social mixing in cinemas and restaurants, and on beaches, while introducing increased penalties for sexual intercourse between different races. The Population Registration Act established a racial register, and the decade witnessed the humiliating spectacle of 'reclassifications' (see *Drum*'s article, 'A Native by Mistake', July 1956). The Group Areas Act set out to enforce separate residential areas for the different races, and of especial pertinence to the *Drum* generation was the allied Natives Resettlement Act (1954). This began the process that would culminate in the forcible removal of 57 000 Africans from Sophiatown, Martindale, Newclare and Pageview, the so-called black spots in the western areas of central Johannesburg, to Meadowlands and Diepkloof, over fifteen kilometres south-west of the city. The terms 'removal' and 'endorsement out' began to take on sinister connotations. With Minister of Native Affairs Dr H. F. Verwoerd assuming responsibility under the Bantu Education Act (1953) for African education, mission schools came under severe pressure to conform to government syllabuses which, in introducing vernacular instruction, were designed to 'retribalize' Africans and limit their role in the 'white cities' to 'certain forms of labour'.[8] As a result of the Defiance Campaign in 1952, when members of the African National Congress (ANC) and the South African Indian Congress (SAIC) courted arrest on a massive scale in defiance of 'unjust laws', the government promulgated severe penalties for the breaking of any law as a political protest, and provided for rule by decree in a state of emergency. Bannings and arbitrary police searches became a common feature of political life. Smarting at *Drum*'s investigations of prison conditions, the state in 1959 imposed heavy restrictions on the reporting of information about South Africa's gaols. Of the many acts of security legislation, the Suppression of Communism Act of 1950, besides outlawing the Communist Party, offered a wide definition of 'statutory communism' and spearheaded the state's sustained attack on civil liberties. (Its present-day form is the Internal Security Act.) The decade was to end tragically with the shooting at Sharpeville (the result of police action in response to the Pan Africanist Congress anti-pass law campaign), and shortly afterwards the Unlawful Organisations Act empowered the Governor-General to ban the ANC and the PAC. The list of apartheid-inspired laws continued. For present purposes, however, we need only note further the Suppression of Communism Amendment Act of 1965, which prohibited the publication of speeches and writings by banned persons who had left South Africa. Under this amendment, the *Drum* writers Mphahlele, Modisane, Themba, Nkosi, Matshikiza and Nakasa, all of whom have at times been accused of bourgeois-individualist dependencies, were silenced as 'statutory communists', and their writings have only in the last decade again been made available in South Africa.

In helping to shape and convey the textures of the 'black experience', *Drum* provided a social barometer of the decade. It did this by tapping the most urgent currents of life in the townships of the Witwatersrand, from soccer and boxing to the politics of African nationalism. If it often presented the 'events' of cultural life as opposed to an analysis of historical causes, this defined its purpose as an illustrated periodical, and ensured its popular appeal. While the rival pictorial *Zonk!* (1949) continued to offer a diet of soccer, sex and sin, and while *Bona* (1956) acted as a propaganda medium for pro-government views, *Drum* after its first few issues managed to combine a commercial image with journalism of heightened awareness. Ironically, Jim Bailey and his successive editors (Anthony Sampson, Sylvester Stein and Tom Hopkinson) felt justified in calling, respectively, for more 'cheesecake' and more social commentary. Controversial pieces such as the report of the Defiance Campaign and the exposé of slave-like conditions on the potato farms of Bethal caused circulation figures to increase dramatically (suggesting a relatively developed political consciousness among urban dwellers); *Drum*'s popularity, however, could be traced equally to its crime investigations, its sporting features, its cover girls and its stories of shebeen adventure. In possibly the most perceptive critique to date of *Drum* in the 1950s, Graeme Addison explains that

> *Drum* was neither a political paper nor a newspaper of record but was an entertainment-exposé-picture periodical crammed with fiction and muckraking, busty broads and huckster advertising, superficially rather like *Scope* magazine today. The curious thing about *Drum* – the *problem*, one could say – was that it appeared to function as a political instrument in spite of its tawdry, irresponsible air; – that its commercial guise somewhat belied its importance as an articulator of the black experience and black aspirations.[9]

Drum came into existence in Cape Town as a monthly magazine in March 1951, under the title *The African Drum*, and was financed by a three-man consortium, which would soon be headed by Bailey, who had inherited part of the fortune left by his father, the Randlord Sir Abe Bailey. In spite of the original finances in mining capital, however, Bailey would remain something of an independent spirit, part shrewd businessman, part quirky idealist, who was as prepared to act the rebel son as to show a sense of commercial caution about overstepping some difficult-to-define mark of socio-political tolerance. While he was concerned that *Drum* should not be narrowly identified in the 1950s as a mouthpiece for the ANC, Bailey agreed with editor Sampson that the magazine must be seen to be witnessing the most crucial political events of the day, as well as capturing the 'real' feelings and tones of black urban living.

Initially, the 'authenticity' of the magazine was a cause of worry. Under its first editor, the South African tank commander and Springbok cricketer Bob Crisp, *Drum* adopted an educative, even a moralizing air. It included features on religion, farming, and soil conservation, as well as cultural articles on African art and 'Music for the Tribes'. Although the first cover designs, in counterposing silhouetted figures of a tribesman and a city-dweller, showed some alertness to the transitional nature of black life, Crisp did not grasp the full extent of the urbanizing process. This had accelerated tremendously during the war years when shortages of white labour (as many men joined the army) led to a temporary relaxation of influx control. (According to the estimate of the Johannesburg Department of Non-European Affairs, the urban African population in the Witwatersrand area in 1946 was half a million and, despite severe controls during the fifties, an extra 50 000 people had managed to take permanent root in the Johannesburg townships by 1959.) After the first four issues (March-June 1951), the circulation of *Drum* was only 20 000 and Bailey was losing £2 000 a month. The proprietor's commercial instinct saved the magazine and the reading market began to dictate its urban character. Perceiving the need for a more 'modern' approach Bailey had a disagreement with Crisp, who resigned in November 1951. His position was taken by Anthony Sampson, whom Bailey had met at Oxford and who would later become famous as 'Pendennis' of *The Observer* (London) and author of *The Anatomy of Britain* (1962). At the time, Sampson had no working experience of newspapers; he did, however, possess something more valuable: a fascination and sympathy for the African world he saw about him, especially in Sophiatown. Together with the journalist Henry Nxumalo, Sampson and Bailey visited African clubs and homes and talked about *Drum*. One of the responses, quoted by Sampson in his book, *Drum: A Venture into the New Africa* (1956), summarizes the feelings of many black people that the magazine had on it 'the white hand':

'Ag, why do you dish out that stuff, man?' said a man with golliwog hair in a floppy American suit, at the Bantu Men's Social Centre. 'Tribal music! Tribal history! Chiefs! We don't care about chiefs! Give us jazz and film stars, man! We want Duke, Satchmo, and hot dames! Yes, brother, anything American. You can cut out this junk about kraals and folk-tales and Basutos in blankets – forget it! You just trying to keep us backward, that's what! Tell us what's happening right here, on the Reef!'[10]

Against the practice of Verwoerd's Department of Native Affairs, such comments were politically loaded. Although *Drum* during the fifties would continue to have white editors ('at the time,' Bailey believed, 'whites were mostly better organisers'),[11] an African Advisory Board was appointed. It consisted of Job Rathebe, secretary of the Bantu Men's Social Centre, Dan

Twala, sportsman and broadcaster, Dr A. B. Xuma, ex-President-General of the ANC and a prominent medical practitioner in Sophiatown, and Andy Anderson, a coloured printer who prepared pamphlets for Congress. One of the Board's first actions was to advise the axeing of 'Music for the Tribes'. At its inception *Drum* had only one African journalist, Henry Nxumalo, who had progressed from a poverty-stricken childhood to a job as a messenger on the daily *Bantu World*. He graduated to sportswriter, became friendly with the novelist Peter Abrahams (whose novel *Wild Conquest* would follow Alan Paton's *Cry, the Beloved Country* in *Drum*'s serialized fiction), and after he had served in Cairo and London during the Second World War, he worked in Johannesburg as a freelance reporter until joining *Drum* as sports editor. But Nxumalo was essentially a reporter, and his articles on Bethal (March 1952) and prison conditions ('Mr Drum Goes to Jail',* March 1953) set the high standard of *Drum*'s social and political reportage. As 'Mr Drum', Nxumalo represented the magazine's 'crusading mission' and, after having transferred to news editor of Bailey's *Golden City Post*, he was murdered in 1956 while pursuing a story about a white doctor who had performed illegal abortions in the Western Native Townships, and after whose interventions several women had died. (As George Magwaza, the name he used when investigating conditions of farmworkers at Bethal, Nxumalo also displayed some gifts of humour in the column 'Talk o' the Rand'.) Todd Matshikiza, the well-known musician and composer, was persuaded to contribute a regular page of record reviews and jazz features, and his style of Matshikeze can be seen to have influenced the manner and idiom of several of *Drum*'s investigative reports and opinion pieces. (Towards the end of the decade he would write a regular column, 'With the Lid Off'.) Arthur Maimane arrived from St. Peter's School in Rosettenville – the institution established and run by the Anglican monks of the Community of the Resurrection. Recommended by Father Trevor Huddleston, Maimane was wholly urbanized; he wrote boxing commentaries and, under the pen-name Arthur Mogale, a series of crime stories.

After winning the first *Drum* short-story competition in 1953, Can Themba joined the magazine and, in 1957, became assistant editor. In succeeding Nxumalo as 'Mr Drum', he would produce several important 'opinion pieces', such as 'Let the People Drink'* (March 1956), (with Matshikiza) 'A Country Marching into Trouble' (April 1957), 'Terror in the Trains' (October 1957), 'Why Our Living's So Tough' (June 1958), and 'Our Hungry Children' (August 1958). While contributing the column 'Talk o' the Town' Themba was sacked in February 1959, but returned to the *Drum* office in 1960 as a reporter

---

* An asterisk indicates that the article or story has been reprinted in the present anthology.

Henry Nxumalo – 'Mr Drum'

Arthur Maimane

on *Golden City Post*. Like Maimane, Themba claimed that he could speak no African language. Born in Marabastad in 1924, he graduated with a first-class degree at Fort Hare and taught English at Western Native High School to, among others, Casey Motsisi and Stanley Motjuwadi, well known as the editor of *Drum*, who died in 1989. From his Sophiatown home, known as 'The House of Truth', Themba entertained writers, journalists, white liberals and gangsters alike, with his style of worldly cynicism. As a cult figure of Sophiatown, he more than any other single member of the *Drum* staff typified the 'new urban culture'. A story sent to *Drum* by Moses ('Casey') Motsisi attracted the attention of Themba, who was at the time editing the short-lived magazine *Africa*, and Motsisi was offered a job on *Africa* before moving over to *Drum*. Born in 1934, Motsisi after leaving school embarked on but did not complete a teacher-training course at Normal College, Pretoria, and it was not until 1958 that he won wide recognition for his monthly column 'On the Beat', which grew out of an earlier attempt called 'Bugs'. Other notable members of the *Drum* staff were Bloke Modisane, who joined the magazine in the early 1950s, Lewis Nkosi, who joined as a nineteen-year old in 1957 during the editorship of Sylvester Stein, Nat Nakasa, James Matthews (in the Cape Town office) and, as a reporter and the fiction editor in 1955 until he left for Nigeria in 1957, Ezekiel Mphahlele. Reinforcing the features with photographs were Jurgen Schadeberg, Bob Gosani and, subsequently, Ian Berry (as a free lancer) and Peter Magubane. Offices also operated in West Africa and, later in the fifties, in East Africa, from where special copy was despatched to Johannesburg to be included in an 'international' edition of *Drum*, which was aimed at the African market outside South Africa.

The effects of Sampson's editorship were felt almost immediately in the features on crime. The first report, 'Inside Johannesburg's Underworld', appeared in October 1951. It was followed by 'The Birth of a Tsotsi'* (November 1951), and by innumerable others. As Sampson recalls:

> Chatting with gangsters at the Cosy Café I grew to understand the pressure towards crime . . . the eternal humiliation of black life in a white city – the constant rejection and exclusion. Gangster films, street corner gambling, drinking to get drunk, were open to all. Theatres, decent houses, open spaces, libraries, travel abroad, were for Europeans only.[12]

Implicit in these comments are the ambivalences of African/European attraction and repulsion which, in the *Drum* era of the 1950s, were to characterize a great deal of literate black society no less than its 'white-liberal' counterpart. Nkosi could say, 'The European *presence* in us has contributed to a feeling of self-consciousness; a desire to be judged and rewarded by our European critics.'[13] At the same time Sampson, drawing on his experiences of the shebeens, was helping to create 'Sophiatown' in the pages of *Drum* as an inspirational myth. In 1897 an investor, H. Tobiansky, had bought 237 acres of land four miles west of the centre of Johannesburg. After failing to sell it to the government as a 'coloured location', Tobiansky planned a private leasehold township for low-income whites and named it after his wife, Sophia. But the distance of Sophiatown from the city, poor drainage, and the proximity to the municipal sewage depository at Newlands, made it difficult to attract tenants and buyers. By 1910, lots were being sold without discrimination, creating a racially mixed area that became increasingly black. With the factories of the Reef hungry for labour, the government specifically exempted Sophiatown from the ownership restrictions of the Urban Areas Act, but did not designate it as a recognized location, so that municipal services failed to keep pace with the expanding population. In 1934 Sophiatown was 'proclaimed' (that is, marked for removal); but the government was not at the time prepared to absorb the cost of rehousing its residents.[14]

When he visited Sophiatown, Sampson saw the rudiments of a community rather than a drab 'location'.[15] Freehold ownership had given Sophiatown a sense of identity. While the bulk of the inhabitants were working class, whose reality was illiteracy or semi-literacy, grinding poverty, rack-renting landlords and harsh police actions, the 'new African' – the clerk, the schoolteacher, the nurse, the journalist – constituted a petty-bourgeois grouping which often had relatively 'elite' aspirations as well as experience of the levelling-down effects of discriminatory racial and economic controls. At the fringes the writer-intellectual, the musician, and the gangster all pictured themselves as 'outsiders', even as they shared the shebeens and cinemas with the 'common people'. In fact, one of the major contributors to Sophiatown cultural life was the cinema, or bioscope, where American B-movies were hits, and the rhythms and hyperbole of movie-language enriched the tsotsi-taal of the era. Sophiatown also provided a centre for music[16] with Dolly Rathebe (a *Drum* cover girl) specializing in African versions of American jazz favourites, and appearing in the films *Jim Comes to Jo' burg* (1949) and *The Magic Garden* (1950), both of which dramatized in a highly sentimental way a South African black man's story in the big city.[17] In the fifties, too, Miriam Makeba made her name with *mbaqanga*, as the lead singer with the jazz band, the Manhattan Brothers. While choral singing and ballroom dancing offered 'respectable' middle-class example, kwela developed from improvised penny-whistle street music, and gave rise to the stars Spokes Mashiyane and Lemmy Mabuso. It was Strike

Vilakazi's kwela-song 'Meadowlands' that would be sung by Sophiatown residents as their belongings were hauled away, during the removal of 1955, to the government township of the same name. Again, gaiety and destruction are seen to be inextricably intertwined.

Violence, even sudden death, in Sophiatown could emanate from both official and unofficial sources. In his autobiography, *Blame Me on History* (1963), Modisane describes the brutality of police raids while, like Themba and Motsisi, he is inclined to glamorize the tsotsi as a superior villain: one who had made the city yield its pleasures of flashy clothes and V-8 motor cars. Like so much else about Sophiatown life, however, the tsotsi had an ambiguous presence. Themba may have employed his command of literary English to compose love letters for members of the 'Americans' gang, and the Americans may sometimes have been referred to as Robin Hoods (they sold their stolen goods in Sophiatown at prices which were more reasonable than similar items could be purchased in the shops); nevertheless, the tsotsis' lack of social conscience or sense of community was typified in the name of the gang the Gestapo (the name adopted in ignorant admiration of German war-time viciousness). Trevor Huddleston, prior of the huge Church of Christ the King which dominated the skyline of Sophiatown, referred out of compassion to the demythologized version of the tsotsi: 'The tsotsi is youth rotting away . . . the tsotsi is symbolic of something other than a simple social evil common to all countries . . . Like them he is aggressively anti-social; but unlike them he has a profound reason, as a rule, for being so. He is a symbol of a society which does not care.'[18]

In a society which did not care, the church had an important spiritual and social function. Following Huddleston's example, the more socially conscious members of the Anglican clergy in particular gave many people in Sophiatown a sense that Christian love and unity were real possibilities. While church schools and church workers could sometimes convey a rigid code of Europeanized morals and manners, Huddleston's St Cyprian's Mission sought to nurture the individual qualities in the people among whom it worked. To Huddleston, the unique value of Sophiatown was that it was a community. Writing of the utter determination of the Nationalist government to brand the area a slum and to remove the inhabitants together with those from the adjacent suburbs of Newclare and Martindale, he says: 'Sophiatown could have been replanned but for the pressure of white opinion and the political force it represented . . . the existence of freehold tenure and the threat of permanence it implied . . .'[19] As early as 1953, Sophiatown had been marked for removal. Two days before the first removals were scheduled to take place, in February 1955, 2 000 police armed with automatic rifles invaded the streets and in pouring rain started moving the first families. Talk of resistance by the ANC failed to materialize as the events exposed problems of organization and direction within black political leadership. As Tom Lodge observes, 'The Congress movement was changing but its transition from an elitist to a popular movement was a complicated, gradual and often painful process . . . But in the ultimate analysis, the decisive factor was the massive force the state was prepared to deploy to destroy Sophiatown. This was no slum clearance scheme.'[20] With the destruction completed by 1963, the Nationalist government erected on the rubble the white working-class suburb of Triomf.

By the beginning of 1952 *Drum* had altered its appearance. Covers regularly showed pin-ups rather than the symbolic designs of the first issues. Inside, the magazine used more and larger pictures. Copy was shorter, but better written. Educational articles, except for the women's and children's pages, had disappeared. The main features were typically concerned with crime, music, township news, or – as indices of success – news of Negro America and of moves towards independence in tropical Africa. Advertisements promoted correspondence colleges, mail-order clothing, radios, and skin-lightening lotions. Circulation rose to 35 000, but remained below that of *Zonk!*. In March 1952, on the anniversary of the first issue, *Drum* broke new ground with Nxumalo's special feature which exposed conditions of farm workers and convict labour on the potato farms of Bethal in the Transvaal. In 1947 the Revd Michael Scott had prepared a report on similar conditions,[21] but *Drum's* report was written by an African out of first-hand experience. Showing the courage and enterprise which earned him the title Mr Drum, Nxumalo had spoken to labourers on the farm and gained access to their prison-like living quarters. Reinforced by the dramatic pictures of the photographer Jurgen Schadeberg, which had been obtained by various ruses, the feature caused a sensation. In response to demands for an official enquiry a report was prepared for the Minister of Native Affairs, but never published. In October 1952 a photo-feature on the Defiance Campaign pushed the circulation figures to 65 000, and an exposure of prison conditions, 'Mr Drum Goes to Jail'* (March 1954), by Nxumalo who had deliberately got himself arrested on a trivial pass offence, saw the readership top 70 000. *Drum* was outselling the politically non-contentious *Zonk!*.

The tactic of the social exposé was to remain fairly consistent. The magazine did not adopt a revolutionary voice, but appealed to authority in the name of civilized values and better race relations. This was in consonance with the ANC's long tradition of Christian-humanism which, despite the Africanist resolve of the Youth League's Programme of Action in 1949 and some perceptible Marxist stirrings, was again by the early 1950s in the ascendancy.

(In the world arena, of course, the democratic cause, as codified in the Atlantic Charter, seemed to have been vindicated by the Allied victory over dictatorship.) In 'Mr Drum Goes to Jail', for example, Nxumalo's personal testimony focuses the issue – the ill-treatment of African prisoners – on a particular prison, The Fort (Johannesburg), and the accompanying photographs (taken secretly from the roof of an adjacent high-rise block of flats) are sufficiently unusual as to suggest a 'special case': under the eyes of a white warder, naked male African prisoners dance the 'tausa', a humiliating high-stepping run which was meant to reveal any articles concealed in the rectum. In part, Nxumalo's approach reinforces his own liberal-journalistic predisposition of depicting racism as a human aberration rather than as a manifestation of a total social-historical situation. (In sharp contrast to the aggressive behaviour of individual members of the prison service and their 'trustees', we are given the correct procedures of the Prison Regulations and reminded of the enlightened recommendations of the Lansdowne Commission on Penal Reform.) At the same time Nxumalo, whatever his predilections, could not have adopted anything other than an ameliorative voice of social conscience (like other *Drum* writers, he had to indict white-ruled society while accepting the gatekeeping of 'responsible' white entrepreneurship). Nevertheless, the readers who rushed to buy issues on Bethal and the 'tausa' dance obviously recognized in Nxumalo's chilling personalized accounts a typical version of their own South Africa. The plea to the authorities for orderly reform, which so often concluded the exposé, hardly negated the implications of the story: that the forces of law and order in South Africa were part of the problem rather than offering any real solution. When *Drum* adopted its high moral tone against crime, the voice in the subtext was apt to transform folk-heroes into folk-devils, and vice versa, suggesting a crisis of hegemony in a society where a substantial proportion of the population did not subscribe to the norms imposed upon it by whites. As we shall see, 'disjunctures' of narrative intention also occur in short stories dealing with protagonists who hover on the margins of so-called social respectability.

By including 'Mr Drum Goes to Jail' in a volume of short stories, I am obviously stretching any single definition of the short story: the entire *Drum* writing exercise forces us to examine assumptions about story-telling forms and purposes. Nxumalo is probably also the author of 'The Birth of a Tsotsi'* (November 1951). Is this a 'short story'? Unlike Alan Paton's 'Death of a Tsotsi', [22] it does not consistently focus upon a character or a set of interlinked characters in an ideal action, and it is primarily concerned with information rather than experiential insights. Yet it includes several conventions of the fictional approach, such as the colloquial story-teller's opening remarks, descriptive evocations and the introduction of particular testimony. What is interesting, however, is that by decentring individualized experience, the writer ensures that we 'place' his tsotsis as typical figures (black juvenile crime in Johannesburg is not exceptional; it is widespread), and a chilling irony is allowed to frame the small boy's story: 'When I leave Diepkloof I am going straight. I hope to get a good job. I have stabbed 15 or 16 people . . . It's not our parents' fault. They don't even know we are doing it.' By virtue of the surrounding context of information ('Of course, tsotsis are made as well as born: they are made every day on the Reef'), the reader – if not the small boy himself – knows that the weight of 'sociology' will crush his personal resolves. This is not meant to be a tale of individual liberation. People are not essentially free: 'the roots of crime are to be found in the deep social evils that breed wickedness . . .' Just as Paton's story ends with a moral plea ('And this death would go on too, for nothing less than the reform of society would bring it to an end'), so does 'The Birth of a Tsotsi'.

But, to return to the initial question: is the latter a 'short story'? One of the most influential theorists of short fiction, Frank O'Connor,[23] might say that we can get verisimilitude from a newspaper report; what the story offers is an action worked out in terms of verisimilitude. If he could argue that 'The Birth of a Tsotsi' had failed to honour this distinction, he might have more difficulty in deciding whether only our 'moral judgment' has been stimulated and not our 'moral imagination' (the story depends on 'how much information the writer gives in order to enable the moral imagination to function'). O'Connor could not deny that 'The Birth of a Tsotsi' has as its subject a 'submerged population group': 'Without the concept of a normal society, the novel is impossible. In the story we don't have a hero; we have a submerged population group . . . an attitude of mind that is attracted by submerged population groups . . .' To which James Cooper Lawrence might say that stories insist only on the simple limitations of 'brevity and coherence': 'they can be told *historically* (in seeking primarily to record the matter-of-fact nature of things, just as they happened); they can be told *dramatically* (in seeking a single effect); or they can be told *didactically* (in the effort to teach a lesson).'[24] And the story-writer H. E. Bates, in his frustration at defining the story, is led to say that the 'short story can be anything the author decides it shall be . . . it is something shaped also by readers, by social expansion and by [what Elizabeth Bowen] calls "peaks of common experience"'.[25] To the readers of *Drum*, Nxumalo's social features were accurate 'stories' of peaks (or troughs) in their common experience, and in his attempts in the 1970s to narrate other peaks of common experience Mtutuzeli Matshoba has turned in 'A Glimpse of Slavery'[26] to the pattern of Nxumalo's Bethal exposé. In Matshoba, the categories of 'fact' and 'fiction' are again seen to be necessary corollaries to the black story-writer concerned as much with educating his readers as with aesthetic satisfactions.

Drum during the 1950s recorded most of the major political events of the decade, including the Sophiatown removals, the adoption of the Freedom Charter by the Congress Alliance at Kliptown in 1955, and the consequent indictment of Alliance leaders on charges of treason (The Treason Trial of 1956). *Drum* reported on the bus boycotts, the action of apartheid in churches, the rise of the PAC and the shooting at Sharpeville. It also published a 'Masterpiece in Bronze' series: short biographies which praised the achievements of Africans ranging from jazz singers to politicians. The common denominator was the glorification of individual mobility in relation to the class values of the 'New African'.[27] And the New African, as a concept and an inspiring example, was often viewed in terms of a united black front. Langston Hughes's several contributions to *Drum* served, for example, as a reminder of the successful Negro American. In compiling his *African Treasury* (1960), an anthology of articles, essays, stories and poems dedicated to the 'young writers of Africa', Hughes himself spoke of 'African pride'. This was symbolized most dramatically by Ghanaian independence and the stirring concluding response to the Accra Conference: *Mayibuye, Afrika!* (Come back, Africa!). Under the editorship of Sylvester Stein in 1955 and Tom Hopkinson in 1958, the policy of illustrated features on socially and politically topical events, both in South Africa and Africa as a whole, continued to be extended.

Pride in black people did not necessarily mean 'black pride'. As I have said, the language and perceptions of the multiracial ideal informed the magazine as well as the oppositional social and political life of the 'fabulous decade', and gradualism tended to absorb the radicalized challenge. The police harassed members of the *Drum* staff (Modisane was requested by Major Spengler of the Special Branch to find out in return for a passport the names of which writers had written what articles);[28] nevertheless, Sampson could still say that 'the most exciting event of these people [his urban African readers] was not the Defiance Campaign in which 8 000 Africans went to jail . . . but the discovery of a *tokoloshe* – a kind of Zulu imp – in a location in Johannesburg'.[29] As a part of the socializing process, therefore, *Drum* could lead its crusades at the same time as evidencing the limitations not only of commercial constraints, but also of prevailing forms of popular consciousness. Its romance was part of the real world; its reality often manifested itself in acts of romantic possibility and, in this respect, David Coplan's account of the genesis and impact of the musical play *King Kong* is instructive.[30]

Appearing at the culmination of the decade, *King Kong* was based on the tragic career of the South African heavyweight boxing champion, Ezekiel 'King Kong' Dhlamini (see Nat Nakasa's story in the present anthology). Its creators, Union Artists, had begun as an interracial effort to protect the professional rights of black performers, and intended the play to be a model of fruitful co-operation between blacks and whites in the international entertainment field. With production, direction, script and musical direction by whites, but using black musical actors and musicians and a score by Todd Matshikiza, the show proposed to put on stage a kind of paradigm of the partly real, partly symbolic artistic-intellectual contacts, between Sophiatown and Houghton, which had characterized the decade: the polish and style of Broadway would be combined with the cultural 'vitality' of the townships. The play did not make a strong political statement, but showed something of the hardships, violence and frustration of township life. At the University of the Witwatersrand Great Hall *King Kong* was an immediate success with 'progressive' Johannesburg people of all races, and the producer Leon Gluckman naively imagined it might create a more sympathetic attitude among whites towards blacks ('Any white person who has seen the show will think twice before he pushes an African out of the way on a street corner. It's not politics, but a question of human relations').[31] Yet, outside of South Africa in 1960 African nationalism and independence were already dominant movements; and although it ran for a year in London, the show was branded as '[politically] dynamic as a bag of of laundry'.[32] (But see Glen Skelton's recent comments.)[33] Most of the black actors received atrocious wages; nevertheless, as Coplan says, 'implicit in the production was the dream, no less than the illusion, of a better, more humane South Africa . . . In Johannesburg of 1959 *King Kong* represented at once the ultimate achievement and final flowering of Sophiatown culture'. But, perhaps Nkosi touches the true significance when he says that 'the finished product [of *King Kong*] did not – could not have succeeded in mirroring half the conspiratorial excitement, the tremendous amount of underground planning, the rehearsals in a large Johannesburg warehouse for lack of non-segregated theatres, and finally the physical hazards to musicians and actors nightly travelling home from the city to the crime-infested African townships – an easy prey to both thugs and police'.[34]

As I have suggested, *Drum* – as much as *King Kong* – can be seen as a contextualized phenomenon. It was not a militant journal like *Fighting Talk* or *New Age* (both of which used more political commentary than reportage), and – like the African nationalism of the time – it displayed both the strengths and the limitations of understanding persuasion more thoroughly than power. Yet its valuable relationship to the political scene was astutely recognized in 1955 by the former theorist of the ANC Youth League, A. P. Mda, who retained his sympathy for the Africanist idea of psychological revaluation. On the debit side, Mda believed that *Zonk!* and, to a lesser degree, *Drum* 'reflect a spineless liberalistic philosophy which lacks dynamic power and creative drive . . . The journals glorify the fads and foibles of the most degenerate classes among the Western nations'. On the other hand:

> the introduction of pictorials and monthly journals in which Africans feature prominently [has] revolutionised the entire field of journalism among Africans . . . [and has] struck deep into the social life of the African people in towns in particular . . . These welcome changes [have] had an immediate impact on the psychological make-up of our people, more especially the youth. The resultant feeling among vast sections of our people [is] that of self-importance . . . This . . . fact has been of immense value. When people begin to realise their own intrinsic importance as human beings, they are on the road to full nationhood. It is only a little step to a consciousness of rights, and to an awareness of the anomalous position under which vast sections of the people are denied elementary democratic rights. No doubt the monthly journals and pictorials have served in no small way to destroy the sense of inferiority and futility which have eaten into the very vitals of our national life, generation after generation.[35]

In the 1970s the Black Consciousness movements would need to return, more uncompromisingly, to the question of 'consciousness-raising'. In the mid-1950s, however, Mda's remarks would have had something equally valuable to say to the short stories which also constituted a regular aspect of *Drum*'s response to the black urban experience. Like the journalism the stories, to which I now want to turn, arose from a particular context of human and literary opportunity, so that Sampson could say: 'How easy to understand those short stories I read and discovered every day, obsessed with race and violence, in single-minded bitterness. How compulsory was this floating cabin of jazz and jive.'[36]

When *Drum* appeared in March 1951 the only publications open to African story-writers were *The Native Teachers' Journal*, which was subject to strict censorship, and *Fighting Talk* (1946), the magazine of the Springbok Legion, a liberal ex-servicemen's organization. In the March issue *Drum* announced its intention of encouraging the writing of short stories and poetry. Besides H. I. E. Dhlomo's English-language poem 'Lindiwe Laughs' (June 1951), however, little verse was to appear. The first stories leant towards tribal or rural themes, and a Folklore page appeared in the first few issues. The March issue included Alfred David Mbeba's 'Rhodesia Road',* which was accompanied by the following description:

> 'Rhodesia Road', such as we present it here, is a condensation from the
> original MS written in one of the Nyasaland languages. Mbeba wrote
> 'Rhodesia Road' so that his country-folk would be aware of the
> difficulties as well as the attractions and excitements of the journey to the
> south in search of work. We think that the story may have a wider appeal,
> for it tells of an experience common to all Africans.

Readers were invited to submit stories.

'Rhodesia Road' introduced the 'Jim comes to Joburg' (in this case, Harare)
motif, and at the end the characters return to their village and to a reaffirmation
of traditional ways. Such a journey, back to the tribes, was not to persist, even
though several of the early stories reveal interesting hesitations between city
and rural attractions. In 'The Harvest Is Waiting' (June 1951) and 'Under the
Blue-gum Trees'* (April 1954), for example, Dyke H. Sentso sets his stories
on white farms, and depicts the hardships and insecurities experienced by his
black farm-worker protagonists, whose simple, honest responses probably owe
something to the pervasive influence on several authors not only of their
mission schooling, but also of *Cry, the Beloved Country*. (As I have indicated,
Paton's novel was serialized in *Drum*.) Interestingly, however, Sentso's
narrative patterns show signs of collapsing under the pressure of the human
story-experience. There seems to be no satisfactory form of 'closure' in a world
of poverty and death, and the older tradition of the parable provides the frame of
Sentso's 'The Sun Stood Still' (November 1951), where drought either
undermines or fortifies human resilience and moral integrity. Like several
early contributors, Sentso turned to writing in English after having published
African-language works (his Sesuto book *Matlakala* had already appeared with
Morija Publishing Co.). Educated at Tigerkloof Training Institute, Sentso, a
teacher at Vredefort, said that he wrote 'simply because I love it and I owe
everything to the influence of my father who was a minister of religion'.[37]
Nevertheless, his story 'Pay Back' (May 1952) would begin to acknowledge the
force of an alternative city experience. In fact, the urban scene had appeared as
early as the second issue (April 1951), where Randolph Ben Pitso's 'Nomoya!
Of the Winds' offered an awkward glimpse of a 'new' style of life.

When, in June 1951, *Drum* published Sentso's 'The Harvest Is Waiting', it
drew attention, in the editorial column, to its aim of 'discovering' and
encouraging writers: 'Have no doubt about it we have discovered in Dyke
Sentso an outstanding writer whose prose can be measured up to that of any
contemporary of any race.' The element of self-congratulation is understand-

able. Sentso's stories, however, reveal a formality of expression, an almost learned English, which at the time was characteristic of the 'educated' African writer. A similar stiffness of syntax had informed much of H. I. E. Dhlomo's work in the 1930s and 1940s, and Mphahlele in his first volume of stories, *Man Must Live*, also sometimes sounded 'schoolmasterish' in a way that betrayed his university studies of English literature.

By contrast, William 'Bloke' Modisane, whose story 'The Dignity of Begging'* was published in September 1951, was the intellectual schooled in the university of life, Sophiatown. Born in the township in 1923, he lived there until he left South Africa on an exit permit in 1959. Forced to leave school by the brutal murder of his father, he worked in the leftish bookshop, Vanguard Booksellers, until joining *Drum*, and the opening lines of his story marked the first appearance of the *Drum* style, racy, agitated, cynically amused by its own urban air:

> The magistrate raises his eyes above the documents and plunges them like daggers into my heart. His blue eyes are shining with a brilliance that sets my heart pounding like the bass of a boogie woogie.
>
> 'I'm sick to death of you . . . heartily sick. There is not a native beggar on the streets whose full story I do not know,' the magistrate said . . .
>
> These are fighting words, the magistrate sounds as though he is going to put us away for a few weeks.

The Americanized 'tough tale' is signalled by the historical present tense as the local environment dictates the character and subject of petty crime. The slick sophistication acts in defiance of the retribalizing mentality. Yet when 'The Dignity of Begging' is set against some of the earlier *Drum* stories of folk-tale derivation, Modisane's tsotsi recalls an ancient precedent: the trickster-figure of folklore, where guile provides a psychic escape from convention while acting as a warning of anarchy. In the 'city experience' the older lessons are lost, and the new code demands the triumph of the superior cheat. Interestingly, the revised form of this story, as printed seven years later in Peggy Rutherfoord's anthology *Darkness and Light*, remains consistently within the ironic mode of the street-wise beggar, and ends with the words: 'Deep down I know that I will want it [the room in Sophiatown] again . . . I have to come back. I owe it to the profession.' In the original version, in *Drum*, the story-line appears less 'unified', but in terms of theme and structure perhaps indicates a more deeply problematic response to the conventional polarities of the city and the country. Here, the 'urban' son and 'rural' father conspire at some not fully articulated level to introduce new 'city' expectations and gratifications to the (literary-mythical) 'innocence' of the pastoral landscape.

Modisane clearly does not regard himself as deriving from story-telling patterns of old. In seeking 'Soweto' group-identity in 1976, Mtutuzeli Matshoba might have wanted to effect the continuing communal voice;[38] Modisane, by contrast, aspires to be the literate individualist, only half comforted by, only half amused by the oral residue of African life, where face-to-face contacts are still a reality. The tough tale may have allowed his folk-devil to become a folk-hero, but Modisane's relentless, urbanized intelligence is bound to be frustrated. His two subsequent stories in *Drum*, 'The Fighter Wore Skirts' (January 1952) and 'The Respectable Pickpocket' (January 1954), brazenly affirm the black city-presence, but lack the human observation of 'The Dignity of Begging', and it is interesting to read, in *Blame Me on History*, what seemed to Modisane to be his motivation for turning to writing.[39]

Having been stirred in 1949 by the ANC Youth League's Programme of Action (an Africanist assertion of pride and militancy), Modisane looked on with dismay as the Youth Leaguers (who included Nelson Mandela, Oliver Tambo and Walter Sisulu) 'went respectable' at the time of the Defiance Campaign. (See Mandela's statement in *Drum*, 'We Defy', August 1952.) What was bothering Modisane was that, in its various co-operations (with the SAIC, with members of the by then banned Communist Party, and, later in the decade, with the Coloured Peoples Organisation and the white Congress of Democrats), Congress had tempered the Africanist manifesto of its Youth League and was appealing, by way of passive resistance, to the principles of a 'multiracial' alliance. Hating white arrogance, Modisane saw African power becoming blunted. When the Congress leaders were indicted in 1952 under the Suppression of Communism Act, President-General Dr J. S. Moroka, who was subsequently replaced by Luthuli, employed separate counsel to conduct his personal defence, to submit a plea of mitigation in his case. Displaying anger and disillusionment with African political leadership, Modisane burned his Youth League membership card and 'retreated into a political wilderness':

> I assumed a mask of political innocence and established a reputation for being apolitical. I turned again to my writing, but this time there was a broad omission of the commitment to fight against the prejudice against my skin, to speak out against injustice and wrong. I wrote innocuous stories about boxers with domestic problems, respectable pickpockets, hole-in-the-wall housebreakers, private detectives and other cardboard images of romanticism, and yet against this background my escapist hero was seldom, if ever, on the side of formal law and order. Like me, my

Bloke Modisane [1954]

Ezekiel Mphahlele

characters were invested with a contempt for the law, their efforts were directed towards a flaunting of the law; my heroes were social maladjusts in a society where heroism is measured by acts of defiance against law and order. I did not then recognise the sociological significance of what I was doing, that with a central idea behind them I could use my stories as a reflection or a study of our society.

But the yellow African magazines encouraged and paid for short stories which presented an image of the African as an uncomplicated sentimentalist with an addiction for pin-ups, nice-times, violence in love and temper, which made one wonder whether the Africans lived in a candy floss of vulgarity, in the make-up for their women, their advertised hair straighteners and skin lotions.

In similar vein Mphahlele – as fiction editor of *Drum* – would complain that serious fiction was not regarded by the proprietor as the magazine's 'mission';[40] and, when viewed as discrete texts, many of the stories do convey a sense of 'cardboard romanticism'. When seen as products of a complex social and literary process, however, different illuminations become apparent. Possibly Modisane, as a participator in the partly real, partly symbolic history of Sophiatown, could not at the time appreciate the full sociological significance of what he was doing. For just as *Drum* evoked images of 'pin-ups, nice-times and violence in love and temper', so did Sophiatown: one interacted with the other, and distinctions between fantasy and socially determined ploys of self-definition are complex. Recollecting the old Sophiatown, Modisane writes in his autobiography:

> Walking down Good Street and up Gerty Street was like walking through a ghost town of deserted houses and demolished homes, of faded dreams and broken lives, surrounded by rousing memories, some exciting, others terrifying; for Sophiatown was like our nice-time parties or the sound of the penny whistle, a mounting compulsion to joyousness, but always with the hint of pain . . . It was a complex paradox which attracted opposites.[41]

Evincing anger at the failure of the ANC to oppose the Sophiatown removals, Modisane almost simultaneously wants to shift his experiences out of the material concerns of any class and, as the writer-intellectual, to posit an 'aesthetic' of freedom and constriction. He for one would refuse to acknowledge the ANC's real difficulties in deciding on tactics of mobilization (when parents are given the choice by Verwoerd of endorsing Bantu Education or removing their children from school, what advice – Luthuli sanely asks – does one proffer?).[42] Modisane, however, was impatient with such 'caution', and he increasingly expressed sympathy for Robert Sobukwe's break-away PAC. As a 'situation' (a term of abuse for members of the African petty bourgeoisie trying to 'situate' themselves above the masses), Modisane shows both envy and scorn for white intellectual society. At the same time as he was labelled by apartheid as a kaffir, he sought to stand apart from what he saw as the undifferentiated mass of black people and cultivate his individuality. 'The Dignity of Begging' gives the first hint of his need to adopt masks of survival; *Blame Me on History* would explore the harrowing alienation of the 'situation' in the 1950s, as Modisane came to recognize that he was as much a figure of history as any other inhabitant of Sophiatown.

While Modisane was seething inwardly with bitterness and frustration, Arthur Maimane (writing under the pen-name of Arthur Mogale) seemed to have absorbed thoroughly the European manners and modes of his 'British' education at St. Peter's. With a nonchalant disdain he created his series of crime stories, featuring an Americanized black private detective, Chester O. Morena (see 'Crime for Sale!',* January and March 1953). As another trickster-figure, Morena outwits all comers. Yet like the trickster of folk tradition, he cannot be allowed finally to triumph over the contracts of society. What does one do, however, when the contracts of South African society are not regarded as fair or just? Maimane's answer might be: remove your protagonist from the demands of social dynamics, create a fictitious 'Golden City', and as an afterthought in the last paragraph pop Morena into prison ('I couldn't escape, I reckon that will teach me to play everything straight . . . Well, I better be getting along. Here comes the prison warder!'). Mimetically, the story is 'escapist trash'; as an imitation of style – one involving Maimane's own brief respites from a demeaning life – 'Crime for Sale!' is a kind of 'bourgeois-individual' reaction.

The other 'thriller' represented here – Mboko Manqupu's 'Love Comes Deadly!'* (January 1955) – reveals something of the hybridism that is a feature of many of the *Drum* stories. In writing about either bad conditions or bad women (one is uncertain which is meant primarily to direct the action), Manqupu is unable to integrate his own codes of realism and pulp. Pointing to the way in which gangster dialogue ('I'm levelling a torpedo at your spine') incorporates phrases of contemporary South African political reportage ('a revolt to overthrow the established government of that joint'), David Rabkin in his doctoral study of *Drum* reminds us of the meagre literary resources which would have been available to many of the writers.[43] A major part of their acquaintance with narrative craft, dialogue, setting, etc., would have come from an assortment of school 'classics', popular magazines, and primarily from the cinema and press. Manqupu worked as a civil-service clerk and is not recorded to have matriculated. Mphahlele, the best educated of the writers, admits that when he began writing his stories in *Man Must Live*, he had never studied the short-story form: 'I was just writing as my feelings dictated.'[44] The reality of an 'unevenness of literacy and learning' in itself presents a challenge of critical response to South African literature, and we should note that combinations of disparate influences need not always necessarily lead to a failure of tone or poise. James Matthews's 'Dead End!'* (September 1954), for example, tags what we might initially feel to be clumsy frames of social explanation on both ends of a compelling narrative about a small-time crook. On reflection, however, the device serves a useful purpose as a 'popular' means of extending the implications of the 'thriller'.

The 'popular situation' lent impetus to the prize-winning story in the first of an annual short-story competition, announced in the October 1951 issue as a 'Great African International Short Story Contest'. It offered £50 for the winning story and £4 for each entry published. Stories were to be up to 3 000 words in length and in any language, and the judges were announced as Peter Abrahams, Alan Paton and R. R. R. Dhlomo (who was at the time editor of *Ilange Lase Natal*). 'Owing to a tremendous response' the period of the competition was extended to the end of the year, and in April 1953 the results were published with the editor remarking that 'stories in English and every African Language have poured into the *Drum* office from every part of the world . . . there were over one thousand stories for the judges to read'. Commenting on the general quality, the judges noted that 'one of the difficulties was to find stories that combined a good plot and a good style'. They remarked on the high proportion of entries from West Africa, and in announcing the winner as 'Mob Passion' by D. Can Themba, Peter Abrahams believed that 'we have in this story notice of an unusual talent'.

Basing his story on the topical issue of Basotho-Nguni tribal fights in Newclare, Themba in the tradition of 'Romeo and Juliet' focuses on two lovers from rival sides. Exploiting ironies of expectation and a melodramatic foreshortening, the death of the boy Linga provokes a lament that inter-tribal divisions are destructive of a people's humanity. In emphasizing the love relationship, however, Themba avoids exploring the 'sociological record'. The position was that 'raw' Basotho mineworkers were easy victims for city-slick tsotsis, and for self-preservation had grouped themselves into a gang, the Russians (they believed that Russia had really won the war). As it happened, the Russians soon took initiatives in violent robbery, in protection rackets among vulnerable squatters and, according to Trevor Huddleston, in vigilante actions on behalf of the authorities.[45] In Themba's story such details are ignored, and individual humanity is simply placed in opposition to 'mob passion'.

Themba's writing frequently presents this problem, which is common in the stories of the decade. Several have been seen in fact as politically naive or, at least, disdainful of politics.[46] White society has always been eager to brand so-called black-on-black violence as non-sociological and evidence of innate African savagery, and 'Mob Passion' appears not to refute the contention. Nevertheless, the overall effect is to depict the 'human condition' of African urban life with a force of emotion and compassion that had not been felt before in fiction. Similarly, Themba's first story in *Drum*, 'Passionate Stranger' (March 1953), had championed modern love over traditionally arranged weddings, and 'Forbidden Love' (November 1955) would quite shamelessly manipulate events in order, again in the name of common humanity, to expose coloured and African prejudices. The reader is reminded of the value of love, children, parentage and people. In all of these stories (including 'The Nice Time Girl!' – May 1954) 'yellow press' situations are pushed towards serious confrontation, and in noting Themba's plot manipulations we should remember that, despite an element of 'literariness' in his language and reference, he was appealing not to some 'literate' readership, but to an ill-defined yet actual 'popular' audience, where the needs of communication would have outweighed the subtleties of Eng. Lit. In raising the question of his neglect of sociological analysis, we need to place his stories in the end firmly against the racial-classification laws of the 1950s. In this context, Themba's unalloyed humanism has considerable social import, as – together with *Drum* – he turns sharply away from race divisions in his 'venture into the new Africa'.

In 'Marta'* (July 1956) Themba's interest in ironies of events continues to shape the action. With their baby and their home in a state of neglect, Jackson and Marta are victims of 'all the tawdry, vulgar, violent recklessness of their lives'. When Marta is tempted by her friend to the shebeen, she suddenly sees behind the bravado of a young man all the trampled feelings of her own almost forgotten youth. In innocence she takes him home. Jackson, however, arrives back early, imagines the worst, and kills the boy. Yet the 'strong' plot has been fused with Themba's developing gifts of atmosphere, dialogue and character creation. The opening description – 'Marta came along, still drunk. Her baby was hanging dangerously on her back' – is given tragic resonance in Marta's closing comment, in which she refers to the dead boy from the shebeen: 'Yes. The drunk woman's child has fallen.' And in the interim Marta has been brought vividly alive as a vulnerable person behind her social devastation:

'Maybe it's true I was fed up with Jackson. Maybe I did want in my heart to make Jackson feel that other men could like me. But not with that boy . . .'

Possibly Themba, who was steeped in English literature, cultivated the image of the dandy (he often lugged around the *Complete Works of Oscar Wilde*) as he struggled with perceived divisions of roles between the 'journalist' and the 'author', in which the former was expected to deal with the facts of social life and the latter with the psychology of human experience. As in the case of Modisane, such a New African 'situation' was as explicably part of socializing activity as were earlier, more confident identifications: Sol T. Plaatje immediately comes to mind as the singular figure of the writer-journalist, who registered the crucial movements of African public life. By contrast Themba, as the 'u-Clever' of Sophiatown, increasingly effected a style of coinages and idiosyncratic turns of phrase, in which English was wilfully distorted and made to mock and challenge any conforming view. As a journalist, he intruded into his reports a recognizably fictionalized texture, and I have included an example of his flexible approach to the telling of the facts. In 'Let the People Drink'* (March 1956) the issue ('They're drinking anyway. Why not make it legal?') is 'dramatized' as Themba, like a latter-day Baudelaire, journeys into the shebeens to hear dialogues of personal testimony. The drinking dens are evoked; narrative markers, which are designed to arouse 'curiosity', ensure that we read on; 'human interest' is sustained in quirky details and personal anecdote, while we are allowed to share the writer's intimate knowledge of the workings of the illegal liquor trade. Themba the journalist and Themba the imaginative writer become completely intertwined. It is not that he follows Plaatje's author-journalist practice where, as in *Native Life in South Africa* (1916), emotive incidents are used to illustrate the attack on government legislation. Rather, Themba the author becomes caught up in the fascination of the shebeen life, and his journalistic self, which is supposed to be adopting the high moral tone of *Drum*'s crusading mission, is forced reluctantly to extricate itself from the 'ruptures' of the story. In this connection, an interesting point was made by Hopkinson, the editor, when he said that *Drum* would have benefited had the quality of its journalism equalled that of its writing.[47]

Like Nxumalo's 'The Birth of a Tsotsi', many of Themba's stories are cognisant of antithetical links between what Walter Benjamin has termed the 'information' of modern, social reportage and the 'experience' of story-telling.[48] Becoming increasingly documentary in form, the stories written in the early 1960s, such as 'Crepuscule', 'The Will to Die', 'Requiem for Sophiatown' and 'The Bottom of the Bottle',[49] have as their subject the precariousness of the Sophiatown writer-intellectual. In making a plea for the independent spirit, Themba often turns to tsotsi-camaraderie in an attempt to find the comfort of his 'people', and in 'The Bottom of the Bottle' he accentuates his drunkenness when reminded by ANC elders of the need for social example. In 'The Will to Die' Foxy, the schoolteacher-Themba figure, breaks all the rules that sustain the fragile securities of a member of the black middle class, while in real-life Themba, as assistant editor of *Drum*, had increasingly defied Hopkinson's expectations of sobriety and responsibility from his journalists. One confrontation involved far more than the issue of political commitment:

> 'When the shooting war starts – which side will you be on then, black or white? Because the whites will start it one day for sure.'
> I made no answer [writes Hopkinson], but Can pressed on.
> 'Which side will you be on?'
> 'Depends who starts it, and what the issues are, and where I'm standing at the time.'
> Can snorted and went out. Our talk had been as unsatisfactory to him as it had to me.[50]

In 'Crepuscule' the 'document' of the Immorality Act frames a series of ironic events, in which Themba's relationship with a white woman in Sophiatown is allowed to measure how far blacks and whites alike are conditioned to see human beings in terms of racial categories. 'Why,' asks the journalist and the author, 'do we have to be in reaction all the time?', and his own voices of sociological significance and human aspiration speak as one: 'It is a crepuscular, shadow life in which we wander as spectres seeking meaning for ourselves.'[51] Indicating their own broadly Marxist-ideological sympathies, Rabkin and Kelwyn Sole see in the *Drum* writers an alienation that is both personal and historical in that their petty-bourgeois dispositions did not allow them to face the shift of social forces which, even in the 1950s, was slowly moving the ANC away from its somewhat elitist leadership towards a mass-based movement.[52] This may be so, but need not detract from the poignancy of Themba's expression, in all its ambivalences. Here, Themba as a man of the fifties reacts to the same process that could lead Modisane to condemn the surface manifestations of 'pin-ups, nice-times, violence in love and temper'. A full response to the *Drum* stories includes a recognition not only of the 'candy floss of vulgarity', but also of the underlying, barely concealed abyss.

In the July 1953 issue the editors commented that 'since our great contest last year we've discovered a whole school of writers'. This may have been an exaggeration; nevertheless, by 1955 *Drum* was publishing stories by Peter

Can Themba [1956]

Richard Rive [*c.* 1952]

Clarke, Richard Rive, Mphahlele and Themba. A second short-story competition was won by Sentso's 'Under the Blue-gum Trees'* (April 1954), and the winner of the 1954 contest (judged by Nadine Gordimer, Themba – now working for *Drum* – Jordan Ngubane and Langston Hughes) was Peter Clarke. Published in the April 1955 issue, his story 'The Departure'* touches on racial sensitivities and prejudices among coloureds in his depiction of childhood perception and experience. By and large, however, the action gains its power from the 'personal' rather than the 'political', and the fact that the story should have been adjudged the best is a reminder of the importance, in literary education of the time, accorded to the notion that the inner life was somehow the privileged domain of imaginative art. (By 1955 Gordimer herself had published only one novel, *The Lying Days* (1953), in which political concern intrudes only intermittently on a white South African girl's growth of personal consciousness.)

Under the editorship of Sylvester Stein, who had joined *Drum* from the *Rand Daily Mail* and who in 1958 would publish a political satire *Second Class Taxi*, Mphahlele was appointed as fiction editor, reflecting a new importance attached to this aspect of *Drum*'s activities. Two further short-story contests did not produce particularly notable winners (Nimrod Mkele's 'The Devoted Leeches' was published in May 1956, and Ritchie Maber's 'The Way of the Prodigal' in May 1957); nevertheless, Mphahlele set out with conviction to encourage a new level of seriousness. Born into poverty in 1919 and educated at St. Peter's ('slowly I realised how I hated the white man outside the walls of St. Peter's'),[53] Adams College and the University of South Africa (where he was awarded the MA degree for his study of the 'non-European' character in fiction),[54] Mphahlele had been involved in organized protests against the report of the 'Commission on Bantu Education' (according to which the Bantu Education Act was framed). As a result, he was barred from practising as a schoolteacher, and he arrived at *Drum* as a reluctant journalist:

> My whole outlook resisted journalism: my attitude towards the white press; towards the double stream of newspaper policy in South Africa where there is a press for whites and a press for non-whites; towards *Drum*'s arbitrary standard of what the urban African wants to read: sex, crime and love stories; its use of Sophiatown as the yardstick of what South African non-whites should read.[55]

That Sophiatown should have been the yardstick was inevitable given the relationship of *Drum* to urban African source material and commercial enterprise. And Mphahlele's remarks about his three years with *Drum* reveal an interesting clash between his sometimes austere standards of African worth and the susceptibilities of a popular press. If Stein was sympathetic to the pursuit of literary merit, Bailey was not and, in his writings on *Drum*,[56] never mentions the magazine as a ground for fiction. By 1958 *Drum* had almost ceased publishing short stories; during Mphahlele's spell as fiction editor, however, significant developments did occur. After some contentious debate it was decided, as a matter of general policy, to broaden coverage, and submissions were encouraged from coloured writers. (James Matthews worked in the Cape Town office.) Themba's 'Forbidden Love' had implicitly questioned the commitment of coloureds to identify with the oppression of African people, but by 1955 the Coloured Peoples Organisation had joined the ANC, SAIC and the COD in adopting the principles of the Freedom Charter. In May 1955 Richard Rive made his first appearance in *Drum*. Influenced like several other black writers at the time by the language and sentiments of the Harlem Renaissance and subscribing to Mphahlele's beliefs in non-racialism, Rive's 'Black and Brown Song'* (May 1955), 'Willie-Boy!' (which included independent sections by Peter Clarke and Matthews – April 1956) and 'African Song'* (June 1956) all dedicate themselves to the ideal of a unitary South Africa. (Up until his violent death in 1989, Rive continued to explore the same theme with increasing subtlety and complexity, most notably in his stories 'Riva' and 'Advance, Retreat' as well as in his autobiographical writing.)[57]

Despite his commitment to non-racialism, Mphahlele has always accepted the facts of African history in any interaction with European culture. Consistently revealing a more coherent understanding than other *Drum* writers of his responsibilities to his own community within the larger society, he would in his critical study *The African Image* (1962) continue to uphold realism: the importance of confronting the reality of South Africa in all its complexity.[58] In this respect, it is interesting to note the shift of language and tone in two editorials ('Mr Drum's Letter') which, in June and October 1956, focused on the subject of fiction in the magazine. The first employs the style of the 'yellow press'. In announcing a forthcoming anthology of stories from *Drum* ('African Parnassus. It's a classic')[59] it concludes: '. . . so far only *Drum* has the sensitive snail-horns to feel and understand the deep gusto that lies intermingled with the naïveté, the laughter and the mystery that is Africa.' If this is the pen of Themba, as assistant editor, then the October comment is closer in temper to Mphahlele:

> Almost everybody these days is interested in reading and writing about Africa. That's good. But what we'd like to see is more Africans writing about the lives of Africans. Think of the teeming life and the mass of vital

material that lies hidden somewhere in the backyards and the back-bushes and the back-eddies of the African mind. We could easily build up a literature like that of anywhere in the world . . . And there can be no doubt about it, we would teach the world more than a thing or two in that wonderful experiment called human life.

Surrounding both editorials are the familiar advertisements aimed at a 'levelled-down' nascent petty bourgeoisie and appealing to the aspirations of success and respectability: 'Mummy uses Rinso for all our clothes'; 'Did you Maclean your teeth today? Of course I did! says Simon Cox Hlapa (African golf champion living in Johannesburg)'. In the example of his own fiction, however, Mphahlele set out to 'deromanticise' black urban life, and his stories in *Drum* introduce the pattern of his literary development. As he himself accurately described it in 1959: 'In ten years my perspective has changed enormously from escapist writing to protest writing and, I hope, to something of a higher order, which is the ironic meeting between protest and acceptance in their widest sense.'[60]

With 'Blind Alley' having appeared in September 1953 and 'Reef Train!' (under the pen-name Bruno Esekie) in August 1954, Mphahlele as fiction editor published (again under the name, Esekie) 'The Suitcase'* in February 1955 and, in August 1955, 'Across Down-Stream' (which was later collected as 'The Coffee Cart Girl'). To a greater or lesser degree, all of these stories employ the compulsive twist of events in highly-wrought urban situations. Esekie's 'Down the Quiet Street'* (January 1956), however, initiated a new departure. Instead of the hyperbole of jazz and infidelity in Sophiatown, we are introduced in Mphahlele's sober, sometimes even angular prose to Nadia Street – the quietest street in Newclare. The 'unusual' event – a funeral procession in which, as we discover, the coffin is used to transport illicit booze – is simultaneously an ordinary event of life lived under 'prohibition' laws. Only Tefo the policeman is surprised, and fails to make an arrest. But then Tefo, who is also part of the township, is in love, and his marriage causes more of a stir than the illegal 'funeral'.

Written under Mphahlele's own name, a series of self-contained episodes introducing the Lesane family appeared from December 1956 to April 1957.* Here, too, the spectacular event (the sudden attack by severely frustrated Newclare residents, for instance, on the Indian fruit-and-vegetable hawker) is interspersed with smaller, equally credible frustrations, which might also momentarily erupt. An episodic structure, however, continues to impose the rhythms of greater and lesser importance in the daily round, and what would be Mphahlele's abiding concern – the capacity of ordinary people to survive –

begins to make itself felt. As Ursula Barnett has said, Mphahlele's use of the term 'acceptance' is not 'acceptance of township conditions or of life in South Africa; rather acceptance of the fact that human values of love, trust, and loyalty can continue even under impossible living conditions'.[61] In September 1957 Mphahlele resigned from *Drum* and began twenty years in exile. With the 'Lesane' stories pointing the way, his story-telling art would reach summation in the collection *In Corner B* (1967), particularly in the title story, in 'A Point of Identity', and in 'Grieg on a Stolen Piano'.

Soon after Mphahlele's resignation, Stein resigned as editor and left for England, and after Humphrey Tyler had acted as caretaker-editor, Tom Hopkinson arrived from England in April 1958.[62]As founder and editor (1938–1950) of *Picture Post*, Hopkinson was one of Britain's most experienced journalists, and his editorship saw vast improvements in the lay-out of the magazine while, as I have said, the trend towards feature articles was encouraged to continue. In the meantime, Nat Nakasa had been employed as a junior reporter and would develop into a competent and respected journalist who, before his sudden death in 1965, had in 1963 begun the literary journal *The Classic* (named after a shebeen) and won a Nieman Scholarship to Harvard. His skills of 'objectivity' and ironic perception are well illustrated in 'The Life and Death of King Kong'* (February 1959), where the township hero, 'King Kong' Dhlamini, is firmly demythologized even as he is allowed to retain his vulnerability as a human being behind the bravado of his public presence.

Displaying a professional integrity in his dealings with his staff and interceding on individual members' behalf with both the management of *Drum* and the police, Hopkinson retained a just but measured relationship with Sampson's 'Sophiatown culture'. In seeking to make *Drum* a full-blown picture magazine, however, he never did manage to dispense with its reliance on flamboyant literary copy. Like Bailey, he was not inclined to defend space for short-story writers, and his editorship was distinguished by the investigative reporting of the rise of the PAC and the Sharpeville shooting. He saw the future of *Drum* most tellingly in the rest of Africa (the Congo troubles were graphically recorded), and he correctly perceived that literacy among South African urban blacks was spreading widely and thinly, so that social and political reporting would increasingly become the province of the daily press. Alex La Guma's only contribution to *Drum*, 'Battle for Honour',* appeared in November 1958. (As a political activist, La Guma, who directed other stories to the 'committed' journals *Africa South* and *Fighting Talk*, would soon be under house arrest and 'silenced' as a writer in his own country.)[63] Hopkinson's only concession to fiction was to spot the humorous potential of Casey Motsisi's column, 'Bugs',* and to help initiate the popular 'On the Beat',* which ran continuously for the three and a half years of his editorship.

The result was the creation of a small mythology of township life, as characters such as Kid Cucumber, Aunt Peggy (the shebeen queen) and Kid Booze (Casey himself) sprang to life in Motsisi's inventive language (an English variant on township slang in vocabulary and syntax). Events, in contrast, unfolded by a rigorous logic and were compressed into the 600–700 words which the column was permitted. The literary precedents are Langston Hughes's *Simple Speaks his Mind* and Damon Runyon's threatened bar-room worlds of America, where authority is outwitted and the challenge to grey uniformity erupts in drink and laughter. As the 'fabulous decade' entered the grimmer repressions of the 1960s, Motsisi's shebeen characters suggest, simultaneously, the resilience and the fragility of the black urban culture which seemed to be symbolically battered into the ground by the bulldozing of Sophiatown; and, under the Black Consciousness imperatives of the 1970s, the poet Mongane Serote would acknowledge Nat Nakasa, as a representative figure of the 'Sophiatown days', with a mingling of sympathy and condescension: 'Poor Nat, he died still believing that he was a non-white.'[64] By 1960 'On the Beat' had lost the informing power of its original context; so had *Drum*.

Except for a period between April 1965 and 1968 when it was banned and appeared as a fortnightly supplement to *Post* (Bailey's renamed *Golden City Post*), *Drum* has continued to be published each month to the present day. In April 1984 Bailey finally sold the magazine to the Cape-based Afrikaans publishing giant Nasionale Pers. Referring to the fact that the magazine was never a lucrative venture Bailey, who is approaching 70, has spoken of the sheer time, the personal financial commitment and the frustrations ('locked in between Harry Oppenheimer's Argus group . . . and two government presses')[65] that his 'beloved publishing mistress' has exacted from him. In 1982 Bailey's African Photo Archives began producing a series of books on *Drum* of the fifties.[66] *Drum* itself, together with *City Press* and the magazine *True Love*, today spearheads the attempts by Nasionale Pers to tap the audience growth-market of black print-media readers. In addition, it is meant to answer Nasionale's perception that 'verligte' Afrikaner nationalism needs a credible voice with which to win the hearts and minds of the country's black (African) townships.

If *Drum*'s social mission reached its peak in the journalism of Nxumalo, Themba and others at the time, then its role in South African literary developments remains an issue which can prompt considerable debate. That the *Drum* writers constituted something 'new' has variously been recognized. Writing in 1960, soon after exiling himself from this country, Mphahlele displayed the disenchantment which had characterized his years as fiction editor, when he said that '*Drum* magazine has over the last decade of its existence been shouting for and promoting a tough superficial prose'.[67] Yet Mphahlele's response has undergone modifications in relation to his own changed needs of reconstructing a viable past. After having returned to South Africa in 1978 and thus ending almost twenty years in exile, he reiterates the fact that the proprietor decreed that fiction was a 'hardsell', but adds that although the imaginative writing courted no political confrontation, it spoke of the drama of black life: 'The black writer was asserting his sense of permanence.' He 'helped to fashion a township culture':

> To the extent that black politics were dramatized and indeed displayed theatrical style, the masses developed an awareness. They had found a political language suited to their own time. Similarly, the writer had found his tongue, a language, and relative freedom of expression that matched the political expression of the decade.[68]

In recognizing this new confidence of expression, however, we should not ignore the difficult links which *Drum* writers had with earlier modes of response. As I have been emphasizing, *Drum* did not pop out of a vacuum, and Tim Couzens in his study of H. I. E. Dhlomo's life and writings in the 1930s and 1940s makes comments on the linguistic-social opportunities available to Dhlomo which are pertinent to our identifying further contours that help to define *Drum*. Locating Dhlomo's often derivative, literary-romantic idiom as the failings of his mission-school educated group, Couzens reminds us of the 'protected worlds' of Lovedale, Adams College, St. Peter's and other similar institutions:

> The aspirations of this educated class were frustrated and, as Luthuli wrote of himself and his generation, 'roughly between the late thirties and the middle forties, an awakening was taking place'.[69]

The fact that several of the *Drum* writers − such as Modisane and Motsisi − were streetwise reinforces, rather than detracts from, Couzens's main point: 'The language break began to come when the forces which produced the "available idiom" failed to deliver on the expectations raised and disillusionment set in.'[70]

Continuity may be seen, by way of example, in two particular areas. Like Dhlomo, many *Drum* writers reveal what on the surface could be described as a petty-bourgeois contradiction between identification with a specific local

Casey Motsisi

Nat Nakasa

reality and the desire to find in art a universalizing, even a transcending image of experience. (Such a response is delineated by Nat Nakasa in 'Writing in South Africa'.)[71] Yet, in the context of the writers' lives, 'universality' was itself a historically precise concept, in which the 'universal' was pitted not against the 'local', but against segregationist policies and practices. Just as Dhlomo reacted closely to the Hertzog Bills of 1936, so *Drum* writers inherited Malan's apartheid. The second area concerns Dhlomo's disillusionment and recourse to alcohol. In this, he also prefigures the *Drum* generation, and nowhere is the fragility of shebeen camaraderie recognized more harrowingly than in Themba's last stories: 'The conflict between the opposed forces seems inevitable: the (roughly) white nationalism poised before the (not too roughly) black nationalism. The dilemma is so complete! As I brood over these things, I, with my insouciant attitude to matters of weight, I feel a sickly despair which the most potent bottle of brandy cannot wash away. What can I do?'[72] After publishing a few stories in the early 1960s in *Drum* ('The Urchin', April 1963, in *Africa South* and *The Classic*, which Nakasa had begun with the intention of providing a continuing publishing opportunity for black writers), Themba, as a schoolteacher in Swaziland, drank increasingly and died in 1968 of thrombosis. (Selections of his writings were collected and became freely available in South Africa only in 1982.) Like Mphahlele, Modisane had left this country as an exile and, as I have suggested, *Blame Me on History* is probably the most disturbing extended study of the alienated black writer-intellectual of the fifties. Two months before his autobiography was due to be republished in 1986, and made available for the first time in South Africa, Modisane died in West Germany. Matshikiza left Johannesburg with *King Kong* and was never to return. He died in 1968, and his autobiography *Chocolates for My Wife*, which had been published in London in 1961, appeared in South African bookshops for the first time in 1982. Nkosi and Nakasa also left this country on exit permits, and the latter would commit suicide in 1965 by jumping from a building in New York. Nkosi's essays, collected as *Home and Exile* (1965), were republished in 1983 and released in South Africa shortly before the appearance of his first novel, *Mating Birds* (1986). A selection of Nakasa's writings first appeared in 1975. Motsisi, who continued to live in Soweto, died in 1977 of an alcohol-related illness, and his writings were collected in 1978. Only after Mphahlele had been allowed to return to South Africa in 1978 was the ban on his writings lifted (*The African Image* remains proscribed), and a South African edition of his stories, *The Unbroken Song*, appeared in 1981.

When Minister of Justice Vorster, in April 1966, gazetted a list of 46 people living abroad as statutory communists, thus 'silencing' them, he is commonly held to have delivered the final blow to the *Drum* generation. Certainly, as Nick

Visser says in his article 'South Africa: The Renaissance that Failed',[73] the combination of bannings, premature deaths and despair severely curtailed the literary output of these writers. Yet I want to suggest that it is possible to look at other ways in which the 'renaissance' has not simply failed. First, however, we need to take account of the fact that most of the prognoses are, understandably, gloomy ones. I have already mentioned a tendency among some cultural analysts to study the limitations of the *Drum* writers in terms of their status as a 'repressed elite'.[74] This is useful in helping us to understand the constraints placed upon them by socially determining factors; the approach, however, is inclined to elevate 'ideology' over 'experience' in a fairly rigid way. Whereas *Drum* is typified as middle class, the only true move forward is regarded as mass-based. Although Sole says that meaningful criticism merely begins with considerations of class and ideology and should then elaborate on these to show the individuality of the writer's response to his or her context, he himself is not prepared to give a great deal of attention to the particular 'shadings' of any single work. There is also the tendency of formalist criticism to identify 'good' and 'bad' texts and, in consequence, to dismiss many of the stories in *Drum* as thrillers or true confessions. This is more or less the practice of Bernth Lindfors and Don Dodson. Although both claim to be viewing the effects of environment on literature, the former has difficulty in scrutinizing his own New Critical expectations of relatively autonomous, morally complex artefacts,[75] while the latter privileges Western-categories pertaining to a hierarchy of truth-value in the modes of irony, realism, humour and romance.[76] In confining his examples, unaccountably, to stories written between 1960 and 1964 Dodson concludes that because *Drum* rarely used irony – a destabilizing device – it must have acted mainly as a stabilizer of social control. In looking, more pointedly, at the matter of continuities and discontinuities, we also need to consider the nature of the literary and ideological break which has seemed to separate the world of Sophiatown from that of Soweto in the 1970s. Even had *Drum* writers continued to be active, or had their works remained freely available, however, decisive shifts of sensibility and intention would have been guaranteed by the rise of Black Consciousness in the wake of the temporary defeat, by the state, of the oppositional movements of the fifties.

All of this notwithstanding, my own emphasis has been to look back to the 1950s primarily as the informing context, in its expansions as well as its constrictions, of a previous generation's imaginative life. It is interesting, therefore, that two of the more recent story-writers, Mbulelo Mzamane and Njabulo S. Ndebele, have rediscovered in the 1980s what Themba and Mphahlele also knew: that the imaginative landscapes of the human story are often only indirectly related to the programmes of political protest. Just as

Themba reminded his audience of its fundamental humanity, so does Mzamane as he seeks to reconstruct a literary as well as a social-historical dialogue with these earlier writers. Like Modisane's trickster-figures in the township, Mzamane's Jola is another 'Jim' who comes to Joburg, and who beats the city at its own games. Or, we are invited to re-enter Themba's Dube train in 'Dube Train Revisited'.[77] If Themba has influenced Mzamane, Mphahlele seems to have given considerable direction to Ndebele, whose story 'Uncle',[78] for instance, has several affinities of theme and style with the earlier writer's 'Grieg on a Stolen Piano'. In fact, Mphahlele's concern with the 'ordinary' in black life has re-emerged in a recent debate, initiated by Ndebele, about the need for the black writer to reject the story of spectacle in favour of a 'rediscovery of the ordinary' textures and processes of the urban experience.[79]

Neither Mzamane nor Ndebele is concerned with easy imitation of content or technique. The world of South Africa in the 1950s is not simply transferable to our day, in either socio-political or literary terms. Nevertheless, just as the *Drum* publication *The Fifties People of South Africa* has the power to set up a memory of material for recognition and debate, so have the *Drum* stories, as long as we are prepared to agree with the Argentinian writer Jorge Luis Borges and see the story as more than a verbal structure of experience: it is also 'the dialogue' it establishes with its reader, and the 'intonation it imposes upon his voice' and the 'changing and durable images it leaves in his memory'. 'This dialogue,' Borges maintains, 'is infinite.'[80] I hope that the present essay has suggested several strands of a continuing dialogue with the fifties. It is not just that any real understanding of the writers of the 1950s needs to take account of the conditions and possibilities of their original publishing opportunity. More generally, it is that in allowing the text and context to inform each other, we are setting up a dialogue between *Drum* and the historicist criticism of our own decade. The implications for retrieval and revaluation are important ones, and the basic ethical criterion becomes not what behaviour a text will prescribe, but what qualities it can make available for a variety of practical stances. On this model, works do not necessarily always address political life directly, but elicit fundamental forms of desire, admiration and critical recognition that can motivate efforts to produce social change. One might want to say that an aura similar to the 1950s will never appear in South Africa under any future black government, since the imperatives of a revolutionary state are expected to rule out individuality of style; it is worth noting, however, that the extra-parliamentary opposition of the Mass Democratic Movement (MDM), which comprises a 6:4 ratio of workerist and petty-bourgeois members, has rooted its own historical memory to the mass campaigns of *Drum*'s heyday. It was in 1955, at Kliptown, that the principles of a non-racial, democratic South Africa were codified in the Freedom Charter. Looking back to *Drum*, Mzamane (like several black writers and commentators today) is willing to down-grade theories of ideological 'reproduction' (which can often present people as Althusserian *tragers*, or passive bearers of a social position) and to give credence instead to difficult, even tenuous 'culturalist' relationships between alternative forms of participation and actual historical change. In consequence, he is prepared to see in Themba an idealizing example, in whom a black person can seek both continuities and discontinuities in the long march of struggle.[81]

In mentioning in the course of this essay stories by Paton, Matshoba, Mzamane and Ndebele, I have drawn on only a few examples of the continuing inspiration of the *Drum* years on South African writers. If the 'renaissance failed' in that its writing talent was abruptly curtailed, we need to keep in mind how poorer would be our literature had it not been for the 'personal style' of the 1950s. Nadine Gordimer's novel *A World of Strangers* (1958), for example, uses Anthony Sampson and Can Themba as models for, respectively, the characters Toby Hood and Steven Sitole, as Gordimer explores the possibilities and limitations of private and public opportunities against the nexus of Sophiatown-Houghton. And the influence of Sophiatown was to persist in the work of Athol Fugard, so that ideological ambiguities in the presentation of the character Styles (in *Sizwe Bansi Is Dead* (1972))[82] cannot be fully understood outside of the legacy of fifties 'individualism'. The play *Sophiatown*, by the Junction Avenue Theatre Workshop Company, was produced in 1986, Don Mattera's autobiography of his early years in 'Kofifi' or Sophiatown, *Memory Is the Weapon*, was published in 1987, and William Kentridge's film *Freedom Square and Back of the Moon* was screened in 1988. I could continue to list later works which are indebted, either directly or indirectly, to the *Drum* ethos. I could also continue to raise points of debate with issues of our own time. As a further example, the depiction of women in the *Drum* stories should be worth investigation. Against the march by 2 000 women to Pretoria in 1956 in protest against the extension of the pass laws to African women, Mphahlele (in the monthly 'Masterpiece in Bronze' series) raised the brief biography to the level of persuasive life-experience, as he paid tribute not to a 'master' in bronze, but to Lilian Ngoyi, Vice-President of the South African Federation of Women, the first woman on the National Executive of the ANC, orator at Freedom Square (Sophiatown) and Treason Trial defendant (see 'Guts and Granite'* – March 1956). Rather than seeing the anti-pass campaign as genderless (wholly as a matter of political dehumanization) we glimpse, in Mphahlele's partly idealizing portrait, Ngoyi's struggle against economic marginalization as well as against the difficulties of mobilizing women in their capacities as home-makers and mothers. Despite this, *Drum* stories were written exclusively by men (a few 'true love confessions' used female pseudonyms), and often depict women as fickle temptresses, shebeen queens or models of dull domesticity. Finally, however, I want to return to a 'dialogue' which I mentioned above, concerning the 'correct' way of depicting the black urban experience.

In reacting against what he sees as predominating 'spectacles' of protest in stories by black South Africans, Ndebele has reminded his readers in the 1980s that black people, on their way to work, do not sit on buses endlessly discussing politics, but that marital infidelity, soccer, superstition and shebeen life are all part of the gradations of any community. Undoubtedly *Drum* writers would have concurred; the argument, though, has a further dimension. In praising the stories which appeared in *Staffrider* in the early 1980s, by Michael Siluma, Joel Matlou and Bheki Maseko (who discover 'complexity in a seemingly ordinary and faceless worker'),[83] Ndebele makes it clear that he could not have approved many of the *Drum* stories. For too many offer the spectacular display of individual talent rather than the analytical response to prevailing conditions. The crux of the problem for Ndebele is that the 'event' can easily be foregrounded at the expense of processes of recognition (we are reminded of Themba's singular human interests in 'Mob Passion'); the writer might, in consequence, offer only a limited understanding of the dynamics of the South African social formation and thus end up confirming, rather than seeking to transform, current relations.

Generally, we can allow Ndebele's argument to stand. In his determination to make a case for the 'ordinary', however, he is inclined to deny degrees of difference in stories, and see Themba and Mphahlele together, for example, as writers who reveal the 'spectacular ugliness'[84] of the South African scene. But Mphahlele would no doubt object to being classed as a writer of the 'surface' reaction. As fiction editor of *Drum*, his personal mission was, after all, to return stories to what he at the time also saw as the processes of 'ordinary experience', and he said dismissively in 1960 that Can Themba 'is basically *Drum*: romantic imagery, theatrical characters, Hollywood, with a lace of poetic justice'.[85] Such a debate may be unsolvable in any way that refuses to take into account the writer's and the reader's own ideological predispositions; nevertheless, it encourages us to attend, afresh, to the many and complex ways in which stories can convey and help shape experience. What Mphahlele and Ndebele have in common is an understandable tendency to justify the story as an imitative 'selection' from real life, as a kind of miniature realist novel. One consequence is to notate the story merely as a mode forced on black writers because their own lives are attenuated ('I am now more confirmed than ever before,' said Mphahlele after having left the country, 'that I wrote short fiction in South

Africa because the distance between the ever-present stimulus and anger was so short').[86] The implication is that a freer, fuller life would have required the larger work, the novel, with its space for complex explorations, and it is interesting that both Mphahlele and Ndebele later tended towards 'long' stories.

Such an argument, however, can too easily underplay the 'meaning' of convention in a story. Further, it assumes a passive reader who, whether trained or untrained in literary understanding, is sufficiently naive as to take stories as transfers of actual incidents in life. But, as Themba realized, stories (like human lives) are as much about imaginative habitation, archetype, symbol, and even luck, as about social causes. They seek to engage us in 'infinite dialogue' with enlivening perceptions and possibilities. If we were to follow too rigidly the demand of the 'ordinary', for instance, we would probably dismiss as melodramatic (and, therefore, not socially 'true') the story which I have included here by Jordan Ngubane. In 'Man of Africa'* (July 1957) a Zulu turns against the collective hatred of his fellow dock-workers in order to save the baby of an Indian woman from a burning dwelling. In his action, he is killed. It is not simply that the 'stock situation' has been prompted by the 1949 riots in Durban between Zulus and Indians; rather, it is that the symbolic memory of 'Cato Manor' persisted, its horror persuading the ANC and the SAIC that courses of multiracial co-operation should shape the path of political opposition in the fifties. As a former member of the Youth League, Ngubane had joined the Liberal Party, and his story is concerned quite unobtrusively, behind its spectacular events, with the nature of group actions (tribal or socio-economic?), the qualities of heroism, and relationships between individual and social identity and responsibility – ideas which informed the most crucial struggles of the day. If the incident which Ngubane describes did occur in life, his shaping of the action reminds us of the permanent capacity of short fiction to return to ancient origins of folk-tale and legend, and to make new uses of apparently unsophisticated literary conventions. As its title suggests, 'Man of Africa' is an exemplary tale, in which 'spectacle' and 'instruction' are indivisible. In foregrounding the dramatic event, Ngubane, who has written astutely on African literature,[87] does not ignore the processes of society. As any reader familiar with the environment of *Drum* would have recognized, 'Man of Africa' is one of a number of stories written during the 1950s; its text isolates a moment of greater intensity from the general movement of the age.

In initiating the search for a black urban voice, the *Drum* stories, especially when taken together, can be seen to be involved, inescapably, in difficult procedures of definition and intervention. If urbanization has often seemed 'spectacular' in its violence and crime, as well as in its political mobilizations, how adequate is the label 'melodrama' as a judgment of literary worth? If heroes and myths remain a necessary part of an oppressed people's struggle, where does realism begin and romance end? Or, conversely, if the dislocations of black urban life are so unexceptional as to demand 'non-spectacular' presentations, then did Sophiatown in the 1950s not seem to offer something 'really' distinct from the drabness of Meadowlands, Orlando or, in our own day, the hundreds of unimaginatively designed government townships? In defending Themba against Mphahlele's charges of theatricality, for example, we need to attend also to his underlying matter. As Elizabeth Bowen has said generally of the short story: it has to work on immense matter – 'the disorientated romanticism of the age',[88] in which little may be certain beyond the episode. It is an observation which succinctly sums up the temper of the 'fabulous decade', and reminds us that if Themba still speaks to us today, he does so, paradoxically, because he is so true to his own milieu. Given our need for memory, idealization and dialectical enquiry we may continue, in the 1980s, to enter into processes of both identification and exchange with his stories.

In making available to readers of today this selection of stories from *Drum*, therefore, I do not see myself as merely preserving a record of another time. We can, in retrospect, respond to more than a 'renaissance that failed'. At issue are the possibilities of black urban life in a restrictive socio-political system. The style may have epochal delineations; the human and literary pursuit constitutes an ongoing challenge.

Notes

1   Dhlomo's stories are conveniently available in *English in Africa*, Grahamstown, Vol. 2, No. 1, March 1975. His brother, H. I. E. Dhlomo, had published a single story, 'An Experiment in Colour', in *Bantu World*, 3 August 1935, and several stories which remained unpublished at the time appear in *H. I. E. Dhlomo: Collected Works*, ed. Nick Visser and Tim Couzens. Johannesburg, Ravan Press, 1985.

2   Abrahams, P. *Dark Testament*. London, Allen and Unwin, 1942.

3   Mphahlele, E. 'History and Change in Black Literature: Landmarks of Literary History in South Africa'; reprinted as 'Landmarks' in *Umhlaba Wethu: A Historical Indictment*, ed. Mothobi Mutloatse. Johannesburg, Skotaville Publishers, 1987, pp. 11–12.

4   See David Rabkin's *'Drum* Magazine (1951–61): And the Works of Black South African Writers Associated With It'. Ph.D. thesis, University of Leeds, 1975, p. 104.

4   See David Rabkin's *'Drum* Magazine (1951–61): And the Works of Black South African Writers Associated With It'. Ph.D. thesis, University of Leeds, 1975, p. 104.

5   See Mphahlele's chapter, 'Drum', in *Down Second Avenue*. London, Faber and Faber, 1959, pp. 187–200, and J.R.A. Bailey's 'Letting the Genie Out of the Bottle' in *The Beat of 'Drum': The Rise of Africa*, ed. Angela Caccia. Johannesburg, Ravan Press, 1982, p 123. (*Drum* Publications.)

6   Nkosi, L. 'The Fabulous Decade: The Fifties' in *Home and Exile and Other Selections*. London, Longman, 1965, p. 17.

7   See Bunting, B. *The Rise of the South African Reich*. Harmondsworth, Penguin, 1964, pp. 158–93.

8   Verwoerd, H. F. Statement to the Senate, 1954.

9   Addison, G. 'Drum Beat: An Examination of *Drum*', *Speak*, Cape Town, Vol. 1, No. 4, July–August 1978, pp. 5–6.

10 Sampson, A. *Drum: A Venture into the New Africa*. London, Collins, 1956, p. 20.

11 Bailey, 'Letting the Genie Out of the Bottle', p. 125.

12 Sampson, *Drum: A Venture into the New Africa*, p. 99.

13 Nkosi, L. 'A Question of Identity' in *Home and Exile and Other Selections*, p. 33.

14 See André Proctor, 'Class Struggle, Segregation and the City: A History of Sophiatown, 1905–40' in *Labour, Townships and Protest: Studies in the Social History of the Witwatersrand*, ed. Belinda Bozzoli. Johannesburg, Ravan Press, 1979.

15 See Bloke Modisane's *Blame Me on History*. London, Thames and Hudson, 1963 and Johannesburg, Ad. Donker, 1986. Also the Junction Avenue Theatre Company's programme notes to the play *Sophiatown*. Johannesburg, 1986, and Pippa Stein and Ruth Jacobson's *Sophiatown Speaks*. Johannesburg, Junction Avenue Press, 1986.

16 See David Coplan, 'Sophiatown: Culture and Community, 1940–60', *In Township Tonight!: South Africa's Black City Music and Theatre*. Johannesburg, Ravan Press, 1985.

17 Other sentimental screen portrayals were *Song of Africa* (1953) and the film version of the *Zonk!* Show. By contrast, Lionel Rogisin's *Come Back Africa* (1957) portrayed not only the reality of Sophiatown but also the desperate plight of black workers in South Africa's cities, and was promptly banned. (Rogisin's 'classic of the Sophiatown era' was released for public viewing in South Africa in 1988.) The film *Freedom Square and Back of the Moon*, directed for BBC's Channel 4 by William Kentridge, appeared in 1988. In 1989 Jurgen Schadeberg's *Have you seen 'Drum' lately*? was first shown at South African film festivals.

18 Huddleston, T. *Naught for your Comfort*. London, Collins, 1956; Fount Paperbacks, 1977.

19 Ibid., p. 143.

20 Lodge, T. *Black Politics in South Africa Since 1945*. Johannesburg, Ravan Press, 1983, pp. 91–113.

21 Scott, M. 'A Memorandum on Compound Labour Conditions in Agriculture – Bethal District'. Unpublished typescript, 1947.

22 Paton, A. *Debbie Go Home* (1961). Harmondsworth, Penguin, 1965, pp. 49–69.

23 O'Connor, F. *The Lonely Voice: A Study of the Short Story*. Cleveland, World Publishing Co., 1963; extract reprinted in *Short Story Theories*, ed. Charles E. May. Athens, Ohio University Press, 1976, pp. 81–93.

24 Lawrence, J.C. 'A Theory of the Short Story', *North American Review*, No. 205, February 1917; reprinted in *Short Story Theories*, ed. May, pp. 274–86.

25 'The Modern Short Story: Retrospect' in *The Modern Short Story: A Critical Survey*. Boston, The Writer, Inc., 1941; reprinted in *Short Story Theories*, ed. May, pp. 72–79.

26 Matshoba, M. *Call Me Not a Man*. Johannesburg, Ravan Press, 1979, pp. 27–64.

27 See Tim Couzens, 'The Concept of the New African and the Literature of the Nineteen Thirties', *The New African: A Study of the Life and Works of H. I. E. Dhlomo*. Johannesburg, Ravan Press, 1985.

28 Modisane, *Blame Me on History*, pp. 271–74.

29 Sampson, *Drum: A Venture into the New Africa*, p. 121.

30 Coplan, *In Township Tonight!: South Africa's Black City Music and Theatre*, pp. 173–75.

31 *The Star*, Johannesburg, 7 August 1959.

32 Robert Muller, quoted in Muff Andersson, *Music in the Mix*. Johannesburg, Ravan Press, 1981, p. 34.

33 In comparing *King Kong* and Dawn Lindberg's *King Afrika* (1988) Skelton says: '*King Kong* takes this story [and Ezekiel Dhlamini] of the myth that surrounds it and places it in a historical context. The tragedy of the piece is the tragedy of apartheid. *King Afrika* takes the trappings of the tale, loses the history and offers a glamorous presentation of an African Rocky with a conscience.' *Weekly Mail*, Johannesburg, April 22 to April 28 1988, p. 25.

34 Nkosi, 'The Fabulous Decade: The Fifties', p. 16.

35 Mda, A.P. 'African Youth and the Pictorials', *The Africanist*, May–June

1955. Quoted in Gail Gerhart's *Black Power in South Africa*. Berkeley, University of California Press, 1974, p. 129.

36 Sampson, *Drum: A Venture into the New Africa*, p. 154.

37 '*Drum* Authors', *Drum*, May 1952, p. 25.

38 See Matshoba, *Call Me Not a Man* and Mike Vaughan, 'The Stories of Mtutuzeli Matshoba', *Staffrider*, Johannesburg, Vol. 4, No. 3, November 1981, pp. 45–47.

39 Modisane, *Blame Me on History*, pp. 88–89 and pp. 137–39.

40 Mphahlele, *Down Second Avenue*, p. 188.

41 Modisane, *Blame Me on History*, p. 9.

42 Luthuli, A. *Let My People Go*. London, Collins, 1962; Fount Paperbacks, 1980.

43 See Rabkin's discussion of Manqupu's 'Love Comes Deadly!' in '*Drum* Magazine (1951–61)', pp. 98–100.

44 Mphahlele, *Down Second Avenue*, p. 164.

45 See 'Shanty Town', Huddleston, *Naught for your Comfort*, pp. 76–88.

46 See for example Ezekiel Mphahlele, 'Black and White', *New Statesman*, London, 10 September 1960, pp. 342–46; Don Dodson, 'The Four Modes of *Drum*: Popular Fiction and Social Control in South Africa', *African Studies Review*, East Lansing, Vol. 17, No. 2, September 1974, pp. 317–43; Kelwyn Sole, 'Class, Continuity and Change in Black South African Literature, 1948–60' in *Labour, Townships and Protest: Studies in the Social History of the Witwatersrand*, ed. B. Bozzoli, Johannesburg, Ravan Press, 1979, pp. 143–82; Njabulo S. Ndebele, 'The Rediscovery of the Ordinary: Some New Writings in South Africa', *Journal of Southern African Studies*, Oxford, Vol. 12, No. 2, April 1986, pp. 143–57.

47 Hopkinson, T. 'The Knight's Tale' in *The Beat of 'Drum': The Rise of Africa*, p. 21.

48 Benjamin, W. 'The Story-teller: Reflections on the Works of Nikolai Leskov' in *Illuminations*, ed. Hannah Arendt. New York, Harcourt, Brace and World Inc., 1968, pp. 83,109.

49 See 'Crepuscule' in *The Will to Die*. Cape Town, David Philip, 1982, pp. 2–11, and 'The Will to Die', 'Requiem for Sophiatown' and 'The Bottom of the Bottle' in *The World of Can Themba*, ed. Essop Patel. Johannesburg, Ravan Press, 1985, pp. 47–52, pp. 237–44 and pp. 227–36 respectively.

50 Quoted by Hopkinson, T. *In the Fiery Continent*. London, Gollancz, 1962, pp. 109–111.

51 Themba, *The Will to Die*, pp. 8–9.

52 See Rabkin, '*Drum* Magazine (1951–61)', p. 104 and Sole, 'Class Continuity and Change . . .', p. 143–82.

53   Mphahlele, *Down Second Avenue*, p. 126.

54   Published as *The African Image*. London, Faber and Faber, 1962; revised ed. 1974.

55   Mphahlele, *Down Second Avenue*, p. 188.

56   See Bailey, 'Letting the Genie Out of the Bottle', 'The Potter and the Pots', 'Worship of Mammon: Betrayal by the Educated' and 'The Great Conspiracy', *The Beat of Drum: The Rise of Africa*, pp. 123–168.

57   See Rive, R. *Advance, Retreat: Selected Short Stories*. Cape Town, David Philip, 1983, and *'Buckingham Palace': District Six*. Cape Town, David Philip, 1986.

58   See also the essays in *Voices in the Whirlwind*. New York, Hill and Wang, 1972.

59   The reference is probably to the anthology of African writing, *Darkness and Light*, ed. Peggy Rutherfoord and with a preface by Fr Trevor Huddleston, which appeared in 1958 under the joint imprint of The Faith Press, London, and *Drum* Publications, Johannesburg. It includes from *Drum*, Sentso's 'Under the Blue-gum Trees', Themba's 'Mob Passion' and Modisane's 'The Dignity of Begging'.

60   Mphahlele, *Down Second Avenue*, p. 217.

61   Barnett, U. A. *A Vision of Order: A Study of Black South African Literature in English (1914–80)*. London, Sinclair Brown; Amherst, University of Massachusetts Press; Cape Town, Maskew Miller Longman, 1983.

62   See Hopkinson's account of his years as editor of *Drum* in *In the Fiery Continent*.

63   Some of La Guma's stories appeared in *Quartet: New Voices from South Africa*, ed. Richard Rive, London, Heinemann, 1963, and his short novel *A Walk in the Night* (1962) was reissued, together with a selection of stories, by Heinemann African Writers Series, in 1968.

64   Serote, M.W. 'The Nakasa World', *Contrast*, Cape Town, No. 31, 1973.

65   Bailey, 'The Great Conspiracy', *The Beat of Drum: The Rise of Africa*, p. 161.

66   See *Drum* Publications in the Bibliography.

67   Mphahlele, 'Black and White', p. 342.

68   'Landmarks', in *Umhlaba Wethu: . . .*, ed. Mutloatse, p. 12.

69   Couzens, *The New African: A Study of the Life and Works of H. I. E. Dhlomo*, p. 353.

70   Ibid., p. 353.

71   Nakasa, N. 'Writing in South Africa', *The Classic*, Johannesburg, Vol. 1,

No. 1, 1963; reprinted in *The World of Nat Nakasa*. Johannesburg, Ravan Press, 1975, pp. 187–94.

72   Themba, 'The Bottom of the Bottle', *The World of Can Themba*, p. 236.

73   Visser, N. 'South Africa: The Renaissance that Failed', *The Journal of Commonwealth Literature*, Leeds, Vol. II, No. 1, August 1976, pp. 42–57.

74   See Rabkin's, '*Drum* Magazine (1951–61)', p. 104, and Sole, 'Class, Continutiy and Change . . ., pp. 143–82.

75   Lindfors, B. 'Post-war Literature in English by African Writers from South Africa: A Study of the Effects of Environment upon Literature', *Phylon*, Atlanta, No. 27, 1966.

76   See Dodson, 'The Four Modes of *Drum*'.

77   See Mzamane's 'Jola' stories (pp. 3–73) and 'Dube Train Revisited' (pp. 146–152), *Mzala: The Stories of Mbulelo Mzamane*. Johannesburg, Ravan Press, 1980.

78   Ndebele, N.S., *Fools and Other Stories*. Johannesburg, Ravan Press, 1983, pp. 53–123.

79   See Ndebele, N. S. 'Turkish Tales and Some Thoughts on South African Fiction', *Staffrider*, Johannesburg, Vol. 6, No. 1, 1984, pp. 24–25 and pp. 42–48, and 'The Rediscovery of the Ordinary: Some New Writings in South Africa', *Journal of Southern African Studies*, Oxford, Vol. 12, No. 2, April 1986.

80   Borges, J.L. 'A Note on (toward) Bernard Shaw' in *Labyrinths: Selected Stories and Other Writings*, ed. Donald A. Yates and James E. Irby. New York, New Directions, 1975, p. 213.

81   See Mzamane's Introduction to his volume of stories, *Mzala*. Johannesburg, Ravan Press, 1981.

82   Fugard, A. *Statements: Three Plays*. London, O.U.P., 1974. See also Fugard's early 'Sophiatown' plays, *No-good Friday* and *Nongogo* in *Dimetos, and Two Early Plays*. London, O.U.P., 1977.

83   Ndebele, 'The Rediscovery of the Ordinary', p. 153.

84   Ibid., p. 145.

85   Mphahlele, 'Black and White', p. 343.

86   Mphahlele, *Down Second Avenue*, p. xxi.

87   See for example Ngubane, J. 'An Examination of Zulu Tribal Poetry', *Drum*, August 1951.

88   Bowen, E. Introduction to *The Faber Book of Modern Short Stories*. London, Faber and Faber, 1936; reprinted in *Short Story Theories*, ed. May, p. 152.

Select Bibliography

A *Drum* Archives and Index

Drum magazines for the period 1951–60 are housed at the Killie Campbell Africana Library (University of Natal, Durban), the Natal Society Library (Pietermaritzburg), the Johannesburg Public Library and the South African Institute for Race Relations (Johannesburg).

Bailey's African Photo Archives, Johannesburg.

Woodson, Dorothy C. *Drum: An Index to 'Africa's Leading Magazine', 1951–65*. Madison: University of Wisconsin, 1988.

B *Drum* Publications

The Beat of Drum: The Rise of Africa, ed. Angela Caccia. Johannesburg: Ravan Press, 1982.

The Beat of Drum: Foundations of the Future in Africa, Volume II, ed. H. Lunn. Johannesburg: J.R.A. Bailey, 1983.

Profiles of Africa, ed. H. Lunn. Johannesburg: J.R.A. Bailey, 1983.

The Beat of Drum: The Bedside Book, Vol. IV, ed. H. Lunn. Johannesburg: J.R.A. Bailey, 1984.

The Finest Photos from the Old 'Drum', Jurgen Schadeberg. Johannesburg: Bailey's African Photo Archives, 1987.

The Fifties People of South Africa, ed. Jurgen Schadeberg. Johannesburg: Bailey's African Photo Archives, 1987.

In preparation: *The Agony of Uganda*; *Tanzania: A Classical Tragedy; The Success of Kenya*; the stories of Nigeria and Ghana (3 volumes); *Kippie: The Sad Man of Jazz; Dolly by Dolly by Can Themba; Tandie's Talkin' Blues; Henry 'Mr Drum' Nxumalo*.

(See also Rutherfoord, below.)

C Individual Volumes of Stories

(by writers associated with *Drum*)

Matthews, James. *The Park and Other Stories*. Johannesburg: Ravan Press, 1983.

Motsisi, Casey. *Casey & Co.: Selected Writings of Casey 'Kid' Motsisi*, ed. Mothobi Mutloatse. Johannesburg: Ravan Press, 1978.

Mphahlele, Ezekiel (now Es'kia). *Man Must Live and Other Stories*. Cape Town: African Bookman, 1946.

— *The Living and the Dead and Other Stories*. Ibadan: Ministry of Education, 1961.

— *In Corner B*. Nairobi: East African Publishing House, 1967.

— *The Unbroken Song: Selected Writings of Es' kia Mphahlele*. Johannesburg: Ravan Press, 1981.

Nakasa, Nat. *The World of Nat Nakasa*, ed. Essop Patel. Johannesburg: Ravan Press, 1975.

Rive, Richard. *Selected Writings*. Johannesburg: Ad. Donker, 1977.

— *Advance, Retreat: Selected Stories*. Cape Town: David Philip, 1983.

Themba, Can. *The Will to Die*. London: Heinemann African Writers Series, 1972; Cape Town: David Philip, 1982.

— *The World of Can Themba*, ed. Essop Patel. Johannesburg: Ravan Press, 1985.

D Social and Literary Background, and Criticism

Addison, Graeme. 'Drum Beat: An Examination of *Drum*', *Speak*, Cape Town, Vol. I, No. 4, July–August 1978.

Andersson, Muff. *Music in the Mix*. Johannesburg: Ravan Press, 1981.

Barnett, Ursula A. *A Vision of Order: A Study of Black South African Literature in English (1914–80)*. London: Sinclaire Browne; Amherst: University of Massachusetts Press; Cape Town: Maskew Miller Longman, 1983.

Bishop, Solomzi. *Channel 48*. Play utilizing the figure of Henry Nxumalo. Performed at the Funda Centre, Soweto, 1988.

Coplan, David. 'Sophiatown: Culture and Community, 1940–60', *In Township Tonight!: South Africa's Black City Music and Theatre*. Johannesburg: Ravan Press, 1985.

Couzens, Tim. *The New African: A Study of the Life and Works of H.I.E. Dhlomo*. Johannesburg: Ravan Press, 1985.

Creative Camera, London, Nos. 235/236, July–August 1984, Issue '*Drum* – South Africa's Black Picture Magazine'. Contains: Editorial 'The Muffled Drum'; '*Drum*: An Introduction' by Colin Osman; 'I carried a gun for *Drum*' by Arthur Maimane; 'The Men in the Centre: Sylvester Stein and Jurgen Schadeberg' (interview); Photographs by Peter Magubane and Ian Berry; 'Drum Beat: An Examination of *Drum*' by Graeme Addison; '*Drum* – The Later Years' by Kerry Swift; '*Drum* in East Africa' by Shamlal Puri; 'The Future of *Drum*'; and 'Some Books on *Drum* and Apartheid' by Colin Osman.

Dodson, Don.   'The Four Modes of Drum: Popular Fiction and Social Control in South Africa', *African Studies Review*, East Lansing, Vol. 17, No. 2, September 1974.

'*Drum* Writing in the Fifties', two articles, *New Nation*, supplement *Learning Nation*. Johannesburg, Vol. 1, Nos. 9 & 10, 1988.

Fugard, Athol.   *No-good Friday* and *Nongogo*; in *Dimetos, and Two Early Plays*. London: Oxford University Press, 1974.

— *Tsotsi*. Johannesburg: Ad. Donker, 1980; Penguin, 1983.

Hart, Deborah M.   'South African Literature and Johannesburg's Black Urban Townships'. Masters thesis, University of the Witwatersrand, 1984.

Hopkinson, Tom.   *In the Fiery Continent*. London: Victor Gollancz, 1962.

— *Under the Tropic*. London: Hutchinson, 1984.

Huddleston, Trevor.   *Naught for your Comfort*. Collins, 1956; Fount Paperbacks, 1977.

Hughes, Langston.   *An African Treasury: Articles/Essays/Stories/Poems by Black Africans*. New York: Crown Publishers, 1960.

Junction Avenue Theatre Company. *Sophiatown*. Play performed at Market Theatre, Johannesburg, 1986.

— *Sophiatown* (programme notes). Johannesburg: Market Theatre, 1986.

— *Sophiatown* (playscript), ed. Malcolm Purkey. Cape Town: David Philip, 1988.

Karis, Thomas and Gwendolin M. Carter.   *From Protest to Challenge: A Documentary History of African Politics in South Africa, 1882–1964*. Stanford: Hoover Institute Press, 1972–77; Cape Town: David Philip, 1986.

King Kong: An African Jazz Opera. Book by Harry Bloom; Lyrics by Pat Williams. London: Collins Fontana, 1961.

Kirkwood, Mike.   'Fifties People', *Leadership*, Cape Town, Vol. 5, No. 6, 1986.

Lindfors, Bernth.   'Post-war Literature in English by African Writers from South Africa: A Study of the Effects of Environment upon Literature', *Phylon*, Atlanta, No. 27, 1966.

Lodge, Tom.   *Black Politics in South Africa Since 1945*. Johannesburg, Ravan Press, 1983.

Luthuli, Albert.   *Let My People Go: An Autobiography*. London: Collins, 1962; Fount Paperback, 1982.

Makeba, Miriam.   *My Story: Makeba*. Johannesburg: Skotaville Publishers, 1988.

Matshikiza, Todd.   Chocolates for my Wife. London: Hodder and Stoughton, 1961; Cape Town: David Philip, 1982.

Mattera, Don.   *Memory Is the Weapon.* Johannesburg: Ravan Press, 1987.

Matthews, Z.K.   *Freedom for my People*, with a memoir by Monica Wilson. London: Rex Collings, 1981; Cape Town: David Philip, 1983.

Mda, A.P.   ('Sandile').   'African Youth and the Pictorials', *The Africanist*, May–June 1955.

Modisane, Bloke.   *Blame Me on History.* London: Thames and Hudson, 1963; Johannesburg: Ad. Donker, 1986.

Moloi, Godfrey.   *My Life: Volume One.* Johannesburg: Ravan Press, 1987.

Morris, Patricia,   'The Rise and Fall of *Drum*', *New African*, No. 205, October, 1984.

Mphahlele, Ezekiel (now Es'kia).   'The African Intellectual', *Africa in Transition*, ed. Prudence Smith. London: Reinhardt, 1958.

— 'The Dilemma of the African Elite', *Twentieth Century*, April 1959.

— *Down Second Avenue.* London: Faber and Faber, 1959.

— 'Black and White', *New Statesman*, London, 10 September 1960.

— *The African Image.* London: Faber and Faber, 1962; revised ed. 1974.

— *Voices in the Whirlwind and Other Essays.* New York: Hill and Wang, 1972.

— *The Voice of the Black Writer in Africa.* Johannesburg: Witwatersrand University Press, 1980. (Senate Special Lectures/History and Change in Black Literature: Landmarks of Literary History in South Africa)

— 'Landmarks' in *Umhlaba Wethu: A Historical Indictment*, ed. Mothobi Mutloatse. Johannesburg: Skotaville Publishers, 1987.

Mzamane, Mbulelo.   'The Short Story Tradition in Black South Africa', *Donga*, Johannesburg, September 1977.

— 'The Fifties and Beyond: An Evaluation', *New Classic*, Johannesburg, No. 4, 1977.

— 'The Uses of Traditional Oral Forms in Black South African Literature', *Literature and Society in South Africa*, ed. Landeg White and Tim Couzens. Cape Town: Maskew Miller Longman, 1984.

— Introduction to *Hungry Flames and Other Black South African Short Stories*. London: Longman, 1986.

Nakasa, Nat.   'Writing in South Africa', *The Classic*, Johannesburg, Vol. 1, No. 1, 1963; reprinted in *The World of Nat Nakasa* (see C. above).

Ndebele, Njabulo S. 'The Rediscovery of the Ordinary: Some New Writings in South Africa', *Journal of Southern African Studies*, Oxford, Vol. 12, No. 2, April 1986.

Nkosi, Lewis. *Home and Exile and Other Selections*. London: Longman 1965; 1983.

— *Mating Birds*. London: Constable, 1986.

Paton, Alan. *Cry, the Beloved Country*. London: Jonathan Cape, 1948; Harmondsworth, Penguin 1958.

Powell, Ivor. 'A Trip Down Memory Lane – Which Ends in Death Row'. Review of the Exhibition 'The Finest Photos from the Old *Drum*' at the Market Photo Gallery, Johannesburg. *Weekly Mail*, Johannesburg, 30 April – 7 May 1987.

Proctor, André. 'Class Struggle, Segregation and the City: A History of Sophiatown, 1905–40' in *Labour, Townships and Protest: Studies in the Social History of the Witwatersrand*, ed. Belinda Bozzoli. Johannesburg: Ravan Press, 1979.

Rabkin, David. '*Drum* Magazine (1951–61): And the Works of Black South African Writers Associated With It'. Ph.D. thesis, University of Leeds, 1975.

Rive, Richard, ed. *Quartet: New Voices from South Africa*. London: Heinemann, 1963.

— ed. *Modern African Prose*. London: Heinemann, 1964.

— '*Buckingham Palace*': *District Six*. Cape Town: David Philip, 1986.

Roux, Edward. *Time Longer than Rope: The Black Man's Struggle for Freedom in South Africa*. Madison: University of Wisconsin Press, 1948.

Rutherfoord, Peggy, ed. *Darkness and Light: An Anthology of African Writing*. London: The Faith Press; Johannesburg: *Drum* Publications, 1958.

Sampson, Anthony. *Drum: A Venture into the New Africa*. London: Collins, 1956.

— *Drum: An African Adventure – and Afterwards*. London: Hodder and Stoughton, 1983.

Serote, Mongane Wally. 'The Nakasa World', *Contrast*, Cape Town, No. 31, 1973.

Smith, Rowland. 'Le Magazine *Drum*: Voix des Townships Noires', tr. André Viola, *L'Afrique Littéraire*, Paris, No. 75, 1985.

Sole, Kelwyn. 'Class, Continuity and Change in Black South African Literature, 1948–60' in *Labour, Townships and Protest: Studies in the Social History of the Witwatersrand*, ed. Belinda Bozzoli. Johannesburg: Ravan Press, 1979.

Sophiatown. Play. See Junction Avenue Theatre Company, above.

Stein, Pippa and Ruth Jacobson, eds. *Sophiatown Speaks*. Johannesburg: Junction Avenue Press, 1986.

Stein, Sylvester. *Second Class Taxi*. London: Faber and Faber, 1958; Cape Town: David Philip, 1983.

Themba, Can. 'Through Shakespeare's Africa', *The New African*, 21 September 1963.

Tlali, Miriam. 'Interview with Bra Luke of Sophiatown', *Staffrider*, Johannesburg, Vol. 4, No. 4, 1982.

Trump, Martin. 'Literature against Apartheid: South African Short Fiction in English and Afrikaans since 1948'. (Ph.D. thesis, University of London, 1985.

Visser, N.W. 'South Africa: The Renaissance that Failed', *The Journal of Commonwealth Literature*, Leeds, Vol. II, No. 1, August 1976.

E. Films Pertaining to *Drum*
See Note 17, on p. 228.

Appendix
Stories in *Drum*

Although my selection has deliberately blurred distinctions between 'stories' and 'reportage', I have confined this list to stories which employ fictional characters and situations.

1 March 1951, 'Rhodesia Road', Alfred Mbeba.
2 April 1951, 'Nomoya! Of the Winds', R. B. Pitso.
3 May 1951, 'The Wicked Adventures of KenKebe', Guybon Ben Sinxo.
4 June 1951, 'The Harvest Is Waiting', Dyke H. Sentso.
5 July 1951, 'The Cup Was Full', C. O. D. Ekwensi.
6 September 1951, 'The Dignity of Begging', William Bloke Modisane.
7 November 1951, 'The Sun Stood Still', Dyke H. Sentso.
8 December 1951, 'The Answer He Wanted', Jordan K. Ngubane.
9 January 1952, 'Farm Boy', E. A. P. Sixala.
10 January 1952, 'The Tie Pin', Sanduza Bavu.
11 January 1952, 'The Fighter Wore Skirts', William Bloke Modisane.
12 February 1952, 'Tomorrow Never Came', E. Rhezi.
13. March 1952, 'Ntombo Gets A Job', Douglas Sidayiya.
14 April 1952, 'Duma Comes Homes', D. G. Tsebe.
15 May 1952, 'Pay Back', Dyke H. Sentso.
16 June 1952, 'The Boomerang', Guybon B. Sinxo.
17 . July 1952, 'The Bride Price', A. S. Massiye.
18 August 1952, 'The Boy Who Painted Christ Black', John Henrik Clarke.
19 September 1952, 'Blood between Us!', Sam Mokgalendi.
20 November 1952, 'Forbidden Love!', C. O. D. Ekwensi.
21 December 1952, 'Night of Passion!', Kyle Mdenge.
22 January 1953, 'I was in Dream Land . . . until I told him . . .' (A True Love Confession), Rita Sefora.
23 January 1953, 'Crime for Sale!', Arthur Mogale.
24 February 1953, 'Dangerous Love!', K. E. Ntsane.
25 February 1953, 'Crime for Sale!', Arthur Mogale.
26 March 1953, 'Crime for Sale!', Arthur Mogale.

27   March 1953, 'Passionate Stranger!', D. Can Themba.
28   April 1953, 'Hot Diamonds!', Arthur Mogale.
29   April 1953, 'Mob Passion!', D. Can Themba.
30   May 1953, 'Hot Diamonds!', Arthur Mogale.
31   May 1953, 'My Husband Was a Flirt!' (A True Love Confession),
      Joan Mokwena.
32   June 1953, 'Hot Diamonds!', Arthur Mogale.
33   June 1953, 'Loving Two Men!', E. E. Mkize.
34   July 1953, 'Hot Diamonds!', Arthur Mogale.
35   July 1953, 'Live Man's Blood!', C. O. D. Ekwensi.
36   August 1953, 'I Broke Their Hearts!' (A True Love Confession),
      Dorris Sello.
37   August 1953, 'You Can't Buy Me!', Arthur Mogale.
38   September 1953, 'You Can't Buy Me!', Arthur Mogale.
39   September 1953, 'Blind Alley!', Ezekiel Mphahlele.
40   October 1953, 'You Can't Buy Me!', Arthur Mogale.
41   November 1953, 'You Can't Buy Me!', Arthur Mogale.
42   December 1953, 'You Can't Buy Me!', Arthur Mogale.
43   December 1953, 'Love's a Gamble!', Alexander Hlazo.
44   January 1954, 'The Respectable Pickpocket!', William Bloke Modisane.
45   January 1954, 'The Champ!', James Matthews.
46   February 1954, 'Other People's Goods!', Dyke H. Sentso.
47   February 1954, 'When Boy Meets Girl!', Dyke Ngcobo.
48   March 1954, 'All Love Has Its Price!', C. F. Ogundipe.
49   March 1954, 'Ageless Love', Gabe Offiah.
50   April 1954, 'Under the Blue-gum Trees', Dyke H. Sentso.
51   April 1954, 'His Only Love!', Kenneth Mtetwa.
52   May 1954, 'The Nice Time Girl!', D. Can Themba.
53   June 1954, 'Broken Hearted!', Arthur Mogale.
54   July 1954, 'Never Too Late for Love!', Duke Ngcobo.
55   August 1954, 'Reef Train!', Bruno Esekie.
56   September 1954, 'Dead End!', James Matthews.
57   October 1954, 'Slice Him Down!', Langston Hughes.
58   November 1954, 'Amateur Night in Harlem!', Gene Davis.
59   December 1954, 'Muscle Man's Girl', Peter Clarke.
60   January 1955, 'Love Comes Deadly!', Mbokotwane Manqupu.
61   February 1955, 'The Suitcase', Bruno Esekie.
62   March 1955, 'Leg Man!', Ollie Stewart.
63   April 1955, 'The Departure', Peter Clarke.
64   May 1955, 'Black and Brown Song', Richard Rive.